international
review of
social history

Special Issue 29

When "Adjusted" People Rebel: Economic Liberalization and Social Revolts in Africa and the Middle East (1980s to the Present Day)

Edited by Leyla Dakhli and Vincent Bonnecase

T0349201

Published by the Press Syndicate of the University of Cambridge
The Pitt Building, Trumpington Street, Cambridge, CB2 1RP
1 Liberty Plaza, Floor 20, New York, NY 10006, USA
10 Stamford Road, Oakleigh, Melbourne 3166, Australia

© Internationaal Instituut voor Sociale Geschiedenis

*A catalogue record for this book is available
from the British Library*

Library of Congress Cataloguing-in-Publication Data applied for

ISBN 9781009069960 (paperback)

Printed in the UK by Bell & Bain Ltd, Glasgow, UK.

CONTENTS

When 'Adjusted' People Rebel: Economic Liberalization and Social Revolts in Africa and the Middle East (1980s to the Present Day)

Edited by
Leyla Dakhli and Vincent Bonnecase

IRSH 66 (2021), pp. 1–21 doi:10.1017/S0020859021000092

Introduction: Interpreting the Global Economy through Local Anger

LEYLA DAKHLI

Centre National de la Recherche Scientifique
Centre Marc Bloch
Friedrichstraße 191
10117 Berlin, Germany

E-mail: Leyla.Dakhli@cmb.hu-berlin.de

VINCENT BONNECASE

Centre National de la Recherche Scientifique
Institut des mondes africains
5 cours des Humanités
93300 Aubervilliers, France

E-mail: vincentbonnecase@yahoo.fr

ABSTRACT: During the 1980s and 1990s, violent events occurred in the streets of many African and Middle Eastern countries. Each event had its own logic and saw the intervention of actors with differing profiles. What they had in common was that they all took place in the context of the implementation of a neoliberal political economy. The anger these policies aroused was first expressed by people who were not necessarily rebelling against the adjustments themselves, or against the underlying ideologies or the institutions that imposed them, but rather against their practical manifestations in everyday life. This special issue invites reflections on these revolts and what they teach us about the neoliberal turn in Africa and the Middle East.

The echoes between the present and the recent past are as important for the genesis of this work as they are for those that read it. They must not prevent us from investigating the specifics of these uprisings, with a particular emphasis on the intersection between a global political economy and local challenges, while understanding them through their particular circumstances. This issue aims to stimulate a more general reflection on popular feelings and social responses in the face of neoliberalism.

On 18 January 1977, multiple fires broke out in Cairo. Egypt was beset by protests, a day after the Prime Minister had announced the end of government subsidies for consumer goods in order to obtain aid from international financial institutions. On 29 December 1983, protests began at the weekly Douz market in southern Tunisia. The government had ended offsets for basic products resulting in riots against the price increase, which soon spread to the rest of the country. After eight days of conflict between rioters and the military, the official toll was eighty-four dead and more than 900 injured. On 10 March 1994, a few days after the devaluation of the CFA franc and the country's engagement in a round of negotiations with international financial institutions, students in Niamey, Niger, vented their anger at the deterioration in their living conditions. The Nigerien police entered the university campus with brute force. A student was struck in the face by a teargas canister and died the following day.

While each of these violent events had its own logic and resulted in the intervention of different types of actors, what they had in common was that they all took place in the context of the implementation of neoliberal economic policies, generally referred to as structural adjustment reforms. The establishment of this new "financial orthodoxy" as a planning and measurement tool for public policies emerged gradually in a succession of shifts beginning in the early 1970s, most obviously on the initiative of the World Bank and the International Monetary Fund (IMF) and the conditions that were attached to their loans. This new political economy coincided with the end of the post-war economic boom and the beginning of an increasingly significant market integration that was characterized in particular by the entry into the global system of newly industrialized countries following the collapse of the Bretton Woods system in 1973. While the ideas behind neoliberal globalization date back to the Mont Pellerin Society and Friedrich Hayek's teachings in the 1940s, the economic rules came to be defined and implemented first in Latin America in the 1970s. In Africa and Asia, too, one of the principal manifestations of this development can be seen in the structural adjustment programmes (SAPs), which sought to rebalance public accounts by reducing government expenditure, to stimulate business by modifying institutional constraints, and to even out trade balances by lifting protectionist barriers.

These programmes were designed in line with technical and technocratic approaches that the IMF and the World Bank had been fine-tuning since their formation.[1] They were intended to address accumulating national debts in developing countries. Lured into petrodollar-backed spending sprees by the sudden availability of credit from private banks and caught out by rising inflation globally, African and Asian states were at the mercy of the Bretton Woods institutions' open economy dictates. This adjustment policy has gone through several phases, from the most brutal plans imposed by international financial institutions in the early 1980s, to the "adjustments with a human

---

1. Henry Hazlitt, *From Bretton Woods to World Inflation* (New York, 1984).

face" recommended by other international agencies from 1987 onwards,[2] and the World Bank's new focus on poverty in the 1990s.[3] Despite these strategic reorientations and conceptual innovations, SAPs' main lines – reducing state involvement in social services, liberalizing trade and prices, giving priority to fiscal policy discipline – have remained the key pillars of "good governance" as promoted by the Bretton Woods institutions to date.

Criticism of these programmes spread broadly around the world and is well known. It gained strength, and, under the pressure of militant movements, the IMF's and SAPs' responsibility for rising poverty began to be recognized. SAPs were also the trigger for public debate about public services in newly independent states in which education, health, and public transport became neglected as soon as lucrative private markets developed. But anger was first expressed by people who were not necessarily rebelling against structural adjustments, or the ideologies underlying them or the institutions that imposed them, but rather against their practical consequences in everyday life. This issue invites reflections on the eruption of widespread revolts since the 1970s and what they teach us about the neoliberal turn in Africa and the Middle East – and more broadly, the world – as it was experienced by populations.

TOWARDS A SOCIAL HISTORY OF THE ADJUSTMENTS

Structural adjustments have been the subject of extensive literature, but to a large extent that literature has remained focused on the logic (and documentation) of international financial institutions, national governments, and private enterprises, even when the point was to deconstruct the logic or subject it to critical interpretation. Some studies have set out to expose the ideological foundations of policies couched in purely technical external terms.[4] Others have focused on analysing the practices to which the adjustments gave rise, in particular the interactions between the international financial institutions and the national governments of the "adjusted states". It was often a question of identifying the policy that lay at the heart of the technocratic implementations and showing how they were the sites where relations of power, negotiation, or manipulation were developed.[5] Most studies analysed the effects of the adjustments on the living conditions of populations that were supposed

2. Giovanni Andrea Cornia, Richard Jolly, and Frances Stuart (eds), *Adjustment with a Human Face: Protecting the Vulnerable and Promoting Growth* (London, 1987), 2 vols.

3. World Bank, *World Development Report 1990: Poverty* (New York, 1990).

4. See, for example, Béatrice Hibou, *Économie politique du discours de la Banque mondiale en Afrique sub-saharienne. Du catéchisme économique au fait (et méfait) missionnaire*, Études du CERI, no. 39, 1998, and the literature on the "Washington Consensus".

5. Timothy Mitchell, *Rule of Experts: Egypt, Techno-Politics, Modernity* (Berkeley, CA, 2002); Boris Samuel, *La production macroéconomique du réel. Formalités et pouvoir au Burkina Faso, en Mauritanie et en Guadeloupe*, (Ph.D., IEP Paris, 2013).

to be the beneficiaries in sectors such as health and education.[6] Often, the adjustments were subjected to an immanent critique by relying on some of the criteria initially invoked by the international financial institutions to justify their implementation and then showing how they did not work. Naturally, part of this critical literature was written by former promoters of the adjustments who later regretted them – the most celebrated among them being the Nobel Prize winner Joseph Stiglitz.[7] The paradigm shift only occurred once these critics became detached from the issue of structural reforms and macroeconomic equilibria and turned towards the "struggle against poverty" in the early 2000s.[8]

This propensity to look at the adjustments through a prism of "logic" or through the lens of those who had initiated them more broadly is prevalent in the literature on neoliberalism. Some of this literature has sought to explain the genesis of neoliberalism through the trajectory of intellectual communities, which played a major role in the development of a liberal counter-reform project starting in the 1930s,[9] or that of new dominant social classes, who played a decisive role in the implementation of neo-liberalism from the 1970s.[10] In the face of these intellectual histories, others saw neoliberalism as a form of rationality that could be attributed to both intentional and (to a large extent) inadvertent practices. Following Michel Foucault's analysis of modern forms of interactions between institutions and subjectivity – through what he termed "governmentality" – everyone becomes their own entrepreneur.[11] Some studies abandoned the notion of "ideological project" or "conscious world" and focused on the daily practices of individuals who, without necessarily intending to, and for different reasons, participated in neoliberal governmentality. This new governmentality was informed by a collusion of

6. Michael Barratt Brown, *Africa's Choices: After Thirty Years of the World Bank* (London, 1995); Kevin Danaher, *50 Years Is Enough: The Case Against the World Bank and the International Monetary Fund* (Boston, MA, 1994); Marie-France L'Hériteau, *Le Fonds monétaire international et les pays du tiers monde*, 2nd edn (Paris, 1990).

7. Joseph E. Stiglitz, *Globalization and Its Discontents* (New York, 2002).

8. See in particular the discussion papers published in 1998 by the Partnerships Group for the World Bank, available online at: http://documents1.worldbank.org/curated/en/789141468153858137/text/516050WP0Devoi10Box342046B01PUBLIC1.txt; last accessed 12 January 2021; and the document that is sometimes considered to be the most important for this reorientation on the part of the World Bank, *World Development Report 2000–2001: Attacking Poverty* (Paris, 2001).

9. Philip Mirowski and Dieter Plehwe (eds), *The Road from Mont Pèlerin: The Making of the Neo-liberal Thought* (Cambridge, MA, 2009); Quinn Slobodian, *The Globalists: The End of Empire and the Birth of Neo-liberalism* (Cambridge, MA, 2018).

10. Grégoire Chamayou, *La société ingouvernable. Une généalogie du libéralisme autoritaire* (Paris, 2018).

11. Pierre Dardot and Christian Laval, *La nouvelle raison du monde. Essai sur la société néolibérale* (Paris, 2010); Wendy Brown, *Les Habits neufs de la politique mondiale. Néolibéralisme et néo-conservatisme* (Paris, 2007); Idem, *Undoing the Demos: Neo-liberalism's Stealth Revolution* (New York, 2015).

heterogeneous interests rather than a nefarious top-down political pro-gramme.[12] Elites in Africa and the Middle East endorsed reforms in order to assert control over state apparatuses that, in turn, fuelled struggles within national political fields.[13] Most scholarly work, however, remained focused on state administrations and international organizations and ignored the everyday lives and resentments of the population. We believe the shared condition of individuals and the new relations between ideologies and subjectivities must be taken into account in our understanding of the impact of SAPs on people's lives. Hence we use the term "adjusted people", by which we mean there is a range of operations that aim to transform their lives, and that these operations derive from the idea of adjustments to neoliberal policies.

By focusing on the revolts against the SAPs, as well as the absence of revolt, and more generally on the multiple social responses to structural adjustments, such as anger, adaptation, or indifference, we suggest that the perspective should be reversed. The neoliberalization of the world must be understood not only as dispositive of power – whether or not it is considered to be the result of an intentional action – but also through the prism of its popular perception. We want to investigate the ways in which the upheavals brought about by this new liberalization were actually experienced by the people of Africa and the Middle East in their daily and material lives and their shared concepts of fairness and unfairness. Sometimes, these experiences led to the revolts we intend to study here. In addition to moving into the field of (non-)mobilization, this approach also means taking seriously popular representations of economic issues, starting from the notion that populations can be aware of and creative regarding what is actually happening.[14]

This perspective goes hand in hand with an approach that traces social adjustment processes in places other than those where they are most clearly revealed. In addition to the proximity of the events themselves, which makes it difficult to access some sources, this explains why the articles often utilize archival material that is not commonly used in social movement studies but that speaks no less of the real, day-to-day situation in a neoliberal context, including the urban zoning plans explored by Leyla Dakhli in Tunisia, the newspaper cartoons in Togo studied by Robin Frisch, and the ethnography of naming everyday objects in Niger, as studied by Vincent Bonnecase. In addition, almost all the contributions in this issue rely on oral history and face the

---

12. Béatrice Hibou, *La bureaucratisation du monde à l'ère néolibérale* (Paris, 2012).

13. Graham Harrison, *Neo-liberal Africa: The Impact of Global Social Engineering* (London, 2010); Jean-François Bayart, Stephen Ellis, and Béatrice Hibou, *The Criminalization of the State* (Bloomington, IN, 1999).

14. Jane Guyer, Kabiru Salami, and Olusanya Akinlade, "'Kò s'ówó'. Il n'y a pas d'argent!", *Politique africaine*, 124 (2011), p. 48. On this perspective of economic anthropology, see also Jane Guyer, *Marginal Gains: Monetary Transactions in Atlantic Africa* (Chicago, IL, 2004) and Janet Roitman, *Fiscal Disobedience: An Anthropology of Economic Regulation in Central Africa* (Princeton, NJ, 2004).

question of the heteroclite memories of the adjustment period – the "frag-ments of memories" studied by Nayera Soliman. Collectively, we are dealing with memories that are partial in both senses of the word. As they collide, their relationships are rearranged. Sometimes, traumatic recollections reveal that this moment of revolt was a significant temporal point of reference in shared memories, one that can be compared to – or is even a mirror image of – the earlier time of independence. It is essential not to sustain only the most militant forms of these memories, as Mélanie Henry reminds us, so as not to extrapolate a more extensive ideological opposition to the adjustments or to reduce anger to its most explicitly political form, as it might be expressed in the context of protest organizations or collective mobilizations.[15]

Our approach is not unique, but it has mainly been used in other parts of the world that have been subjected to adjustments. In Latin America, for example, the convergence between the installation of authoritarian powers and the implementation of neoliberal policies was sufficiently striking for the historiography to study the links between economic liberalism and political authoritarianism.[16] In these cases, the authorities treated these revolts merely as obstacles along the way, and their wide-scale suppression has often concealed what they introduced and the counter-models that might have been proposed. Pinochet's Chile, which proved to be fertile ground for the implementation of neoliberal policies following the coup d'état of 11 September 1973, was therefore taken into particular consideration, as was Peru, which saw the development of the first great social uprisings against neoliberal policies in the mid-1970s, followed by bloody repression.[17] Other countries, including Argentina, also inspired important studies on social uprisings outside the most expected political spaces.[18] In his ethnography of riots, Javier Auyero invited us to study the "grey zones", where nearly invisible relations are

15. On the importance of considering anger outside the space of mobilizations, see Vincent Bonnecase, *Les prix de la colère. Une histoire de la vie chère au Burkina Faso* (Paris, 2019).
16. There is a significant body of work on the influence of the Chicago School and neoliberal experimentation on the subcontinent: Yves Dezalay and Bryant Garth, *The Internationalization of Palace Wars: Lawyers, Economists, and the Contest to Transform Latin American States* (Chicago, IL, 2002); Marion Fourcade-Gourinchas and Sarah L. Babb, "The Rebirth of the Liberal Creed: Paths to Neo-liberalism in Four Countries", *American Journal of Sociology*, 108 (2002), pp. 533–579; Stéphane Boisard and Mariana Heredia, "Laboratoires de la mondialisation économique. Regards croisés sur les dictatures argentine et chilienne des années 1970", *Vingtième Siècle. Revue d'histoire*, 105 (2010), pp. 109–125.
17. Manuel Gárate Chateau, *La revolución capitalista de Chile (1973–2003)* (Santiago de Chile, 2012); Eugenio Tironi Barrios, *Autoritarismo, modernización y marginalidad. El caso de Chile 1973–1989* (Santiago, 1990).
18. Jane S. Jaquette and Abraham F. Lowenthal, "The Peruvian Experiment in Retrospect", *World Politics*, 39:2 (1987), pp. 280–296.

born among those who mobilize, or between them and the state.[19] Alongside the scientific literature, there is no shortage of images of Latin American uprisings in the neoliberal era, whether they be the occupations organized by the Brazilian Landless Workers Movement in 1985, the occupation of San Cristobal de las Casas by the EZLN (Ejército Zapatista de Liberación Nacional), or Zapatistas as they are more commonly known, on 1 January 1994, or the looting in Argentinian towns in December 2001 following the collapse of numerous banks.

In Africa and the Middle East, repeated social movements, the Arab uprisings, and the recent mobilizations of 2018–2019 in Sudan, Algeria, Lebanon, and Iraq have raised the issues of access to public services and high living costs since 2008. These developments have caught social scientists off guard.[20] Popular discontent with neo-liberalism has appeared less Marxist in Africa and the Middle East than in other parts of the world. Especially in Latin America, numerous uprisings confronted "capitalism", "imperialism", and "international institutions" after the implementation of the first SAPs. The strength of leftist parties, trade unions, and peasants' movements – as well as the proximity of the United States – played a role in this orientation. By comparison, social anger appeared to be less ideologically grounded in Africa and the Middle East and therefore less oriented against neoliberalization itself. In this respect, Latin America must certainly be regarded as the exception, and attending to the dynamics of popular anger in Africa and the Middle East may actually hold more clues to the nature of popular discontent in most of the world.

The principal work examining this question of anti-adjustment uprisings is John Walton and David Seddon's edited volume *Free Markets and Food Riots*. Published in 1994, it laid the foundations for a transnational comparison by associating "food riots" with policies advocated by and adopted on the initiative of international financial institutions in the context of the neoliberal turn.[21] The authors dedicated separate chapters to each of the continents on which these riots occurred and provided a mapping and chronology of these moments of insurrection. Each contribution looked at the protests from a particular angle, particularly by linking structural adjustment to democratization processes in Africa. In the Middle East and North Africa, by contrast, the role of Islamist

19. Javier Auyero, *Routine Politics and Violence in Argentina: The Gray Zone of the State* (Cambridge, 2007). On the failure of the Argentinian state, see also Quentin Deforge and Benjamin Lemoine, "Faillite d'État et fragilité juridique. L'Argentine face à l'ordre financier international", *Actes de la recherche en sciences sociales*, 221–222:1 (2018), pp. 38–63; on the mobilization by the trade unions, see Maurizio Atzeni, *Workplace Conflict: Mobilization and Solidarity in Argentina* (Basingstoke, 2010), ch. 3.

20. Johanna Siméant, "Protester/mobiliser/ne pas consentir. Sur quelques avatars de la sociologie des mobilisations appliquée au continent africain", *Revue internationale de politique comparée*, 20:2 (2013), pp. 125–143.

21. John K. Walton and David Seddon (eds), *Free Markets and Food Riots* (Oxford [etc.], 1994).

movements is considered central. When applied to the regions we are looking at here, these two interpretative keys have often had the effect of folding the social issue into questions of political and/or religious transformations that are intended to direct people's aspirations towards a "return to traditions". "Modern food riots" are therefore claimed to be episodes that mark a form of nostalgia in the face of the transformations under way in the modern world.[22]

The analyses found in Walton and Seddon's book are a product of their time, but for many years they seem to have determined the perspective to be adopted when addressing the question of anti-austerity uprisings and the people involved in them. The outbreak of the Arab revolutions therefore revealed the limited toolkit available to specialists on the region when analysing social movements outside identity- or religion-based distinctions. The protests were seen as a (secular) confrontation between modernists and traditionalists, and between laypersons and religious figures.[23] The history of the uprisings was generally subsumed by these interpretative keys. The abundant literature produced on the uprisings of 2010 and 2011 opened up an extensive area of discussion about the nature of mobilizations in the region and attributed a more important place to the intertwining of political expectations and everyday material aspirations. However, it offered little space to historiography of past mobilizations, in which these uprisings were also anchored. John Chalcraft's 2016 book gave meagre room to the uprisings of the 1980s, which took place in an era he described as "Islamism, Revolution, Uprisings and Liberalism".[24] Social issues were subsumed in recurrent discussions that tended to dominate, such as the causes of the "revolutionary emergence", especially the situation of "unemployed graduates" and obstacles to employment; organizational continuities, which focused on the role of trade unions (especially in Tunisia, Egypt, and Sudan),[25] the new digital activists, and non-governmental organizations (NGOs) in the uprisings; and finally, the disparities between rural and urban worlds, pointing out that the protests were not limited to lower- or middle-class urban sectors of society.[26]

22. Alan Richards and John Waterbury, *A Political Economy of the Middle East: State, Class, and Economic Development* (Boulder, CO, 1990).

23. Michaelle L. Browers, *Political Ideology in the Arab World: Accommodation and Transformation* (Cambridge, 2009). The case of Algeria, where social protests preceded a period of violence similar to a long civil war, is a good example of this. Some helpful reflections can be found in Hugh Roberts, "Moral Economy or Moral Polity? The Political Anthropology of Algerian Riots", Crisis States Programme, Working Papers Series no. 1 (London, 2002); *idem*, *The Battlefield. Algeria 1988–2002: Studies in a Broken Polity* (London, 2003).

24. John Chalcraft, *Popular Politics in the Making of the Modern Middle East* (Cambridge, 2016), ch. 4, 1977–2011.

25. J. Beinin and F. Vairel (eds), *Social Movements, Mobilization, and Contestation in the Middle East and North Africa* (Stanford, CA, 2013).

26. Habib Ayeb, "Social and Political Geography of the Tunisian Revolution: The Alfa Grass Revolution", *Review of African Political Economy*, 38 (2011), pp. 467–479; Habib Ayeb and

By studying the social uprisings against structural adjustments in Africa and the Middle East since the mid-1970s, this Special Issue intends to highlight the long-standing reality of discontent with capitalism in this part of world. But we do not simply claim to make a contribution towards filling a gap. We also aim to stimulate a more general reflection on popular feelings and social responses to neoliberalism beyond the locations under consideration. Some anthropologists have argued that Africa offers a privileged vantage point for understanding neoliberalism from a more global perspective, not because the continent was a laboratory for some plan designed from above, but because the way neoliberal experiments were contested there affected how they were later "upgraded" elsewhere.[27] There is no doubt that the social responses to structural adjustments can be measured there better than they can elsewhere.[28] The contributions in this Special Issue therefore echo other situations that have occurred recently, far from Africa and the Middle East. Was a country such as Greece, which was placed under the tutelage of the IMF and the European Central Bank in 2015, not "adjusted" as other countries further south had been thirty years earlier? Equally, was a problem such as debt – to which Hélène Baillot returns in this issue – not more specifically associated with so-called developing countries by international bodies before appearing today as a problem common to (nearly) all countries?[29]

The echoes between the present and the recent past are important. The underlying resemblances and specificities can be harnessed as a tool for understanding the particular circumstances that gave rise to the revolts we explore in this issue. It is not self-evident that past disorders should be treated as actions taken against the IMF, the World Bank, or the SAPs, just as it is not self-evident that they should be lumped together in the same category. The term "food riots" that Walton and Seddon use in their book was applied too quickly in the media at the time of the uprisings. Although the food issue is at the heart of the conflicts described here, it is, as Charles Tilly wrote, not as the subject of the conflict but as the place for expressing a desire for social justice and dignity.[30] Louise Tilly's work on the ties between conflicts, states, and issues of subsistence clearly shows the complex links among them. In her view, conflicts

---

Ray Bush, *Food Insecurity and Revolution in the Middle East and North Africa: Agrarian Questions in Egypt and Tunisia* (London, 2019).

27. See in particular Graham Harrison, *Neo-liberal Africa: The Impact of Global Social Engineering* (London, 2010); Jean and John Comaroff, *Theory from the South: Or, How Euro-America Is Evolving Toward Africa* (Boulder, CO, 2011).

28. Michael Bratton, Robert Mattes, and E. Gyimah-Boadi, *Public Opinion, Democracy, and Market Reform in Africa* (Cambridge, 2004).

29. As shown by David Graeber's bestseller *Debt: The First 5,000 Years* (New York, 2011).

30. Conflicts "occurred not so much where men were hungry as where they believed that others were unjustly depriving them of food to which they had a moral and political right", in "Food Supply and Public Order in Modern Europe", in Charles Tilly (ed.), *The Formation of Nation States in Western Europe* (Princeton, NJ, 1975), pp. 380–455, cit. p. 389.

emerge in the state of tension between the expansion of the market and state centralization.[31] In the cases that are of interest to us here, new regulation devices were created within the context of adjustment, which apparently dispossesses the state of its functions of providing provisions and regulations. The purpose of our work is therefore to reach a more general understanding of "adjusted societies" and the political economy deployed in them through the protest movements and anger that shook them.

MULTIPLE SOCIAL CONFLICTS WITH A SHARED FOUNDATION

Should we consider the conflicts that took place in the context of structural adjustments in the light of their own particular features? Is each case resistant to our temptation to unify them retrospectively around common categories of analysis? What is the threshold of commonality?

These questions affect the complicated interplay between what really happened; the way events were experienced, written down, remembered, forgotten, and silenced; and how we historians understand these processes. Foucault's genealogical approach invites us to chart the hidden diachronic and synchronic dispersions of knowledge, to demystify master narratives, and to identify our own place in them.[32] Aleatory attention to the apparently irrational actions led us to observe a first principle: the uprisings that are the subject of this work are disparate. There are multiple differences between the protest movements against the high cost of living that broke out in the working-class districts of Egyptian towns in the 1970s (Henry and Soliman); the student protests in Niger (Bonnecase) and the urban riots in Tunisia (Dakhli) in the 1980s; the caustic humour of Togolese cartoonists directed against the government (Frisch) and the more latent criticism of the regime by Ethiopian peasants (Labzaé and Planel); the international debt-cancellation campaign in the 2000s (Baillot); the campaigns to boycott the production of cotton started by Burkinabe peasant farmers (Engels); and the more head-on opposition of Jordanians to the privatization of mining companies in the 2010s (Lacouture). In addition to belonging to different contexts, each of these mobilizations was inspired by different actors who had different

31. Louise Tilly, "Food Entitlement, Famine, and Conflict", *Journal of Interdisciplinary History*, 2:1 (1983), pp. 23–57.
32. Michel Foucault, "Nietzsche, la généalogie l'histoire", in *Dits et écrits*, vol. 2 (Paris, 1994), p. 1009; Paul Rabinow, *The Foucault Reader* (Harmondsworth, 1991), pp. 76–100: "To follow the complex course of descent is to maintain passing events in their proper dispersion; it is to identify the accidents, the minute deviations – or conversely, the complete reversals – the errors, the false appraisals, and the faulty calculations that gave birth to those things that continue to exist and have value for us; it is to discover that truth or being does not lie at the root of what we know and what we are, but the exteriority of accidents." (p. 81)

repertoires of contention and gave different meanings both to their uprisings and to the situation that had caused them to revolt.

The same may be said of the heterogeneity that predominates – to varying degrees – within each uprising. As Leyla Dakhli shows, the riots that broke out in Tunis in January 1984 mobilized young people from the areas affected, women dismayed by measures that impacted their ability to manage their daily lives, students and high school pupils accustomed to going out to proclaim their opposition to an authoritarian regime, and militants from the extreme left whose protests were part of a longer tradition. The question of why all these different groups rebelled at the same time elicited an apparently inconsistent array of recriminations and demands; however, these actors came together to produce an uprising that could draw on yet more actors who had demonstrated in Douz and other Tunisian cities in previous months. The heterogeneous nature of social movements is a key point stressed by Michel Dobry in his analysis of political crises: "It is for different 'reasons', 'motives' or 'interests', or better, under the effect of causal series or determinations that are broadly independent of each other that groups or individuals in different locations are encouraged to take up mobilizations started by others, to invest them with different meanings and, by 'joining the game', give them different historical trajectories."[33] One might even say, counter-intuitively and in contrast to certain approaches that focus on the alignment of the frames from which people view their situation,[34] that this heterogeneity is one of the important conditions for an uprising to prosper and bring together growing numbers of participants.

Finally, the genealogical method also considers the actors' self-interpretations. Usually, a struggle for meaning occurs rapidly around the events. It is perceptible in the contrasting insertions in chronologies: for many militants, the 1977 insurrection in Alexandria seemed to be the last in a cycle of decade-long protests against the gradual disintegration of Nasser's promises, while others (Henry) saw a new form of anger emerging. As a general matter, the uprisings discussed here are often placed "alongside" the normal course of events. They appear as incursions at a particular time that break up the evolution of each of the countries towards economic, social, and institutional reforms and cultural transformations. In some cases, they seem retrospectively to be the symptoms of a social and/or political disturbance that announces more widespread protests. Frequently, they are viewed as benign, episodic outbursts or rebellions that must be overcome in the same way as one overcomes resistance from a piece of machinery that has jammed slightly.

33. Michel Dobry, *Sociologie des crises politiques. La dynamique des mobilisations multisectorielles* (Paris, 2009), pp. 21–22.
34. David Snow, Burke Rochford, Steven Worden, and Robert Benford, "Frame Alignment Processes, Micromobilization, and Movement Participation", *American Sociological Review*, 51:4 (1986), pp. 464–481.

A second empirical finding has led us to conclude that when interpretative unity materializes, it is rarely the starting premise. Rather, it is more often constructed within a framework of mobilizations that can themselves lead to interpretative struggles while they are taking place. In this case, we see that rebels are transformed by the rebellion itself, as part of a process that has been well described by historians of uprisings and revolutions.[35] The main purpose of this issue, therefore, is what we call "the event". We have chosen to place the event at the centre of our analysis, because we contend that, through this perspective, we can capture the field of interpretations that the protagonists themselves have opened up, whether meaning is embodied in concrete symbolic action (street demonstrations or clashes) or in more discreet acts of disruption.

Generally, the dissenting populations we deal with here rarely took to the streets explicitly to protest against neoliberalism or SAPs; rather, they came out to protest against their most practical everyday manifestations: price increases; the brutal nature of public sector reforms; the deterioration of school and health systems; clientelism; poor housing; dependence on the prices of raw materials; or an entire series of combined factors that led to a sense of injustice. The heterogeneous motives and interpretations effectively shape a protest space where this feeling of injustice is expressed collectively, whether it be associated with practices of power, a particular social condition, or the development of the economic situation. When taken together – or even separately – all these reasons constitute a red line, an offence to dignity that can serve as a trigger, but also as a binder for what is a fundamentally disparate popular feeling of anger.

Similarly, unity of action has rarely been achieved against the IMF or the World Bank (whose absolute discretion is noteworthy). In the various uprisings we review here, protests have displayed greater unity against the state, which has de facto played an important role in the implementation of the SAPs, or even relied on them to develop new means of indirect government (as Mehdi Labzaé and Sabine Planel, and Bettina Engels, demonstrate in particular on the subject of rural production, and as Robin Frisch's cartoons also show). The post-colonial context makes it possible to understand this particular relationship with the state. What unites the locations under review is that most of the states are former colonies. The sites are relatively recent independent legal entities, with the exception of Ethiopia, and to a lesser extent Egypt. Post-independence regimes sought to build legitimacy on the idea of popular accountability and an anti-colonial orientation. Sovereignty was thought to have a material component, ensuring dignity for former colonial subjects. SAPs led to dispossession and hit hard the social pact established after independence. Although the reforms tended

---

35. Timothy Tackett, *Becoming a Revolutionary: The Deputies of the French National Assembly and the Emergence of a Revolutionary Culture (1789–1790)* (University Park, PA, 2006).

to dispossess the state of some of its prerogatives, and in particular to erode its role as a protector, the state was (still) found to be responsible for these forced divestments. The state itself took on new contours under SAPs, when read through the lens of these protests: its rules were more abstruse, as were the interests it embodied, when the government authorities formed alliances with those who benefited from the "reforms", as Robin Frisch shows in the case of Togo. Although it cannot be denied today that liberalization policies accentuated disparities in wealth and access to healthcare, education, and social services, it is vital to underline the extent to which their implementation directly contradicted the principles laid down by the new states following independence, as well as the extent to which such policies caused problems – and offered opportunities – for the countries' elites and emerging middle classes. However, in a number of cases the principles laid down by new states in the first flush of independence had already been violated by forms of post-colonial state practices themselves. The persistence of social inequalities, the creation of new bourgeoisies, the repression of dissent – there is a whole range of pre-existing resentments and grievances that were exacerbated by the neoliberal turn. This may also explain why this turn appeared as an opportunity for a good part of the post-colonial elites and why the grievances were often framed as a desire to go back to "the good old days".

Although the interpretations, motivations, and forms of these uprisings were extremely diverse, there are various elements that allow us to restore a common basis and include them in a particular historical moment. On the one hand, these uprisings faced similar realities, such as price increases, unemployment – especially in public services – and hospital and school closures. All these concrete realities were linked to neoliberal policies, albeit this link was not explicitly made by the protesters. The genealogical method allows us to move beyond a nominalist posture that would only consider the categories used by the actors themselves. On the other hand, most of these uprisings were based on the agreed perception that the state was no longer meeting its social obligations. Recourse to E.P. Thompson's notion of moral economy is decisive here, and a number of articles, especially those by Matthew Lacouture and Mélanie Henry, stress the importance of studying articulations of moral economy from actor perspectives. This leads us to question the common representations of what is fair or unfair, of what united – or failed to unite – people in revolt.[36] The emphasis on moral economies makes it possible to demonstrate that the struggle against the IMF may exist de facto (for example, when one breaks the application mechanisms of neoliberal policies), even when the rebels' intention was

---

36. Edward Thompson, "The Moral Economy of the English Crowd in the Eighteenth Century", *Past and Present*, 50 (1971), pp. 76–136. See also Barrington Moore, *Injustice: The Social Bases of Obedience and Revolt* (London, 1978).

not to oppose the IMF. It also makes it possible to show the rationale of the uprising, which is not necessarily the same as that of the international financial institutions or the governments that implement their policies (Bonnecase).

HOW ACTION IS TAKEN: DESCRIBING IN ORDER TO UNDERSTAND

Most of the articles collected here use a similar ethnographic method. They deal with events, many of which take place in a relatively short period of time. Throughout the issue, these events are described and reconstructed. Similarly to Alain Dewerpe reflecting on the repression of the demonstration of 8 February 1962 in Paris, we study uprisings and the state violence that gave rise to them so that we can look anew at their genesis. Like him, we believe that these episodes can be "read as disorder, an abnormal or even unacceptable event, a scandal as short as an affair, [that] are part of a practical history of the *"raison d'État"*.[37] These events leave a trace because they carry collective emotions within them, especially through death, but also through the micro-resistances that can lead to victories. We have brought together specific cases and have assumed the role of historians of events, making it possible to think about more general phenomena that might be called the *"raison d'état* of neo-liberal states".

This descriptive, events-based approach involves a number of challenges. The first is to understand the moment when widespread anger turns into open revolt. It is often the meeting point between a favourable context for anger, as a result of situations of suffering and injustice that are experienced as such by those who are subject to them, and triggering events and disruptive accidents that cause things to tip over.[38] When taken individually, neither of these two terms would be enough to explain the path to revolt. As far as suffering is concerned, it has become commonplace, following the works of E.P. Thompson, to abandon any kind of objective criteria.[39] It is not because populations are suffering that they revolt – as if above a certain threshold of unsustainability one necessarily moves to mobilization – but it is possible to go even further: it is no longer enough to feel that suffering is unfair in order to mobilize. This can be seen in the case of Ethiopia, which teaches us that non-mobilization is not the same thing as consent. For historians who

37. Alain Dewerpe, *Charonne, 8 février 1962. Anthropologie historique d'un massacre d'état* (Paris, 2006), p. 16.
38. Edgar Morin, "Pour une sociologie de la crise", *Communications*, 12 (*La prise de la parole*) (1968), pp. 2–16, p. 5.
39. Thompson, "The Moral Economy of the English Crowd".

are paying close attention, non-mobilization enables other forms of "low scale criticism" or resistance at an individual level (Labzaé and Planel). In Niger, too, mobilizations against the powers-that-be thinned out when the level of perceived injustice and popular incomprehension regarding the government seemed to reach a peak (Bonnecase).

Situations of perceived suffering and injustice are not inherently enough to trigger events or to explain the passage to an uprising. The assembled articles highlight various forms of these events – some of which are dramatic – that have the effect of mobilizing far more diverse categories of people than had driven them initially, as well as others that appear to be more banal, as when the managers of an organization of manufacturers belittle the material expectations of those doing the manufacturing, who promptly amplify their demands in response (Engels). It is neither a question of attributing a single cause to these events, nor of limiting the study to the effects of violent official responses on the development of a particular uprising. An event should be read from an interactionist standpoint regarding the uprising's outbreak and process. These interactions may play out at a very small level around a market where the municipal authorities send the police to confront a group of elderly people expressing their anxiety about a price increase (Dakhli), or around a bridge blockade the police consider to be a red line that cannot be crossed, and the protesters an obstacle to overcome (Bonnecase). Power structures may participate in the narrative of an uprising and the actual event that may develop out of this scripting: in Suez in 1977, communist militants, to whom the government – wrongly – attributed central responsibility for the riots, were imprisoned and retrospectively elevated to leadership of the movement, a role they actually took up at a later date (Soliman).

The second challenge that arises out of this descriptive approach is to interpret the ways in which uprisings occur: they can differ from one country to another and even within the same country, depending on the various profiles of the insurgents. We see common features from one article to another. Strikes and protests, for example, are often treated as part of a "repertoire of collective contention".[40] One also finds older forms, like riots hatched in more limited social spaces such as a district, while also showing a gradation in the use of violence. Clearly, it is important to ask when and how the specific social and political situation gives way to some other form, or why, in certain situations, riots multiply to the detriment of other more peaceful modes of mobilization:[41] in Niger, violence was apparently a normal recourse to collective action from the standpoint of mobilized individuals who had initially expressed their anger within the legal context (Bonnecase). Finally, we find forms of protest that are specific to certain

---

40. Charles Tilly, "Les origines du répertoire d'action collective contemporaine en France et en Grande-Bretagne", *Vingtième Siècle. Revue d'histoire*, 4:1 (1984), pp. 89–108.
41. Alain Bertho, *Le temps des émeutes* (Paris, 2009).

countries or particular socio-professional bodies, such as the boycott of cotton production by Burkinabe farmers (Engels).

The need to take the various forms of rebellion into account goes together with the need to consider everyone's specific forms of participation in an uprising. It is essential to look at the role played by the least visible actors, such as farmers alongside city-dwellers (Engels, Labzaé and Planel); activists from the South next to those from the North in the context of a transnational mobilization (Baillot); and women alongside men. While some of the contributions highlight women's struggles in mobilizations that are essentially managed by men, others illustrate their central role in articulating causes that impact everyday material life or as hardened managers of the household economy, as well as in episodes of direct confrontation with the police (Dakhli, Frisch).[42] Female activists' invisibility seems to be more apparent in structured movements such as the fight against the privatization of joint property in Jordan (Lacouture) or the international debt cancellation campaign (Baillot).

Thirdly, it is also important to look at the role of people who do not belong to political organizations alongside that of those who do. With regard to some of the paradigms of the sociology of mobilizations, there is critical literature on the academic tendency to overvalue the role of organizations in triggering an uprising, the direction it takes, and the meaning attributed to it.[43] The articles in this issue reveal a multitude of configurations: mobilizations that are clearly anchored within an organizational space (such as the debt cancellation campaigns analysed by Hélène Baillot or the defence of a "moral economy of national resources" discussed by Matthew Lacouture); mobilizations in which organizations initially played a leading role before incorporating non-organized individuals (the Association of Nigerian Students at the beginning of the 1990s); mobilizations in which the less visible networks of everyday life were far more important than the organizational base (as was the case with the riots studied by Nayera Soliman, Mélanie Henry, and Leyla Dakhli, or the gestures of resistance highlighted by Mehdi Labzaé and Sabine Planel); or, finally, mobilizations in which organizations that were supposed to mediatize the expectations of those who were mobilizing served more as a screen than a relay (the National Union of Cotton Producers of which Bettina Engels writes, before other protest organizations became part of the struggle). In all these cases, it is important not to take at face value the words and methods of those who were most visible. The militant space may also be a space for a form of relative subordination, which also plays a role in how an event unfolds and the traces it leaves behind, on which historians later rely when they re-examine what occurred.

---

42. See also Véronique Gago, *Economies populaires et luttes féministes. Résister au néolibéralisme en Amérique du Sud* (Paris, 2020).
43. Jean-Gabriel Contamin, "Cadrages et luttes de sens", in Éric Agrikoliansky (ed.), *Penser les mouvements sociaux. Conflits sociaux et contestations dans les sociétés contemporaines* (Paris, 2010), pp. 55–75.

This goes together with a fourth challenge: what does one decide to include and not to include in these descriptions, and in the political space of dissent in general? This question already exists for contemporaries themselves, none of whom would have necessarily embraced the same idea of what is political. It is also standard practice for representatives of a government or security forces to make distinctions between good protesters who express their anger by lawful means and criminals who profit from social mobilization to commit acts of theft or destruction. However, this distinction tends to be part of the practical modes of repression and ultimately the restoration of the status quo ante.[44] Some mobilizations may therefore become disfigured – if not actually deliberately erased – by a *raison d'état* that distorts their meaning. For example, the events in Egypt in 1977 turned into attempted destabilization orchestrated by "communists" (Henry, Soliman), while those in Tunisia in 1983–1984 were portrayed as a power grab started by "Islamists" (Dakhli), and in many cases these groups, which were considered as such, were described as the "usual suspects", to use Matthew Lacouture's term.

Those who mobilize are also shaped by divisive tactics, however, and each of them will have a more or less extensive understanding of the space of mobilization and the practices that ought to be included within it. In Tunis, in 1984, therefore, not everyone viewed looting shops and homes in the middle-class districts as the equivalent of the destruction of places that had direct associations with the state, such as police stations or local town halls. This selective perception of events – or what was considered to be a part of the event – became stronger with the passage of time. Contemporaries recalled the image of bread riots against the government. The privileged also recalled the revolt by the underclass against inequalities that, at the time, led to "a fear of the rich" (Dakhli). The Togolese cartoons studied by Robin Frisch are also narratives. They show us a representation of power relations at work and blend popular representations of the economy with criticisms of the governing elites. More generally, we see in the articles that the memories that follow events are divided. They are retained in the form of stories that often omit certain elements, such as the community nature of mobilizations, local solidarity, or class struggle. Here, the question of selection is also one for the historian using the genealogical method and trying to adapt her/his narrative strategies to relate past insurrections to present audiences.

This also raises the more general question of how we understand what it means to be "political" in situations of heightened social tensions. Many researchers have suggested extending the meaning of the political to "non-movements" or to the "quiet encroachment of the ordinary" as forms of

---

44. Vincent Bonnecase, "Ce que les ruines racontent d'une insurrection. Morales du vol et de la violence au Burkina Faso pendant les journées insurrectionnelles des 30 et 31 octobre 2014", *Sociétés politiques comparées*, 38 (2016), pp. 1–36. Available at: http://www.fasopo.org/sites/default/files/varia2_n38.pdf; last accessed 12 January 2021.

everyday activism.[45] Others invite us to reassess the "weapons of the weak" as tools of resistance in everyday life.[46] Yet others have focused on seeking politics from below, outside its more expected spaces of expression.[47] Here, it has not been a question of seeing politics everywhere, let alone one of resistance to SAPs, which would have removed any specific meaning from the notion: if everything is political in the end, nothing is political in particular anymore. To varying degrees, the contributors to this work have made an effort to seek the social responses to structural adjustments beyond their most visible and noisy dimensions. What was important to us was not to separate the clear – and frequently collective – process methods from a wider range of practices used by people to confront what they see as unjust.[48] The purchase of fertilizers on the black market (Labzaé and Planel) and their diversion for purposes other than those intended by the government (Engels), the way a president is drawn (Frisch), or even the name given to a bottle of beer (Bonnecase) can therefore also speak to us of popular representations of the adjustment policies and an ordinary feeling of discontent towards them that may precede the transition to an uprising.

WHAT REMAINS: IMAGERY, EMOTIONS, AND STORIES

The uprisings studied in this Special Issue have mainly been considered in their contemporary context from the point of view of the actors and those who were involved in them in one way or another. But there is also the question of collective memory that may remain and may still be part of political processes. The issue here is how events live on through the ways different actors continue to grapple with them. William Sewell famously showed that the various means of portraying the taking of the Bastille only a short time after it happened contributed to making it a central event in the revolution. In fact, much can be said in the same vein about how French Republicans picked up the story a century later.[49] How did the various uprisings studied in this work – and their repressions – continue to mark political trajectories in the countries involved, or even beyond them?

---

45. Asef Bayat, "Activism and Social Development in the Middle East", *International Journal of Middle East Studies*, 34 (2002), pp. 1–28, and *Life as Politics: How Ordinary People Change the Middle East* (Stanford, CA, 2010).
46. James C. Scott, *Weapons of the Weak: Everyday Forms of Peasant Resistance* (New Haven, CT [etc.], 1985).
47. Jean-François Bayart, Achille Mbembe, and Comi Toulabor, *Le politique par le bas en Afrique noire*. Nouvelle édition augmentée (Paris, 2008).
48. Michel Offerlé, "Retour critique sur les répertoires de l'action collective (XVIIIe–XXIe siècles)", *Politix*, 81:1 (2008), pp. 181–202.
49. William Sewell, "Historical Events as Transformations of Structures: Inventing Revolution at the Bastille", *Theory and Society*, 25 (1996), pp. 841–881.

Firstly, the potential of uprisings to be remembered and invoked has not been the same in all cases. There is a striking contrast between the 1977 riots, which have remained a central component of revolutionary memory in Egypt (Henry, Soliman), and those of 1983, which are almost forgotten in recollections of revolutionary Tunisia today (Dakhli). Equally, some elements of an uprising may remain more present in the political imagination than others within the same country, even though the political weight of one over the other may not have been clear for contemporaries at the time of the events.[50] The more or less significant presence of one element or another is not the same in the minds of individuals, and the notion of collective memory sometimes leads to minimizing the differences in the issue, as Mélanie Henry notes. For example, the communists in Egypt did not view the conflicts around the Arsenal in Alexandria, which has remained a symbol of their struggle, in the same way as others did (Henry). Similarly, in Niger, the death of three young demonstrators in February 1990 at the end of the one-party regime is not appropriated either in the same manner or by the same people in all cases as that of a student death in March 1994 in the early days of democracy, even though the two events were part of the same cycle of mobilizations against the liberalization of education and showed certain similarities from the point of view of a good number of contemporaries (Bonnecase).

It is therefore important to take a fresh look at the practical challenges posed by these contradictions and to ask why some veterans have good reasons to appropriate one element or episode while others recall another. Different mnemonic mobilizations can also lead to conflict between a militant memory backed by shared symbols, on the one hand, and an ordinary memory that is more informed by personal life or that of the predecessors, on the other hand. There may also be discrepancies between an official memory that has been intentionally constructed for political ends and popular memories that are detached from these stakes. Although we reflect on this aspect, it still needs to be pursued further, especially because the general observation from which we started remains an open one. The fact that anti-austerity uprisings since the 1980s have been somewhat devalued in people's memories – as well as in the scientific literature – in comparison with what they might have represented for contemporaries at the time is no trivial matter: the countries concerned have been expressing the same general orientation towards a neoliberal political economy ever since.

Secondly, if one considers the persistence of a neoliberal political and economic orientation, these various uprisings have, on the whole, been branded a failure. This does not mean they had no political effect. Far from it: for

---

50. To continue the comparison with the French Revolution, if we follow Sewell, "Historical Events", this was the case with the taking of the Bastille and the taking of the Invalides on the same day.

instance, the uprisings against the privatization of higher education led to a more general opposition to the military regime in Niger, culminating in the transition to democracy. However, the uprisings failed to reverse the social and economic policies that were being driven by international financial institutions. This raises the question of post-insurrection disappointment that some of us touch on: some years after the uprisings in the Arab world and in sub-Saharan Africa – beginning with Burkina Faso in 2014 – melancholia still looms large. How can disenchantment be adapted and transformed, and how can defeats bequeath lessons for the future? Through their hopes and disappointments, the revolts we have looked at carry unmet promises that we can see in today's movements. The problem remains to understand and demonstrate how these emotions and their traces develop when memories of the events may have been obscured.

One essential point emerges from a number of the contributions, however: neoliberal reforms were initially implemented by military regimes before being continued either by democratic or pluralist regimes (in the case of Niger studied by Vincent Bonnecase and that of Togo studied by Robin Frisch), or by revolutionary regimes (as in the case of Ethiopia studied by Mehdi Labzaé and Sabine Panel). Democratic and revolutionary disenchantment goes hand in hand with the retrospective enchantment with past authoritarian regimes – "romanticizing the good old days", to use the words of Mehdi Labzaé and Sabine Planel. These regimes were associated with a time when the state took more responsibility for its food- and law-related obligations, including when they took a paternalistic form. This modern process of re-enchantment, which has been noted by E.P. Thompson with regard to Tudor England,[51] remains fairly strong in many countries studied here, so that Kountché in Niger, Nasser in Egypt, and Bourguiba in Tunisia enjoy retroactive popularity today. This raises much more than challenges of reassembled memories or gaps between memory and historical reality: the re-evaluation of authoritarian regimes, which is the flip side of a devaluation of certain democratic and revolutionary experiences, has profound effects even today on the relationships people may have with the institutions or the very idea of democracy. While everywhere in the world democracies may also find themselves under fire when "economic rationality" tells them to go against the wishes of the people, it is important to continue to reflect by looking back on these African and Middle Eastern precedents.

What this means is that the current political stakes of the topic must be underlined. Indeed, we feel obliged to provide a concluding note of self-reflexivity on our choice of subject, if not its direction. We should mention here that the two organizers of this project have participated in anti-austerity

---

51. E.P. Thompson, "Moral Economy Reviewed", in *Customs in Common* (London, 1991), pp. 259–35, p. 298.

protests, mainly in Europe, in what was then called the movement against neo-liberalism and alter-globalization. Since the late 1990s, we have witnessed the increasingly repressive response to mobilizations against the G8, G20, and other financial institutions, as well as the enthusiasm these mobilizations generated at international social forums in the South and North alike. It is no small matter for us to work on this issue twenty years later, when rejection of structural adjustments is more broadly shared in Africa and the Middle East, as well as Asia and Latin America. In our opinion, this backdrop of shared political struggles has not been a hindrance to the need to be scientific, but it has certainly encouraged us to put things more directly, to tackle the topic head on, and to keep our academic superegos in check. We hope that our background has honed our hearing to understand what the rebels were whispering as well as shouting. While the processes described in this Special Issue are still under way well beyond Africa and the Middle East, it seems essential to us to break a lance for committed history.

IRSH 66 (2021), pp. 23–40 doi:10.1017/S0020859021000109
© The Author(s), 2021. Published by Cambridge University Press on behalf of the
Internationaal Instituut voor Sociale Geschiedenis

Remembering the 1977 Bread Riots in Suez: Fragments and Ghosts of Resistance

NAYERA ABDELRAHMAN SOLIMAN

Freie Universität Berlin
Berlin 14195, Germany

E-mail: nayera.ar@gmail.com

ABSTRACT: Most of the existing literature on the 1977 Bread Riots focuses on the protests as an episode in larger national and international political and economic waves of change, either as the end of an era of political mobilization in Egypt, or the beginning of an era of anti-neoliberal struggles in the region and wider world. Moreover, most of the literature focuses on Cairo. Seeking to diverge from the trend even further, this article focuses on the memory of the 1977 uprising in the city of Suez, which it explores through the perspectives of leftist activists and others. It aims to understand how the people of Suez who witnessed and participated in the 1977 protests remember and interpret the event today, asking what memory of the uprising means politically on a local level. By exploring the memory of the 1977 protests in Suez, this article traces their effects on the lives of the selected interlocutors, and also on their political actions and interpretations. It follows three memory fragments of the 1977 protests in Suez from three different vantage points: the position of people who were members of political organizations before the protests; the traces of protests in Suez's streets; and the position of those who witnessed the protests from home.

On 25 January 1977, the front page of the prominent Egyptian newspaper *Al Ahram* (Figure 1) announced, "the arrest of a student cell headed by a teacher in Suez".[1] The main headline proclaimed the capture of documents that proved members of a secret communist organization had planned the fires that erupted across Cairo on 18–19 January 1977. On 17 January, the Deputy Prime Minister for Financial and Economic Matters, Dr Abdel-Moneim El-Qaissouny, gave a speech in front of the People's Assembly, the lower house of the Egyptian parliament, in which he announced the imposition of economic austerity measures, including substantial cuts to government subsidies on select essential goods.[2]

---

1. *Al Ahram* is one of the main official newspapers in Egypt, founded in 1875.
2. Ahmed Seddik Saad, حاجتنا الي استراتيجية اشتراكية جديدة [Our Need for a New Social Strategy], 2008. Available at https://modernization-adil.blogspot.com/2008/12/blog-post_9762.html; last accessed 2 January 2021.

Figure 1. Front page, *Al Ahram* newspaper, 25 January 1977.

The price of bread, sugar, tea, cooking oil, and rice would rise by between twenty-five and fifty per cent. He described these measures as prerequisites for receiving funds from the International Monetary Fund (IMF) and World Bank. The decision was announced in newspapers and on the radio on 18 January as "proposed" measures, though they were actually an executive order that took effect immediately, and prices increased that same day.[3] Protests against the austerity measures in Cairo started with workers from the city's industrial southern suburb of Helwan,[4] who were soon joined by students and other social groups.[5] Meanwhile, simultaneous protests sprang up in other major Egyptian cities, namely, Alexandria, Suez, Mansoura, Qena, and Aswan.

Most of the existing literature on the 1977 Bread Riots focuses on the protests as an episode in larger national and international political and economic waves of change,[6] either as the end of an era of political mobilization in Egypt,

3. *Ibid.*
4. As part of Nasser's industrialization policy in the 1950s, a large industrial complex was built in Helwan, including steel, iron, textile, and cement factories.
5. Hossam El-Hamalawy, "1977: The Lost Revolution" (Master's thesis, American University in Cairo, 2001).
6. At the international level, both in press coverage and scholarly works, Egypt's January 1977 protests, known as the Bread Riots, have come to be considered one of the first anti-IMF protests.

or the beginning of an era of anti-neoliberal struggles in the region and in the wider world.[7] Moreover, most of the literature focuses on Cairo. In one of the few studies of the 1977 protests that breaks with this Cairo-centric trend, Henry (2018) draws on oral accounts of leftist activists to trace the "treasure" of revolutionary experience and its transmission between three revolutionary events in Alexandria, including the 1977 uprising.[8]

Seeking to diverge from the trend even further, this article focuses on the memory of the 1977 uprising in the city of Suez, which it explores through the perspectives of leftist activists and others. It aims to understand how the people of Suez who witnessed and participated in the 1977 protests remember and interpret the event today, asking what memory of the uprising means politically on a local level. Over the course of a two-month stay in the city in 2018, I asked numerous inhabitants, all of whom could be characterized as middle class by Egyptian standards,[9] how they remembered the 1977 protests in Suez. Where did their memory of the protests start? What stands out in their memory? How do they interpret these events more than forty years later?

The protests were among the biggest seen in Egypt since the July 1952 revolution/coup,[10] Suez was not an exception in this matter. Public and private buildings were attacked and burnt, as well as buses and cars. In response,

See: A.C. Drainville, "The Moral Economy of Global Crowds: Egypt 1977, Brazil 2013", *New Global Studies*, 9 (2015), pp. 101–124.

7. At the national level, the protests became the subject of much analysis regarding the role of Egyptian communists and leftists. See: Hussein AbdelRazik, ٩١ ٨١ و مصر وثائقية سياسية دراسة :يناير (Egypt on 18 and 19 January: A Documentary Political Study) (Cairo, 1984); Saad, "Our Need for a New Social Strategy"; Hossam El-Hamalawy, "1977: The Lost Revolution".

8. Mélanie Henry, "Le "trésor" révolutionnaire. Insurrections et militantismes à Alexandrie en 1946 et 1977, Égypte" (Ph.D., Université D'Aix-Marseille, 2018).

9. This paper is based on oral history interviews conducted with five men and one woman in Suez between November and December 2018. Two men were part of a political organization during the 1977 protests. One was a teacher and the other was starting his career in a governmental institution. Two men who witnessed the 1977 protests in the streets were not part of a political organization, but were close to the local political elite. One participated in the protests, was a government employee and son of a famous local public figure. The other was the son of a famous butcher in Suez and working at a hotel. The last two witnessed the 1977 protests from their homes. The woman was a teacher. The man was a teenager and the son of a government employee. All my interlocutors belong to what we could call the middle class in Egypt, those who work in the public sector or own a small business. As doing fieldwork in Egypt became progressively more difficult and insecure, I was unable to extend my interviews beyond a secure and trusted network of interlocutors. Most of the names have been changed for the privacy of my interlocutors.

10. On 23 July 1952, a group of Egyptian Army officers calling themselves the "Free Officers" seized power by force in Egypt after years of popular resistance against the British occupation in the Suez Canal region, which exercised significant influence over the government in Cairo, including the king and the political elite. This "coup" was supported by protests, hence many Egyptians refer to it as a revolution. Gamal Abdel Nasser established power by 1954, becoming an idol for his promotion of an anti-colonial, pan-Arab nationalist discourse until Egypt's defeat in the Six Day War in 1967.

Sadat ordered the army to intervene to quell the unrest. On the night of 19 January, he imposed a curfew and revoked the controversial austerity measures.[11]

Suez had a special history related to the Arab–Israeli wars between 1967 and 1974. The "teacher" from Suez mentioned on the front page of *Al Ahram* taught philosophy in one of the city's schools after the inhabitants of Suez were finally allowed to return from their forced migration in the late 1960s and early 1970s. In the aftermath of the Six-Day War in June 1967, around two thirds of the Suez population had been ordered to leave the city and relocate to other villages and cities around Egypt.[12] Located on the war's front line, Israeli forces stationed on the east side of the Suez Canal attacked the city several times. On 24 October 1967, the Israeli Air Force bombed the city's petrol factories, setting Suez ablaze. As fires raged throughout the city, the Egyptian government ordered civilians to evacuate. Women, children, and elders, and also factories and their workers, were transferred elsewhere.[13] Defying the order, however, many young men and women decided to join the *fida'yyīn* (popular resistance) and stay in the city, along with a small number of state employees left to run the few remaining governmental institutions.[14] For seven years, Suez was almost vacant.

When conflict erupted with Israel on 6 October 1973, the city of Suez endured a 101-day siege lasting from October 1973 to January 1974. While Egypt considers itself to have won the war, marking its victory annually on 6 October, the city of Suez celebrates a different date: 24 October, which Suezis (the people of Suez) view as "the epitome of popular resistance prevailing over an invading military".[15] In her research on the poems and songs of *Wilad Al Ard* (Sons of the Land), an artistic troupe founded by Suezis in 1967, Alia Mossallam shows how they sought to keep "the struggle in Suez alive in the consciousness of the rest of the country".[16] She argues that some of these songs were a medium for representing *Sawayssa* (Suezi) stories of resistance, which remain underrepresented in the state's official narrative of the 1973 war, according to which the military played the primary role in the fighting.[17]

---

11. Saad, "Our Need for a New Social Strategy".
12. Mohamed Abdel Shakur, Sohair Mehanna and Nicholas S. Hopkins, "War and Forced Migration in Egypt: The Experience of Evacuation from the Suez Canal Cities 1967–1976", *Arab Studies Quarterly*, 27 (2005), pp. 22–23.
13. Ḥamid Hasab, والانتصار الحصار المقاومة؛ :مدينة تجربة السويس [Suez: The Experience of a City: The Resistance, the Siege, the Victory] (Cairo, 2001), pp. 32–39.
14. *Ibid.*
15. Alia Mossallam, "Hikāyāt Sha'b: Stories of Peoplehood. Nasserism, Popular Politics and Songs in Egypt 1956– 1973" (Ph.D., The London School of Economics and Political Science, 2012), p. 207.
16. *Ibid.* p. 210.
17. *Ibid.* pp. 222–248.

When I visited the city in 2018,[18] residents told me that Suez was the last of the three cities along the Suez Canal to be opened so its inhabitants could return. Only in 1975 were Suezis able to go in and out of the city once again without permits. According to the 1976 census, the population of Suez stood at around 193,000 inhabitants, compared to 264,000 in 1966, ten years earlier,[19] in stark contrast to the general upward trend in Egyptian population growth. Thus, when the protests against the government's austerity measures broke out in October 1977, Suezis were still coming back from their host villages and cities after seven years of forced migration (*tahgir*) and Suez was still under reconstruction. Infrastructure had not yet been redeveloped and the conditions of everyday life were unstable. Importantly, however, memories of the city's wartime resistance efforts were still present. The story of how the *fida'yyīn* fought and died to protect Suez from the Israeli invasion was dominant in the collective memory of most of my interlocutors.

In focusing on "memory" in this article, I mean both individual and collective memory. According to Boyarin, "[m]emory cannot be strictly individual, inasmuch as it is symbolic and hence intersubjective. Nor can it be literally collective, since it is not superorganic but embodied".[20] By exploring the memory of the 1977 protests in Suez, this article traces their effects on the lives of my interlocutors, but also on their political actions and interpretations. This is what Charles Tilly defines as the politics of memory, which is both "(a) the process by which accumulated, shared historical experience constrains today's political action and (b) the contestation or coercion that occurs over the [...] interpretation of that historical experience".[21]

In exploring memory, I also draw on Gyanendra Pandey's concept of "fragment", which he describes in the context of studying history with two-fold meanings as "not just a 'bit' – the dictionary's 'piece broken off' – of a preconstituted whole. Rather, it is a disturbing element, a 'disturbance', a contradiction shall we say, in the self-representation of that particular totality and those who uncritically uphold it."[22] Working with this concept of fragments helps

18. This trip comprised one of two fieldwork trips (one in 2017 and this one in 2018) for my Ph.D. research on the memory of forced migration in Suez in the aftermath of the 1967 Six Day War. During these trips, I conducted oral history interviews with thirty-seven interlocutors (fourteen women and twenty-three men). Most of them were former or current governmental employees, though a few were business owners. A small number of the women were housewives whose husbands did not have fixed jobs or were farmers.

19. "Population Census 1976. Detailed Results, Suez Governorate", *Central Agency for Public Mobilization and Statistics*, 1978, p. 14.

20. Jonathan Boyarin, "Space, Time, and the Politics of Memory", in J. Boyarin (ed.), *Remapping Memory: The Politics of Timespace* (Minneapolis, MN, 1994), p. 26.

21. Charles Tilly, "Political Memories in Space and Time", in J. Boyarin, *Remapping Memory*, p. 247.

22. Gyanendra Pandey, "Voices from the Edge: The Struggle to Write Subaltern Histories", *Ethnos*, 60:3–4 (1995), p. 238.

us to acknowledge and consider the "fragility and instability of the 'givens' (the 'meaningful totalities') of history".[23] Therefore, I follow three memory fragments of the 1977 protests in Suez from three different vantage points: the position of people who were members of political organizations before the protests; the traces of protests in Suez's streets; and the position of those who witnessed the protests from home. I argue that these three memory fragments of the 1977 protests show a specific temporality for those who were members of leftist political organizations in Suez before the protests that differs from mainstream literature and discourses on the 1977 event. They also help us to follow the material traces of faceless participants in the streets of Suez, as if following the traces of ghosts. These faceless participants are ghosts not just in the sense that they are invisible, but because a ghost has "real presence and demands [...] your attention".[24] Everyone in Suez spoke about this presence – of the "protesters" – remembering what they did, what they burnt, and what they looked like. Yet, all my interlocutors insisted that they themselves were not among "them"; no one knew exactly who the protesters were. They were subjected to *taghyib*, a concept developed by the Syrian writer Yassin Al Haj Saleh that describes a process by which people are actively made absent in public space, encompassing the impossibility that they might be able to represent themselves. He argues that the vast majority of people in most countries, even democratic ones, are subject to this process. However, he adds that "the stranger or the 'subaltern' is not present unless she breaks into the theater and creates trouble".[25]

The memories of the 1977 protests in Suez are memories that "disturb what we think we know",[26] offering the possibility to fill gaps in our knowledge of what happened during these two momentous days in Egyptian history, particularly in Suez. Moreover, I argue that they are "memories that haunt".[27] By haunting, Salem means "how the legacies of some projects continue to have aftereffects, but not always in visible or measurable ways".[28] Memory of the 1977 protests is attached to an immeasurable, omnipresent legacy of resistance in the city of Suez. However, it is also a memory of chaos and fear of the unknown. It is a memory among other memories in the city that relates to a period when Suez was still recovering from years of war, resistance, and destruction.

23. *Ibid.*, p. 239.
24. Avery F. Gordon and Janice Radway. *Ghostly Matters: Haunting and the Sociological Imagination* (Minneapolis, MN, 1997), p. xvi.
25. Yassin Al Haj Saleh, التفكير الصالح أفكار :الغائبين أصوات (Voices of the Absent: Ideas Towards the Renovation of Thought), *Al Jumhuriya*, 2 April 2020. Available at: https://tinyurl.com/1s8hded1; last accessed 15 February 2021.
26. Roberto Roccu and Sara Salem, "Making and Unmaking Memories: The Politics of Time in the Contemporary Middle East", *Middle East Critique*, 28:3 (2019), p. 223.
27. *Ibid.*
28. *Ibid.*, p. 262.

EXTENDED TEMPORALITY: 1977 PROTESTS FOR POLITICAL ORGANIZATION MEMBERS IN SUEZ

When I asked Mostafa Abdel Salam, the teacher mentioned in Al Ahram, about the 1977 protests, he started with: "when we came back to Suez after 1974, a public movement was founded in Suez headed by a group of young people who belonged to a sub-movement in the Egyptian communist movement named the *Al Tayyar Al Thawry* [the revolutionary movement]".[29] He went on to explain: "These movements were founded after the self-dissolution of the communist political parties",[30] also commenting that "[t]hey didn't join either the vanguard organization or the Socialist Union".[31] Mostafa and the two other colleagues of his I interviewed did not participate in the protests; yet, the authorities accused them of organizing the protests, with some of them also accused of burning buildings in Suez. For the members of *Al Tayyar Al Thawry* in Suez, the memory of the 1977 protests in the city begins with their activism there after the population's return. In this sense, the 1977 protests comprise not only the two days of riots in January, but also what they were doing both before the protests and after.

After the city's inhabitants returned, almost all my interlocutors recalled that Suez was full of rats. Many reasons were given for this phenomenon: the houses that had stood empty for more than seven years; the trash discarded from ships; the corpses during the war; and even a conspiracy theory that the Israelis had left them before finally departing from Suez after their 101-day siege of the city in 1973.[32] The members of *Al Tayyar Al Thawry* met a United Nations expert, who declared that Suez would soon be overrun by pests if the rats were not contained. Under the leadership of Hussein, younger than Mostafa but more experienced in community organizing, young men and women from *Al Tayyar Al Thawry* went door to door offering the residents pesticides, along with instructions on how to use them and other hygiene tips.

The group members also offered free tutoring classes for pupils in schools. According to Mostafa, he was called before one of the authorities in the city and told to stop the classes or to start charging money for them, because the authorities did not want the group to gain a reputation and influence among

---

29. This name was given to them by the authorities. They were a secret group that became more active after Egypt's defeat in 1967 and they were influenced by Maoist ideology. The group had members all over Egypt.

30. In 1955, the Egyptian Communist Party was dissolved and many of its members joined the Socialist Union as a reaction to Nasser's socialist policies; for more details, see Nadia Fawzi "Summary of the History of the Communist Movement in Egypt", *Idaa't*, 2 March 2017. Available at: https://www.idazat.com/brief-history-of-the-socialist-movement-in-egypt/; last accessed 19 December 2020; and Gervasio, Gennaro, *Al-Haraka al-Mārkisiyya fi Misr, 1967–1981* (The Marxist Movement in Egypt, 1967–1981), (Cairo, 2010).

31. Interview with Mostafa Abdel Salam, Suez, 3 December 2018.

32. Interviews with many interlocutors in Suez, November–December 2018.

the inhabitants. He refused, and they continued to conduct their free classes. It is also important to note here that Suez was still under reconstruction and its infrastructure was not fully functioning, including its schools. The group supported the leftist and progressive candidates in the local assembly elections of 1976. When two of the candidates succeeded, they continued to work with them closely. Mostafa and the other two colleagues I interviewed were young men in their twenties and thirties at the time, enthusiastic to be engaged in their local community after seven years away from their city, to which they were attached and had been longing to return. Their activities were visible in Suez's almost-empty streets and they were known to people in specific neighbourhoods. They were also known to the authorities as leftists or communists. Therefore, they were the first to be accused by the authorities of organizing the 1977 protests, as was the case for communists in all Egyptian cities following the Bread Riots.

On 18 January 1977, Mostafa woke up at 9 am in his shared flat located in the heart of Suez's downtown to the sound of protests:

> I went to the local assembly, where I met with the members and discussed the situation. They said there had been an incident at the police station in Al-Arba'in and another at the cultural centre. I committed a serious mistake in that I went with a friend to check on the cultural centre. The State Security took this as evidence and investigated us, accusing me of burning it.[33]

Mostafa and his fellow members of *Al Tayyar Al Thawry* told me they had not known about the protests before they happened. They said they went to the streets only to observe. Allam, a friend of the group, was employed at a hotel on Orabi Street at the time, which was one of the main streets in Al-Arba'in where the protests occurred. He witnessed a major part of the protests because the hotel was so central, and also because he had to help a friend who had been shot. He was summoned to State Security on the day of the protests and asked about another friend who belonged to the *Tagamoa'* (Assembly) party.[34] There, Allam saw the names of his friends on a note in front of the officer. He warned the rest of the group. Initially, some of them said that nothing would happen, but by the end of the day, they had decided they had to escape from Suez in order to avoid arrest. They had to leave their city again, and with it their dreams. They hid for a few months in houses in Cairo, relying on secret means of communication. Eventually, they were cleared of all the accusations against them, as were most of the leftists from other cities who were caught up in the protests.[35] Most of them returned to Suez. However, Mostafa's professional trajectory was directly affected. The

---

33. Interview with Mostafa, Suez, 3 December 2018.
34. One of the main leftist political parties in Egypt.
35. They remained in hiding for a few months, until they learned that the charges against them had been dropped, after which they gradually returned to Suez. The final verdict in which the rest of

decision was made to send him to teach somewhere else, but he refused to move. As a result, he lost his job.

The 1977 protests directly affected the personal lives of this group, as well as their political activism. After 1977, the Sadat regime became more repressive against any form of activism, especially that of leftists and communists. On 3 February 1977, a law was issued to limit many democratic political rights.[36] After this event, Sadat ordered police reinforcements, reluctant to ask the army for help again, as he had been forced to do in response to the January Bread Riots.[37] For Mostafa and his colleagues, the 1977 protests represented the end of an era for potential openness in the political sphere, with the prospect of more freedom for political participation and more spaces for public activities. After escaping arrest and facing the closure of public space, the group was dismantled, as they could no longer get together to meet as they once had. For this group of activists, the memory of the 1977 Bread Riots in Suez includes far more than the two days of protests in January. It includes months of activism in a post-war city, the trials of escaping arrest, and induced changes in their personal, professional, and political trajectories.

This memory fragment shows a prolonged temporality of the events associated with the Bread Riots of 18–19 January 1977. For this group, it is the aftermath of the two days of protest that really matters: how the protests dashed the potential of their local socio-political activism, their dream to change society from below, and their strategy for resisting the corrupt political regime. The protests also marked the start of a new era in which the political regime came to completely control the public and political spheres, and in which its neoliberal policies came to be less and less contested. The 1977 protests mark one of the last mass protests against the neoliberal policies initiated by Sadat after the end of the 1973 war. Meanwhile, the questions of what actually happened in the streets of Suez on 18–19 January 1977 and who was protesting remain unanswered.

TRACES WITHOUT FACES: 1977 PROTESTS FOR PEOPLE WHO MARCHED IN THE STREETS OF SUEZ

The paths of the demonstrations on 18–19 January 1977 in Cairo and Alexandria have been drawn by numerous writers.[38] Hence, I have also tried to draw the path of the demonstrations in Suez from the memories of

communists from all over Egypt were acquitted was not delivered until 1980. See Hussein AbdelRazik, Egypt in 18 and 19 January. A Documentary Political Study, pp. 111–124.
36. *Ibid.*, p. 112.
37. Hazem Kandil, *Soldiers, Spies, and Statesmen: Egypt's Road to Revolt* (London, 2012), pp. 363–364.
38. See: AbdelRazik (1984); Saad (1988); El-Hamalawy (2001).

my interlocutors in 2018, all of whom were middle-class Suezis who witnessed the protests but did not belong to any political organization at the time. Because my interlocutors were uncertain of where the protests in Suez began, the map in Figure 2 sketches the main streets they mentioned and buildings they remember as being burned in the city on 18 January 1977.

According to their memories, the demonstrations mostly took place along the city's main north–south axis, Al Geish Street, extending from Al Mothalath neighbourhood in the north to Suez neighbourhood in the south (Figure 2). They also mentioned Orabi Street, a main thoroughfare in the central neighbourhood of Al Arba'in that connects to Al Mothalath, another neighbourhood where protest action took place. Ahmed, who was a government employee and the son of a well-known politically active local council member, but said he had not been politically active himself prior to the 18 January 1977 protests, participated in the demonstrations that day, recalling that they eventually spread to most of the streets in Suez. Municipal buildings were attacked and even burnt, he recounted, as was the cultural centre that used to be the headquarters of the Socialist Union. This was located in a vibrant neighbourhood that included other public buildings and important Suez meeting places, such as the Department of Education. Ahmed mentioned that the protestors he marched with passed by the Department of Education and threw stones at it, and he recalled that employees in the building threw them back. It was not clear in the interview if he himself threw stones, but it was clear that, to this day, he does not know *why* the Department of Education was attacked.

The two main police stations in Suez – in Al Arba'in and Al Mothalath – were also burnt during the protests. During my visit in 2018, the first station was closed because it had also been burnt during the events of the 25 January 2011 revolution in the city. The Al Arba'in police station is a symbolic reference point in Suez because the Israelis hid there when they tried to occupy the city on 24 October 1973. The *fida'yyīn* of the popular resistance managed to attack the station and it was this incident that prevented the Israelis from entering Suez, leading to their 101-day siege of the city. That the police station in Al Arba'in is burnt every time there is an insurrection in the city highlights what Tilly calls the accumulation of repertoires of contention through memories.[39]

As the protesters traversed Suez's main street from north to south, travelling through the main three neighbourhoods of Suez, Al Arba'in, and Al Mothalath, they attacked and burnt not only the main public buildings, but also private properties belonging to people with close ties to the political regime. For the protesters, these buildings, even the private ones, were material representations of the political regime and its supporters. They were the main target of their anger against the regime's raising of prices on essential goods

---

39. Tilly, "Political Memories", p. 247.

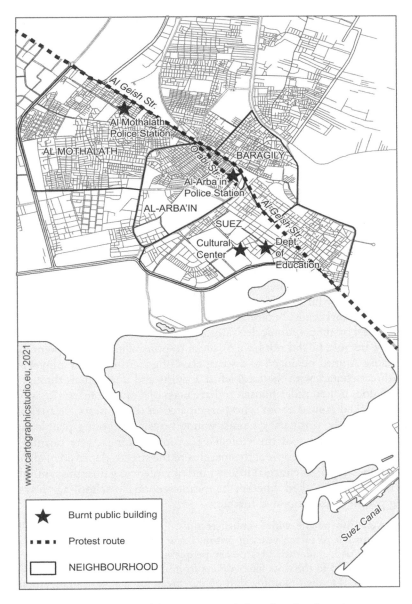

Figure 2. Map showing the sites of the 1977 protests in Suez, based on interviews.

and its switch to Nasserist welfare state policies. Allam, who recalled helping to calm down many of the protesters on this day, declared:

The demonstrations were in Orabi Street. Haj Noor, who was a coffee shop owner and member of the Socialist Union, shot a young boy with his own revolver. I saw him shoot him and then run to his house, the same building as his coffee shop. I told the protestors that it was the owner of the coffee shop who had done it. I had barely finished speaking before they set the coffee shop on fire. How could they just burn it like that? This was the coffee shop we used to all sit in. I knew this guy and his children. Yes, the guy was a jerk and with the regime, but still.[40]

Amjad, currently a history teacher in Suez, who was in his teens during the demonstrations, recalled the same incident:

1977 was very violent in Suez. [...] It was so out of control that it reached the level of sabotage: burning police stations like the one in Al Mothalath, and coffeeshops like the one owned by a famous Suez developer who was a member of Sadat's party. He faced off against the protesters and shot a gun in the air, and the people set the coffee shop he was sitting in on fire. There was also violence against buses and public services.[41]

Allam, who had been active in the streets of Suez before the events of January 1977, told me that he did not know the protesters at all, suggesting they were either people who had not previously been politically active, or had only recently come to the city. Ahmed told me he decided to join the protests without any prior organization because "everyone was in the streets". Though he recalled having been upset by the economic decisions, he insisted that they did not touch him personally, because he did not have financial responsibilities at that point in his life. Because Ahmed belonged to a social class of governmental employees and was in direct contact with the local leftist activists and intellectuals through his father, he does not consider himself to have been one of "the masses".

When I asked Amjad about who participated in the protests, he answered: "Ordinary people, ordinary citizens, young boys. The young people had a role in the spontaneity of the violence [...] many things were burnt." He also mentioned "those people at the margins of the streets, deprived of all privilege, so they would get engaged in any kind of violence against the symbols of authority". When I asked whether he meant secondary-school-age boys by "young people", he elaborated further:

There were also people with criminal records. This guy, Korea, was actually sentenced to five to fifteen years in prison. I saw him once when he got out of prison [...] Also, students and ordinary people in the streets, and people who just got swept up in the riots like workers from the cement factory. They used to catch the bus to their morning shift on our street, just across from us, around 6:30–6:45 in the morning. On that day, the people prevented the buses from moving and so the workers got engaged.[42]

---

40. Interview with Allam, Suez, 22 November 2018.
41. Interview with Amjad, Suez, 7 November 2018.
42. *Ibid.*

In mentioning the spontaneous participation of marginalized people and those who were in the streets – young people and those who were not previously politicized – he echoes the findings of most of the literature on the 1977 events, citing the participation of "the masses" without faces. Amjad's most interesting remark, however, concerns the fact that the person named "Korea" was sentenced to between five and fifteen years in prison for his participation in the riots. While I could find no more details about the criminal record of "Korea" specifically, we do know that, after the protests, around 2,000 people were arrested across Egypt and indicted on accusations related to their participation or potential participation in the protests.[43]

In a long critical analysis of the 1977 uprising published in 2011, communist writer Adel Al A'amry points out that there was significant discrimination in how the state dealt with these "masses" in the judicial system.[44] In a verdict celebrated by the Egyptian left as a victory, the communists and leftists who were chased by the state and accused of being responsible for the protests and their ensuing violence were cleared of all the charges against them. However, those others charged in relation to participation in the riots – those who had not previously been politically active and did not belong to leftist political parties or movements – were convicted and often sentenced to years in prison, just like "Korea".[45]

Al A'amry criticizes the leftist intellectuals for their reaction to the 1977 protests and their aftermath.[46] In refuting the charges against them, the leftists tried to prove that they had nothing to do with the violence that occurred during the protests, or they argued that the protests had started off as non-violent, only changing course when government-ordered "intruders" showed up and began initiating violent acts.[47] Either way, they maintained a discourse that those who set things on fire were "not us". The same tone arose when my leftist interlocutors in Suez remembered the protests. They claimed they had not known about the protests beforehand. They said they did not participate in them, that they just observed, and that they tried to calm down the other protesters, urging them not to burn or sabotage. Those who were in the streets, they said, were "not us". It is here that the process appears of making the masses who participated in these protests absent or as if they did not exist. The *taghyib* of the masses who participated in these protests is not engineered by the State authorities only but also by the leftists who were part of the opposition at the time.

---

43. Adel Al A'amry, "Different Reading of 18–19 January 1977 Uprising", *AHewar Al Motamadin*, 2011. Available at: http://www.ahewar.org/debat/show.art.asp?aid=260472; last accessed 19 December 2020.
44. *Ibid.*
45. *Ibid.*
46. *Ibid.*
47. Hussein AbdelRazik, *Misr fi 18 wa 19 yanayir. Dirasa siyasiyya watha'iqiyya*, p. 112.

Al A'amry argues that those who participated in the spontaneous protests of 1977 used violence as a means to express their anger and dissatisfaction, suggesting that it comprised an important part of their repertoire of action.[48] The fact that Suez was still under construction and just out of a war did not prevent people from adopting this same repertoire of action. The protests on the streets of Suez and other Egyptian cities led Sadat to call in the army to restore order, and ultimately caused him to revoke the austerity measures. Today, we cannot speak with those only remembered as "masses", nor access their personal narratives. We may get to know the traces of those who were present, but not their faces and their voices. They are present in memories of the event, but as ghosts. The memory of these people and what they did on 18–19 January in Suez still haunts the city, warning against chaos, but also reaffirming the city's legacy of resistance.

MEMORY OF FEAR AND RESISTANCE: 1977 PROTESTS AS REMEMBERED FROM HOMES IN SUEZ

When remembering the 1977 protests in Suez, both of my two interlocutors who witnessed the protests from their "homes" emphasized a fear of the unknown, especially in the context of Suez as a city in the process of finding its way back to normality at the time. In 1977, Zinat was a young woman who had just returned to Suez after seven years of forced migration and was working as a teacher. When I asked her if she remembered what happened in 1977, she immediately answered: "Yes, the uprising of the thieves." This was the term used by Sadat in his speech in front of the parliament after the protests. In her memory, the protesters were clearly "the other", not real Suezis, but those who came from other governorates to rebuild and reconstruct the city. For her, "real" Suezis, those who had lived through the war and the city's destruction, would not use violence when protesting. At the same time, however, she made it clear that she understood the people were suffering from the rises in prices and acknowledged that the economic situation was hard. When the protests broke out, she was at school, teaching, but went home and stayed there. As she remembers:

> Yes, we were afraid, afraid and we stayed home. The city was already destroyed. Moreover, those who were active were not peaceful. Whoever was out, was destroying things. They were not protests demanding that the president take back his decision because we are tired or whatever. They were destroying the country, just as on the 25th of January [2011], many things were destroyed in the town, here in Suez, I swear to God. I was remembering today when you called

48. Al A'amry, "Different Reading of 18–19 January 1977 Uprising".

me, how they looted Omar Effendi and the cooperatives.[49] [In 1977 ...] they also broke into and looted cooperatives. By the way, these are not the people of Suez, but people from other nationalities, or how do they call it, tribes? Something like tribes – those who come from Sohag or from Qena, not locals.[50] No, the people of the city cared about it. I mean, the people of Suez who lived through the war and were touched by it.

Moreover, when Suez was opened in 1974, they considered it to be a second Libya, I swear to God.[51] For those who used to come to Suez to work in the construction sector or the companies, they came as if they were going to Libya. For them, it was a source of income and investment. The city was full of people who came to rebuild and reconstruct. Most of them were foreigners, not originally from Suez, not Suezis, I swear to God, because it happened in the area of Al Arba'in.[52]

This excerpt from the interview shows that her memory of the 1977 protests is associated with fear. Zinat stayed at home to avoid the chaos and any potential attacks. She mentions the robberies that happened and, most importantly, she compares events with the 25 January 2011 protests. This is also how the father of my interlocutor Amjad, who was a teenager in 1977 and witnessed the events from his balcony, reacted to the protests. Amjad's father had been a communist in his younger years, and in the 1950s had even been arrested. In 1977, however, Amjad remembers that his father, then a government employee, was sceptical of the protests and prevented his teenage son from going out into the streets, even from going to school, while he himself returned home from work early.

Owing to Amjad's education, reading, and overall influence from leftist ideology, including his activism later in life, his memory of the 1977 events differed significantly from Zinat. Though he also compared the 1977 protests with the 25 January 2011 uprising, he saw both as episodes of resistance, arguing that 1977 was a rehearsal for the 2011 protests. In the latter, he noted, the police station in Al Arba'in was also burnt by the protesters, and the demonstrations took place in almost the same streets. In his analysis of the reasons the 1977 protests broke out in Suez, Amjad stressed the specificity of Suez as a city of resistance. He cited the city's resistance to the Israelis during their 101-day siege of the city three years prior to the 1977 Bread Riots. He also recalled the presence

49. Omar Effendi is a well-known department store chain in Egypt. Cooperatives were state-sponsored markets where the people could get essential goods supported by the State.
50. Sohag and Qena are governorates in Upper Egypt, where harsh living conditions often forced people to emigrate to seek work in big cities. Most inhabitants of Suez have roots in Upper Egypt, which was the case even before the forced migration in 1967. However, this rural–urban exodus intensified after 1975 due to the reconstruction work in the city.
51. In the 1970s, Libya was a prime destination country for Egyptians emigrating to find work, much like the Gulf states. Comparing Suez to Libya emphasizes the city's new role as a destination for job seekers from Upper Egypt.
52. The neighborhood of Arba'in was home to many of the city's immigrants. Interview with Zinat, Suez, 4 December 2018.

of a strong workers' movement in Suez,[53] the lack of infrastructure, and the high expectations that Suezis had after the war, based on the government's promises. For him, the memory of 1977 in Suez comprises one episode in a long tradition of Suezi resistance: from the city's resistance to English occupation and Israeli invasion, to its resistance in the 25 January 2011 revolution.

Several months after my conversation with Amjad, in a statement published in a 2019 article for the Egyptian online news outlet *Mada Masr*,[54] an intellectual from Suez extended the historical trajectory of resistance in the city to include the protest episode that broke out on 19–20 September 2019.[55] He declared:

> The Nasserist regime founded in the city what we call the 'popular university' and a second Socialist Institute [a cultural organization related to the Socialist Union], which have contributed to the continuity of political life in the city. [Suez] has known politics before, through the activities of political movements like the communists, the Muslim Brotherhood, and the *Misr Al Fattah* [party]. This continued even under Mubarak, through the solidarity campaigns with the Lebanese and Palestinian people during the Israeli invasion [of Lebanon] in 1982.[56]

Once again, in the wave of protests in September 2019, Suez was in the vanguard. It was one of the cities where the protests were the most violent and the streets were full of people; many insurrections took place, especially around the Al-Arba'in Mosque, and dozens of people were arrested. The previously mentioned *Mada Masr* article suggests that Suez has a legacy of resistance that always leads the city and its population to be at the vanguard of political opposition movements in Egypt, past and present. Mostafa, the teacher mentioned in Al Ahram, also presented a similar argument:

> Suez is a city that went beyond the line of political movements in Egypt [...] There has always been a general line in Egyptian society, a certain limit, and we went beyond this limit. We became heard to the authorities in Egypt [Cairo]. That's why, in the events of January [1977], the authorities were violent and exercised an excessive level of brutality in following and capturing us [...] To this day, Suez constitutes a red line. For leftists and those who know, it is communist [...], and for those who only have a general idea, it is in the opposition. Suez is a city always in the opposition.

---

53. For more information, see Joel Beinin and Zachary Lockman, *Workers on the Nile: Nationalism, Communism, Islam, and the Egyptian Working Class, 1882–1954* (Princeton, NJ, 1987).
54. Beesan Kassab, "An Entry to Understand What Happened in Suez", *Mada Masr*, 2019. Available at: https://tinyurl.com/1121e25m; last accessed 15 February 2021.
55. A wave of protests broke out in many Egyptian cities on 19–20 September after a series of videos by an Egyptian real estate developer revealed corrupt practices by the Egyptian army. The protests in Suez lasted for two to three days and included many clashes with the police.
56. Kassab, "An Entry to Understand What Happened in Suez".

In these reflections, the 1977 protests in Suez are remembered as one episode in a longer tradition of protest and opposition to the authorities. Kahled Fahmy (2015) argues that Egyptians have always protested against occupation and repression, situating the 25 January 2011 uprising as just one episode in a long history of Egyptian popular resistance.[57] This argument somewhat romanticizes contention, however, as it fails to consider the different motivations of those who were involved in each episode. Suezis who participated in the 1977 Bread Riots have not had the chance to convey their personal motivations for taking to the streets and expressing their anger at the government. At the time, they may not have thought about the protests as an episode in a long line of resistance; they may have only seen them as a means to express their anger at policies that affected their everyday lives. Thus, they may have not given the same answers or interpretations of the protests as those that were advanced by intellectuals and political activists after the fact.

CONCLUSION

The three memory fragments presented in this article help us to understand how middle-class Suezis remember the 1977 Bread Riots in Suez, offering an alternative vantage point for viewing the memories and meaning of this significant event in Egyptian history from the one that is available in the existing and largely Cairo-centric literature on the protests. Then a city just returning from nearly a decade of war and forced migration, Suez was still in the process of reconstruction in January 1977, and its inhabitants held expectations for a better life ahead. The first fragment shows the disappointment of a group of young people who were politically engaged and full of hope after the war. Crucially, it shows how remembering the 1977 protests for this group was not primarily about the protests themselves, meaning what happened on the streets. Rather, their memory of the protests encompassed a much broader temporality than the two days of unrest in January 1977 and centred on the fact that their political activism was being forced to end. The broad criminalization of membership in leftist organizations in the aftermath of the protests, rather than criminalization of actual participation in the events, abruptly dashed their dreams and significantly altered their political and private trajectories.

The second fragment engages with the unknown traces and faces of people who marched in the streets of Suez through the memories of my interlocutors, one who participated in the protests and several who witnessed them, but none of whom had been active in organized politics prior to the event. Owing to the difficulty of conducting fieldwork and accessing archives in Egypt, the main

---

57. Khaled Fahmy, "Opening Politics' Black Box: Reflections on the Past, Present and Future of the Egyptian Revolution", in R. Shehadeh and P. Johnson, *Shifting Sands: The Unravelling of the Old Order in the Middle East* (London, 2015), pp. 69–81.

participants in the protests are not accessible; rather, they are actively absent. They exist as ghosts in my interlocutors' memories. Through these memories and the scant traces left behind in newspapers, articles, and books over the years, we can feel and see their effects, but we cannot see *them*. The people who took to the streets in Suez and across Egypt in January 1977 made the government revoke its decision to impose austerity measures, but today they remain the unknown, the extras, the "other". They only exist in memory as the "masses": the marginalized; the street vendors; day-labourers; workers; and perhaps also foreign migrants to the city who came seeking opportunities after the war.

Finally, the third fragment explores the themes of fear and resistance that predominate in the memories of two interlocutors who witnessed the 1977 protests from their homes in Suez. For the other interlocutor, however, it affirms and further feeds what he views to be a positive legacy of Suez as a city always at the vanguard of oppositional movements and historic progress in Egypt: an esteemed city of resistance. For him and other Suezis documented in media and scholarship, the 1977 Bread Riots represent one revolutionary episode in a broader, ongoing emancipatory trajectory in contemporary Egyptian history.

This article's exploration of memory and the 1977 Bread Riots in Suez has shown that the 1977 protests were a moment in which the absent became present through their actions, sabotage, and physical presence on the streets.[58] Since the actual events, however, they have been subjected to a structured and multilayered process of *taghyib*, starting with their representation in the media, but also including their unequal treatment by the country's judicial system, and even the process of remembering them. Today, they once again appear only as nameless, faceless people, as the "other", as ghosts.

---

58. Yassin Al Haj Saleh, أصوات الغائبين:أفكار نحو تجديد الفكر (Voices of the Absent: Ideas Towards the Renovation of Thought).

IRSH 66 (2021), pp. 41–68 doi:10.1017/S0020859021000110

The Fair Value of Bread:
Tunisia, 28 December 1983–6 January 1984

LEYLA DAKHLI

Centre National de la Recherche Scientifique
Centre Marc Bloch
Friedrichstraße 191
*10117 Berlin, Germany**

E-mail: Leyla.Dakhli@cmb.hu-berlin.de

ABSTRACT: The "Bread Riots" that broke out in Tunisia on 28 December 1983 lasted barely ten days. Yet, they cost the lives of over one hundred people. The revolt studied here centred on two popular neighbourhoods of Tunis in the wake of massive, World Bank-sponsored development plans. This article seeks to understand how the inhabitants in these quarters reacted to the establishment of a new welfare state that was more concerned with fighting poverty – or fighting the poor – than with equalizing conditions or offering the same opportunities for everyone. Based on this case study, I argue that the great Bread Revolt of 1983–1984 marked a break with past practices of state reform and popular protest and suggest that International Monetary Fund and World Bank prescriptions and state implementations reconfigured the political and social landscape of independent Tunisia.

The "Bread Riots" that broke out in Tunisia on 28 December 1983 lasted barely ten days. Yet, they cost the lives of over one hundred people, according to official figures given by human rights organizations. The riots spread rapidly across the country after initially erupting in the south, in the market of the city of Douz. At the time, the newspapers spoke of riots (*ihtijâjât*) and militant publications spoke of revolt (*intifâda*). The narratives told could be inserted into broader chronologies: the history of struggle against neoliberalism;[1] the

* This research was conducted as part of an ERC-funded research programme (ERC-CO 2017 DREAM). Many thanks to Selima Kebaïli and Arwa Labidi for their help in accessing part of the documentation.
1. The bibliography on the origins of neoliberalism and neoliberal policies barely mentions the Tunisian experience, or the regional Middle Eastern side of it. It often starts with an intellectual

end of the reign of independence leader Habib Bourguiba; and the opportunity to consolidate the power of General Zine el-Abidine Ben Ali, who eventually dismissed Bourguiba three years later.[2] But this revolt's inclusion in the long history of social struggles in Tunisia is rarer.[3] It is usually seen through the lens of the arrival of Islamist political organizations,[4] and as indicating their replacement of left-wing forces and organized trade unionism.[5] This article seeks to put this episode into a new perspective, giving it back its many meanings while trying to understand it as a major turning point for Tunisia.

The "spontaneity" and the dissemination of the revolt tempt us to describe what happened as ephemeral "food riots".[6] If we pay attention to the slogans and demands, to the physicality of the demonstrations, we gain a deeper understanding of the political cycle in which this revolt is embedded. Attacks targeting the well-off middle-class neighbourhoods, often seen as collateral damage, suggest a strong element of social conflict, which remains to be interpreted in the context of the withdrawal of redistribution policies and massive urbanization. The aim here is to show how this revolt fits into the repertoire of social struggles in post-independence Tunisia, and, at the same time, show how it contrasts with wider events.

Triggered by price hikes, the revolt was caused by the destabilization of the Tunisian national economy in the wake of global deregulation. More than hunger or poverty, what the demonstrators pointed to was the violation of a

genealogy of the neoliberal turn, mentioning the South American episodes as the earlier key experiments. See David Harvey, *A Brief History of Neoliberalism* (Oxford, 2007); Wendy Brown, *Undoing the Demos: Neoliberalism's Stealth Revolution* (Cambridge, MA, 2015). Abdelwaheb Cherni has written a Master's dissertation for the University of Tunis, but I was unable to access it despite numerous attempts (its title is "For a Sociological Approach of the January 1984 Events and the Place of the Excluded", 1987).

2. This is the major focus of local accounts of the episode, mainly through the memoirs and biographies of the actors. See also Farhat Dachraoui, *Bourguiba. Pouvoir et contre-pouvoir* (Tunis, 2015).

3. Olfa Lamloum, "Janvier 84 en Tunisie ou le symbole d'une transition", in Didier Le Saout and Marguerite Rollinde (eds), *Émeutes et mouvements sociaux au Maghreb. Perspective comparée* (Paris, 1999), pp. 231–242.

4. On Islamism in Tunisia, see Mohamed Kerrou, "Politiques de l'islam en Tunisie", in M. Kilani (ed.), *Islam et changement social* (Lausanne, 1998), pp. 81–102; Frank Fregosi, "La Régulation institutionnelle de l'islam en Tunisie. Entre audace moderniste et tutelle étatique", Policy Paper 4, Ifri, November 2003; Michel Camau, "Religion politique et religion d'État en Tunisie", in Ernst Gellner & Jean-Claude Vatin (eds), *Islam et politique au Maghreb* (Paris, 1981), pp. 221–230; Marion Boulby, "The Islamic Challenge: Tunisia since Independence", *Third World Quarterly*, 10:2 (1988), pp. 590–614.

5. On trade unions, and specifically on the UGTT, see Joel Beinin, *Workers and Thieves: Labor Movements and Popular Uprisings in Tunis and Egypt* (Stanford, CA, 2016); Héla Yousfi, *L'UGTT, Une passion tunisienne* (Paris, 2015); Keenan Wilder, "The Origins of Labour Autonomy in Authoritarian Tunisia", *Contemporary Social Science*, 10:4 (2015), pp. 349–363.

6. John K. Walton and David Seddon, *Free Markets and Food Riots: The Politics of Global Adjustment* (London, 1994).

tacit social contract. These riots constituted a moment of protest in a context of economic crisis and in the face of a state that was deemed incapable of assuming food-producing responsibilities (hence the Bread Riots). They even affected the middle classes, although the inequalities and tensions within Tunisian society subsequently minimized this dimension as peripheral to the event – both in local memory and in historiography. Arguably, this is one reason why the riots are not an important part of the memory of revolutionary Tunisia, even though they constitute one of the moments when protest action was revived.[7]

Investigating the social context in which the riots broke out has led us to look at evidence from different sources. This article is based primarily on the examination of archives related to urban development plans of the late 1970s and early 1980s. This was in order to discover how it was possible for such a social conflagration to occur in neighbourhoods that were in the process of so-called de-gourbification (or slum clearance),[8] and had benefited greatly from national and international development aid. In Tunisia, a particularly active group of urban planners had created a collective that was committed to social responses to urban growth, the Groupe Huit. One of the members, Morched Chabbi, deposited his papers at the Tunisian National Archives, where I was able to consult them. In addition to raw material relating to urban planning, including preliminary studies on the sociology and daily life of the neighbourhoods' inhabitants, the collection includes a number of reports on Tunisia from international institutions such as the International Monetary Fund (IMF) and the International Bank for Reconstruction and Development (IBRD). A few scattered documents were also made available to me at the Urban Rehabilitation and Renewal Agency, created in 1981. In addition, I consulted the national and international press, in Arabic, French, and English, and diplomatic correspondence and reports prepared for the French government. Finally, the testimonies filed with the recent Truth and Dignity Commission (IVD, from the French Instance Vérité et Dignité), and its final report in 2014, made it possible to understand more clearly the viewpoint of the victims of repression and their relatives.[9]

From this documentation, it has been possible to interrogate the nature of what is called the welfare state in a young post-colonial state, along with its

7. In January 2020, a street in the name of Fadhel Sassi was nevertheless inaugurated in Tunis. Available at: http://kapitalis.com/tunisie/2020/01/03/tunis-inauguration-dune-rue-au-nom-de-fadhel-sassi-le-martyr-des-emeutes-du-pain-photos/; last accessed 11 May 2020.
8. Béchir Chebab Tekari, "Habitat et dépassement du droit en Tunisie. Les constructions spontanées", in Pierre-Robert Baduel, *Habitat, État, Société au Maghreb* (Paris, 2003); Lamia Zaki, "L'action publique au bidonville. L'état entre gestion par le manque, 'éradication' des *kariens* et accompagnement social des habitants", *L'Année du Maghreb*, 2 (2005–2006), pp. 303–320.
9. A Commission of Inquiry of the IVD was set up, and reported its conclusions on 23 February 2014. It has opened 1,230 files on the events of December 1983–January 1984, including 932 for facts related to repression after the events, including arrests, torture, and detention.

collapse. By observing the course of brutally crushed riots that took place over little more than a week, we are able to understand the stakes when the IMF's recommendations are applied in a country such as Tunisia. Urban planning is a rich source of documentation for popular residential areas and their inhabitants, and the observation of these urban districts makes it possible to see what the actual implementation of IMF- and World Bank-backed policies looks like at the local level.

Finally, this article looks closely at how demonstrators from these neighbourhoods developed their own criticisms and responses to the price hikes that took place as a result of structural adjustment policies. The demonstrators are taken as an example of what Partha Chatterjee calls "political society", as opposed to the more middle-class, state-tied concept of "civil society":[10] an apparently unorganized and apolitical group of people who, when provoked, appear to do politics in their own way.

THE RIOT IN CONTEXT

In December 1983, Tunisia had been independent for almost thirty years – just one generation. The events of 1983–1984 had no precedent. When the riots broke out in Douz, politicians tried to apply conventional explanations – political manipulation, especially from Libya, or Islamist conspiracy. It was indeed a revolt that set the whole of Tunisia ablaze. Let us reconstruct how it unfolded according to participant voices that have been retrieved from press documents and the proceedings of the IVD.[11]

Tunisians started to mobilize in anticipation of the government's doubling of the price of bread, which was effective from 1 January 1984. The first casualty of the revolt was a young man aged seventeen, Belgassem Belayeb, who was murdered on 29 December 1983 in the southern town of Douz. Eighty more protestors were wounded on this and subsequent days. On 1 January, a peaceful demonstration was held in the city of Gafsa, apparently initiated by Umar Thabet Qadir, head of the Human Rights League branch there.[12] The demonstration was blocked by the arrival of heavy police forces. The next day, another death occurred in the Douz region: a twenty-one-year-old farmer who was assassinated by police officers. That same day, the movement reached the city of Sfax, where shops and buses were set on fire. The police opened fire. Twelve people were killed, and more than twenty others were wounded. On 3 January, riots broke out all over the country and particularly in Greater Tunis, where students and young people from popular neighbourhoods rose up. Fadhel Sassi, a political activist and a student, was murdered by the police

---

10. Partha Chatterjee, *The Politics of the Governed: Reflections on Popular Politics in Most of the World* (New York, 2004).

11. IVD, Final Report, May 2019. التقرير الختامي الشامل , pp. 277–280.

12. *Ibid.*

Figure 1. The ravages in Tunis after the riots (published in the newspaper *La Presse de Tunisie*, 6 January 1984.

in the city centre. There were dozens of deaths and hundreds of arrests. The riots continued in the days that followed, when a curfew was introduced, until President Bourguiba announced the suspension of increased security measures on 6 January. Trials were held in May, relating to theft, looting, assaults on private and public property, damage to property (Figure 1), and participation in hostile and unauthorized demonstrations. Hundreds of people in prison were tortured and abused while awaiting trial, and were then sentenced to long prison terms. The sequence of events was therefore short, but very violent.

For many of the insurgents, going out on the street that day was a "normal" reaction. Moncef Laajimi, from the Kram, who was not used to protest and state violence, told the IVD that he was astonished at the reaction of the forces of law and order. "We went out into the street, at least 3,000 people. We were unemployed." They launched a surprisingly gentle slogan: "Bourguiba, you are generous, leave us the bread at 80 millimes." "The next day, they started shooting at us with real bullets, with a plane above, a helicopter firing." For Moncef Laajimi, it was all about going out for bread, for the price of bread.[13]

13. Special Public Audition of the IVD, January 2016, starting at 23:25. Last accessed on 5 January 2021 at: https://www.youtube.com/watch?v=EaIoyaM1-vs; last accessed 22 February 2021.

This is also seen in the words of the women who were marching in El-Marsa, some 20 kilometres away from the capital. These textile workers shouted the same slogan: "Bourguiba, you are generous, leave the bread at 80 millimes."[14]

Ahmed Ben Massoud, from Douz, remembered market day, when the events began. It was a Thursday like any other, a weekly shopping day. Elderly people were talking about the impending price hikes, and they decided to take their concerns to the mayor. But he refused to receive the delegation and sent for the police. Ahmed, a twenty-seven-year-old teacher, was informed of what was happening when he came back home from school. In his account, he insists that his outburst of anger was motivated by the way his elders were treated with disdain for simply and peacefully wanting to express their concerns. That was when the young people got together, sang *Humât al hima* ("Defenders of the Fatherland", the national anthem), and gathered to demonstrate: "we didn't really have a culture of protest", Ahmed added. He was the one who spoke in public to explain what had happened. Tension mounted as the police started to hit people and push them away with sticks. Shots were heard. The next morning, people gathered again. "It was the first time we had experienced such police violence. In opposition, only stones were thrown." Ahmed was arrested and tortured, and remained in prison for seventeen days. Some of his relatives were injured.[15]

Many other depositions to the IVD confirm this account. They portray a population affected and outraged by measures that impacted family income and purchasing power. The strong presence of women in these movements suggests that it was also a revolt that included housewives and families.[16] They expressed their indignation peacefully and directly, especially in the early days, calling the government to account at a time when pressure on prices had already worsened.

Other demonstrators told a different story. Jamel Sassi, the younger brother of Fadhel Sassi, who was murdered by the police in downtown Tunis on 3 January 1984, testified to the IVD:[17]

> I would like to go back a bit in time to the reign of Bourguiba. Before those days in 1984, there was 26 January 1978, which we lived through. I was eighteen years old, no, sixteen, and we went out, like everyone else, into the streets on Thursday 26

---

14. Abdelaziz Barouhi, "Des Bidonvilles à Carthage", *Jeune Afrique*, 1201 (11 January 1984), p. 32.
15. Special Public Audition of the IVD, 4 January 2018, starting at 35:40.
16. Arlette Farge, "Évidentes émeutières", in Arlette Farge & Natalie Zemon Davis (eds), *XVIe–XVIIIe siècle*, vol. 3 of Georges Duby & Michelle Perrot (eds), *Histoire des femmes en Occident* (Paris, 2002), pp. 481–496.
17. Audition of the IVD, 23 December 2016. Available at: https://www.youtube.com/watch?v=wKZWarNZhdI; last accessed on 5 January 2021.

January, for the general strike. My father was then a union representative, one of those who went on strike. This episode destroyed him. I saw him become, he who was always in a suit and tie, a neglected person, with a beard in a mess, dressed in a *qashabiyya* [a traditional jacket made of wool]. The authorities had given them a one-year work stoppage for their affiliation to the union.

For Jamel, January 1984 was a continuation of earlier struggles, and revenge for the humiliation and degradation suffered by his father. As for the demonstration, it took on a traditional style, taking place downtown. He continues:

. On the day of the demonstration, I was on one route and my brother was on another. We met up at Habib Thameur Avenue, approximately towards the "Passage". We processed. I wasn't a leader, I was young, well, compared with my brother, I was born in 1962, he was born in 1959. We walked towards Rome Street. The police were trying to prevent us from reaching Habib Bourguiba Avenue. They used tear gas and the stick [...] We retreated and went towards Athens Street. I met Fadhel again in Paris Avenue. Again, there was gas. The last thing I remember about my brother was that gesture. He carried a purple tissue, he wiped my tears with it, after that I have not seen him again, since that day. Then there was the shooting, people were a little scattered. Some of them ran away, it was a mess. I came back by myself, like many others, I came home. Fadhel didn't come home.

In his testimony, the Bread Revolt, as it is called in Tunisia (in Arabic and French), is portrayed as part of a chronology of struggles; it is not detached from the rest. Jamel and Fadhel are, of course, special cases, being political activists – specifically, left-wing students and high school pupils. However, this account clearly shows that events took place as a continuation of a confrontation with power, as a routine act in which one goes out to demonstrate and then goes home. In Jamel's speech, bread is not at the centre. He states this explicitly:

Bread was not the problem. It was the drop of water that broke the vase. There was a lot of oppression, of misery. Fadhel didn't come home. We were worried, of course. There is this girl, a student from ENIT [the National Engineering School of Tunis], who saw him die on her knees, next to her in this covered Peugeot 404 in which they took him to the Habib Thameur hospital. He told her, don't be afraid, I leave the student movement in your hands.

This testimony, and the special place of this martyr, brings 1984 into the continuum of Tunisian social struggles, in terms of its pattern of events, the involvement of the "student movement", and in the fundamental aspiration for freedom and social justice (against "oppression" and "misery").

In the rioting, one can read even more narratives, conveyed by the types of action as well as by the slogans that were used. In the crowd, one heard "Power, murderer, is this your policy of openness?" and "We are hungry, and the bread is 170 millimes."[18] On 3 January, the revolt started in the

---

18. These slogans, among others, were mentioned in the press.

popular districts of Tunis, and then reached the city centre. The crowd attacked many symbols of the state, including buses, police cars, and lorries. The two working-class neighbourhoods we are focusing on here are adjacent to privileged or middle-class residential areas (see Figure 2). First, young men from these neighbourhoods marched downtown, where they targeted a number of stores and public property. The account of Anis, from Jebel Lahmar, tells the story:

> This time we really made a killing: on Tuesday 2nd, when we left the city, there were a thousand of us in Bordj Zouara, Bab Lakouès, Bab Sidi Abdelsalem. Lots of kids joined us; they ran like rabbits and came to warn us when there were policemen.

> At Bab Souika, things started to get rough. The BOPs [Brigades de l'ordre public, Public Order Brigades] charged. And we went wild. Bata [the shoe store] had already burned down. We were tearing down all the signposts and using them to smash the windows. Everything that belonged to the state had to be destroyed. Once hit, the state would necessarily react. We stopped motorbikes, we took petrol in yoghurt pots and wham! we threw it away. The bank in the Kallatine district, the CNEL [Caisse nationale d'épargne logement] [...] in passing, we'd break it up, we'd burn it down. We didn't care about money. It's true that some people stole, it's a pity by the way. That allowed Mzali to call us bandits. I saw some of them at Bata's who shouted: "Do you have left foot size 41?" and another one who came back to a TV shop to look for an aerial. On Chedli-Kallala Avenue, at the Party cell, we went upstairs and threw the furniture and TV set out of the window. We went back up to Bab el-Assal. Three cars burned at the Esso kiosk.[19]

The thoughtful nature of these attacks seems obvious, even if we take into account that the interviewee might have taken into consideration the discourse that was expected of him by the journalist: he visibly distinguished himself from robbers, or those who broke things up for fun, but he did not hide the special joy that these moments gave him. We have to rely on the French translation of his words, but the chosen expression "on a fait un malheur" (we really made a killing) captures this feeling well. The rioters created the sense of having choreographed their actions. They wanted to provoke reactions from the authorities, and they targeted the state directly. It may be noted that the bank they attacked was the one that guaranteed and received housing loans as part of urban restructuring plans. It can be assumed that they were familiar with this. Similarly, they pointed to the Party building as representative of the state.

Elsewhere, pitched battles against the police took place, in which women often played a central role. "In Mellassine, they distributed sticks, provided stones and sprayed water on demonstrators asphyxiated by tear gas. In Borj

---

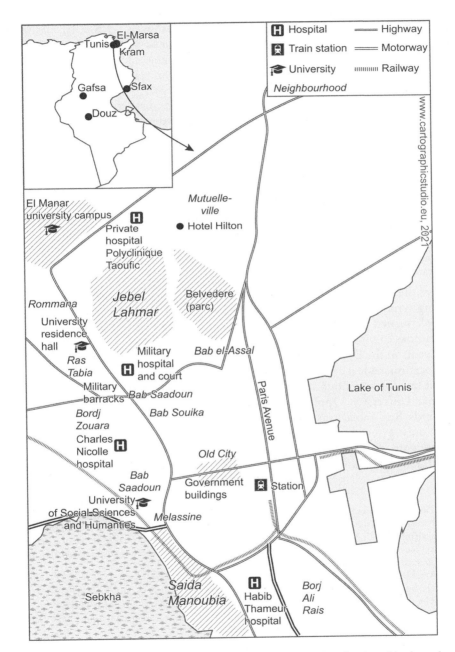

Figure 2. Map of the two neighbourhoods of Djebel Lahmar and Saïda Manoubia, from the reconstruction plans of 1983 (ANT, Fonds Morched Chabbi. Fo. 235 / RHA 716).

Ali Rais,[20] they attacked buses with stones and shovels."[21] Similar clashes could be observed throughout the area, with targeted attacks.[22] Everywhere public transport was attacked, together with branches of the National Bank of Tunisia, the International Arab Bank of Tunisia, and also youth and cultural centres.

On their way back home, it was the middle-class districts and the external signs of wealth that were targeted; for example, a supermarket was looted in El-Menzah. Demonstrators approached the wealthier neighbourhoods and "[terrorized] the inhabitants barricaded in their houses", burning cars. Anis continues:

> Night was falling and the army started shooting; we all scattered. At the *Cité*,[23] we regrouped. But we were not satisfied. So we decided to do something dazzling: burn something big, for example. We went back down in the street. It was a risk. We burned every beautiful car that we came across. Sixteen of them. Pretty good, right? Afterwards, we went to a construction site near the campus, where we dusted off all the equipment. Our goal? To stop the country, until we were heard.[24]

It was therefore on the very edge of their own territory that they attacked, targeting symbols of social wealth, starting with cars, then other goods. Young people turned to their wealthy neighbours, flipping over vehicles, setting up barricades to block traffic.

Events in the Djebel Lahmar neighbourhood are instructive in this respect. Its location made it a place where struggles could converge, as well as it being a front line for street fighting. Djebel Lahmar was on the edge of the Tunis El Manar University. Opposite one of the entrances into the neighbourhood, towards Ras Tabia, was a hostel for female students; the military barracks was only a few hundred meters away. An account transcribed by *Jeune Afrique* on 18 January allows us to grasp part of what was at stake in a street fight. Jamel, a young man from Jebel Lahmar, relates:[25]

---

20. This poor district was partly destroyed in the mid-1960s. During the destruction, the police faced strong opposition from the inhabitants. This was one of the bloodiest episodes of the "de-gourbification". Morched Chabbi, "État, politiques urbaines et habitat spontané. Le cas de Tunis 1960–1980", in Kenneth Brown *et al.* (eds), *Urban Crisis and Social Movements in the Middle East* (Paris, 1988), pp. 258–260, quotation on p. 255.

21. Amel Ben Aba, "Au centre, la femme", *Le Maghreb* (14 January 1984), p. 11.

22. The burning of the Zitouna shops in Sfax was said to be a revenge against the social plan organized by the owner in his Sica factories (which made shoes), which had just put 400 people out of work. In the same city of Sfax, symbols of authority were targeted: police stations, PSD (Parti Socialiste Destourien) cells, and some district municipalities.

23. *Cité* or *hûma* in Arabic are the most frequently used words for district or neighbourhood in Tunisia.

24. Special issue on Tunisia in *Jeune Afrique*, 1202. Interviews by Souheyr Belhassen and Abdelaziz Dahmani, p. 34.

25. *Ibid.*, pp. 29–31.

It was the girls from the hostel [near where Jamel lives] who caused the spark. They joined us. We know some of them. I myself was engaged to a second-year student in the department of French. When we left the *Cité* everyone was with us, including our neighbour, the police officer. You can't imagine how the ululations[26] of women electrified us.

He describes a certain atmosphere in which the unanimity of the revolt – perceived and made visible by the cries of the young women and the police officer's lack of opposition – served to legitimize the struggle. He insisted on the links between the men in the neighbourhood and the female students, clearly going against the evidence of a sharp distinction between these two groups.

Next, there were the tactics employed:

You had to get attention right away. What better way to do that than to block the traffic by lighting a fire. We stopped the first bus, emptied it, and then we lit the fire. Of course, at the university hostel, they hurried to lock the doors and windows and to call the BOPs, who came down on us pretty quickly. But, in the meantime, some students had joined us. And we were the ones who caught the BOPs.[27] The students were at the top of the hill and we were at the bottom. When they came at the students, we chased them with stones, and when they came back towards us, it was the students' turn to harass them. We wrapped our heads in towels or wet scarves to protect ourselves from tear gas and smoke. We didn't stop until 3:00 in the morning. The girls who had been locked inside the Hostel shouted songs and slogans, and we responded to them. Really, it was a party. The BOPs watched us and beat us up when we bothered them too much. At 11 o'clock we started shouting: "Bread for the hungry, with our blood, with our life, we will avenge you, people." Well, all the well-known slogans, I mean …[28]

Here, we can see the way in which the struggle of the working-class neighbourhoods was articulated with that of the students, and also the routine of the confrontations with the police, which took on a particularly strong, and even celebratory, dimension. An element of joy arose from the feeling of having fought a battle, and having won it by managing to surround the police and keep their respect.

The rest of the testimony introduced another dimension. For this young man from the shanty towns, the question of the price of bread did not seem to be central either. When questioned by the journalist, Jamel answered by deploying social analysis, fundamentally challenging the idea of hunger riots and giving events a broader dimension of a struggle for social justice. This was expressed in a mixture of articulated political discourse and the convening of "local thugs", with participants assuming responsibility for their own destiny and not hesitating to resort to violence:

---

26. Ululation (in arabic *zaghrît*) is practiced by women on various occasions of communal ritual events (like weddings) to express strong emotion.
27. The BOP are special police forces.
28. *Jeune Afrique*, 1202, pp. 29–31.

Do I believe in such slogans? It's not important. I'm not really in poverty. Me, my father runs a café, my sister and my two brothers working, we get nearly 700 dinars a month. In the company where I work, the trade union, I don't believe in them. The delegate gets bonuses or benefits. I prefer to fight on my own. In 1977, when I was seventeen years old, I started in this job at 1.5 dinars and then at 2 dinars a week, and it lasted three years. Today I am at 145 dinars a month. From the beginning, I knew how to assert myself. Because I don't fast during Ramadan, the head of department wanted to make me work more than the others. He got my fist in his face. He wanted to fire me, so I spoke a few words to him. "Your daughter Malika, I know her, she's at Carnot High School. If you touch me, I'll give her a treat." Since then, I've had peace of mind. When I need an advance or a vacation, I talk to my boss. I really have no problem but, frankly, I don't like it when the powerful abuse their power.[29]

Challenging what he sees as a corrupt system in which the most powerful give themselves too many privileges, Jamel builds his own place in the system through violence, threats, or riot. He does not seek to change everything, just to regulate his life. In a way, the revolt as a whole can be read in this way. It is also what the end of Anis's testimony seems to say:

It was obvious that we were going to pay the bill. That the kids in our *cités* were the ones who were going to die. But you have to sacrifice a little to get more. […] Did Bourguiba back down? No, it's not Bourguiba, it's Mzali. Bourguiba, he rules the country with the majority. And the majority is who? It's the people. We wanted to reach him. We wanted to blow up everything so he'd hear us. He could have crushed us. He preferred to stand in solidarity with us.[30]

Anis claimed the people's victory. The revolt was the price to pay in order to restore justice. It is striking that he uses the metaphor of paying a bill. In the discussion about a "fair price" versus a "true price", the very existence of the people was at stake. This is what Tunisian government failed to understand in 1983.

NATIONWIDE: FROM PLANNING TO LIBERAL RESTRUCTURING

Independent Tunisia adopted a socialist-oriented economic system in the early 1960s. In 1961, faced with an outflow of capital and a drop in investment, President Bourguiba instructed Ahmed Ben Salah (b. 1926) to impose a national planning policy.[31] Ben Salah had the goal of "creating an objective

---

29. *Ibid.*
30. *Ibid.*
31. This multi-talented minister was a key figure in the 1950s and 1960s. Elected General Secretary of the UGTT at the end of 1952, he made his first steps in trade unionism and the struggle against colonialism. He was the representative of the historic compromise that united Bourguiba with more socialist fringes of the Neo-Destour party, which then included many currents, one of

mystique" around the plan, which was conceived as a comprehensive collective tool that encompassed not only economic objectives, but also "spiritual and moral activities".[32] Such a global undertaking involved transforming the economy, restructuring the social fabric – notably through the establishment of cooperatives – and extending the social transformations known as "modernization", which concerned not only modes of production, but also lifestyles, and even women's bodies (through family planning and birth control). As Ben Salah expressed it in 1965:

> [W]e wanted to break the straitjacket in which we lived. This straitjacket was certainly something we needed to defend ourselves against the spiritual intrusion of colonialism. Yes, we did care about this defence and we were then much more conservative than we are today! [...] For we are now against those same traditions that we used to cultivate to protect ourselves against political, moral, and even metaphysical intrusions.[33]

A complete political and ideological apparatus was then put in place, which aroused opposition and contestation, but called for values of social justice, backed by strong belief in progress, and even, at least rhetorically, in democracy and freedom.

The aim was then to "fight against the emergence of new feudal systems".[34] A global vision of development was at work, aimed at reforming the foundations of the economy and drastically changing society. Ben Saleh expressed great pride in his policy as early as May 1966: "Tunisian society today has largely got rid of nomadism and tribal divisions to become a homogeneous, modern society, rich in all its nuances and diversity, but where these nuances are not breeding grounds for political or sociological division."[35] The model that had been put in place was based on a set of supporting structures built on the school-based meritocracy and on the small-scale property that was supervised by collective units throughout the country. It was firmly oriented towards production and construction, setting up industry that was strongly supported by the state when it was not directly state owned, and was sometimes backed by foreign investment.

The break with Ben Salah and his socialist experiment marked the beginning of the liberal turn of the regime. He was dismissed from his ministerial duties in

which could be described as Labour, headed by Ben Salah. Salem Mansouri, أحمد بن صالح و زمانه (Ahmed Ben salah and his time) (Tunis, 2018).

32. Ahmed Ben Salah "Tunisie de demain. Déclaration faite à la revue Carthage, no. 2, avril–juin 1965", in Ahmed Ben Salah, *Économie et promotion de l'Homme* (Tunis, n.d.), pp. 9–21, quotation on p. 11.

33. *Ibid.*

34. *Ibid.*, p. 12.

35. Ahmed Ben Salah "Vers un avenir meilleur, conférence tenue devant les journalistes d'outre-mer à Paris 11 mai 1966", in Ahmed Ben Salah, *Économie et promotion*, pp. 35–59, quotation on p. 46.

September 1969, excluded from the Destourian Socialist Party, and stripped of his mandate as a deputy. Accused of having breached the president's trust and of having taken advantage of his poor state of health, he was brought before the High Court of Justice and sentenced on 25 May 1970 to ten years of hard labour.

The system that was put in place in the second half of the 1970s called into question some of Ben Salah's initiatives and relied increasingly on private investment and a policy of major works that especially benefited the middle classes and a new business sector. Later, from the second half of the 1970s, it rested on the financial support of the World Bank and the IMF, which set up structural adjustment facilities. Breaking with socialist tradition, Bourguiba appointed Hédi Nouira (1911–1993), a strong proponent of economic liberalism, who was as enthusiastic about it as his predecessor had been about the planned economy.[36] Hédi Nouira proposed what he named the "contract of progress" in 1972. The aim was to boost investment through a variety of mechanisms and institutions and to create wealth, all while securing the middle classes' access to property and public services. This was to be done in particular by freeing up private investment, erasing domestic debt, and implementing a policy of public infrastructure works. He opened up the economy to the outside world by granting tax benefits to companies whose production was exported.[37] The new Tunisian doctrine was a combination of this entry into capitalism and the persistence of a strong state-led politics. The social welfare policy was then drastically transformed and focused more on the promotion and consolidation of the middle class: the two pillars were access to property and the support of younger people, in order to guarantee social peace and the arrival of foreign capital.[38]

Yet, this liberalism was based on clusters of competitiveness, all of which were located on the coastal fringe, contributing to the dramatic accentuation of territorial and social inequalities. As agricultural development was further neglected,[39] vast regions (notably in the north-west) were emptied of their inhabitants in favour of the large cities on the coast, such as Tunis, Sfax, and

---

36. Hédi Nouira comes from the same region as Bourguiba and from a privileged family background. He did not take the usual path of the Tunisian elite, as he did not attend the Sadiki College; nevertheless, he was an important player in student activism in Paris during the colonial period, and a long-time companion of Bourguiba with whom he shared the experience of incarceration in the late 1930s. He was the founder of the Central Bank of Tunisia and its director from 1958 until he became prime minister in 1970, a position he occupied until he was struck by a stroke ten years later. On the 1970 crisis and Nouira's accession to power, see Sadri Khiari, "Bourguiba et les bourgeois. La crise de 1970–1971", in Michel Camau and Vincent Geisser (eds), *Habib Bourguiba, la trace et l'héritage* (Paris, 2004), pp. 357–370.

37. Law of 27 April 1972.

38. Michel Camau, "Chronique politique Tunisie", in Hervé Bleuchot & Maurice Flory (eds), *Centre de recherches et d'études sur les sociétés méditerranéennes, Annuaire de l'Afrique du Nord 1974* (Paris, 1975), Vol. 13, pp. 345–372.

39. René Dumont, *Paysannerie aux abois, Ceylan, Tunis, Sénégal* (Paris, 1972).

Sousse. The domination of the north-eastern coastal area over the inland regions was reinforced by the regional affiliations of most leaders and ministers, most of whom came from this area. Moreover, a new business class became wealthier, relying on this liberal policy, coupled with widespread corruption and nepotism in the deleterious climate of a seemingly endless reign. The era of liberal normalization took place in a context where President Bourguiba, who had been frail for several years, was prey to multiple plots and intrigues. Disgrace, such as that of Ben Salah, fell easily on those who dared to exceed their function or rank.

The authoritarian state had been in place since the early 1960s, and the High Court of State Security was set up to deal with political trials. Having purged the Arab nationalist movements, then the communist left, at the end of the 1970s, the Ministry of the Interior became particularly interested in the Islamist movement.[40] Islamist trials began in 1981, while the regime announced unprecedented democratization under the rule of the new Prime Minister, Mohamed Mzali (1925–2010). This resulted in the legalization of a certain number of banned parties, including the Tunisian Communist Party and the Movement of Socialist Democrats, and the subsequent recognition of a "legal opposition". The Islamist parties, for their part, built their popularity on criticism of the voluntarist and modernizing policy of the Destourian party and its leader, and especially of its cultural secularist side, endorsed both by the Ben Salah era and by Nouira's reforms. Ultimately, Mzali's policies were based on a paternalistic discourse that urged everyone to work hard and to break away from traditions, which were seen as obstacles to development.

The frustration generated by the authoritarianism of the new government and its reforms is perceptible in the student and youth mobilizations that took place during the 1970s.[41] Many students hailed from the working and lower classes and had benefited from the educational boom of the previous decade. Now, they moved from the status of a privileged postcolonial vanguard of the new nation to that of a dangerous class, whose material benefits were conditional on obedience to an increasingly authoritarian order.[42] In addition, the country's wage earners and civil servant elites, especially the

---

40. At the time, Tunisian Islamists were organized mainly around the Mouvement de la Tendance Islamique (MTI), founded c.1970, which is a reformist movement aiming at restoring the place of Islam in modernist Tunisia. It is heavily influenced by the Muslim Brotherhood and followed the same trend of political radicalization in the late 1970s. The MTI structured itself as a political party in 1981, led by Rached Ghannouchi and Abdelfattah Mourou.

41. Mohamed Dhifallah, "Bourguiba et les étudiants. Stratégie en mutation (1956–1971)", in Camau and Geisser, *Habib Bourguiba*, pp. 313–324. Burleigh Hendrickson, "Finding Tunisia in the Global 1960s", *Monde(s). Histoires, espaces, relations*, 11 (2017), pp. 61–78; "March 1968: Practicing Transnational Activism from Tunis to Paris", *International Journal of Middle East Studies*, 44:4 (November 2012), pp. 755–774.

42. John P. Entelis, "L'Héritage contradictoire de Bourguiba. Modernisation et intolérance politique", in Camau and Geisser, *Habib Bourguiba*, pp. 223–248.

youngest, felt neglected by an ever more closed and mafia-like regime. This was expressed, among other things, by the massive general strike of January 1978, which was brutally suppressed and included the arrest of trade union leaders.[43] Although these mobilizations were the target of bloody repression, they remained within the framework of a classic repertoire of social protest. With the "opening" – a word used by the regime for a very light political liberalization in 1981 – the channel of negotiation between these different bodies, and in particular with the Tunisian General Labour Union (UGTT, from the French Union Générale Tunisienne du Travail), seemed to have been relaunched.

In this climate of gradual disintegration of the national unity, which had been inherited from the anti-colonial struggle, pacifying social reforms were attempted in the late 1970s, the effects of which began to be seen when riots broke out in 1983. They were aimed in particular at regulating informal housing on the outskirts of large Sahelian towns and in impoverished city centres, and at improving developing urban areas, roads, electricity and water supply, and sewerage systems. This triggered the policy of "de-gourbification", the watchword for eradicating "urban wounds" that had become a serious problem for health and public order. The neighbourhoods or cities targeted by these development policies represented major challenges when it came to restoring confidence in human and economic development, as government leaders were aware. Loans were granted by the IMF and IBRD from 1977, as well as by Western countries, to undertake this work and carry out reforms. Relations between Tunisia and the international institutions were excellent. At the same time, consumer prices rose sharply and the situation of the most precarious was worsening. Credits allocated to the Compensation Fund were increasingly large, rising from 8.5 million dinars in 1973 to 259 million dinars in the early 1980s. This increase was largely due to the rise in prices on the world market, but also a result of Prime Minister Mzali's adjustment measures, imposed by the IMF and the World Bank.

AT NEIGHBOURHOOD LEVEL: WHAT PRICES MEANT

"Bread was so cheap that it was wasted" was a phrase that was heard repeatedly in 1983, on the eve of the revolt. A television programme had shown in the weeks before the price rise that bread was being fed to animals. It is said that, on seeing this story, President Bourguiba decided to put an abrupt end to bread subsidies. It appears that the decision to put an end to compensation mechanisms on the prices of basic foodstuffs was taken in the autumn of 1983, and was then discussed with labour and management representatives. It was

---

43. The highly complex relationship between political power and the trade union is captured in many accounts. See Dachraoui, *Bourguiba*, pp. 49–102.

presented as a way of consolidating finances and as a means of redistribution. At the time, members of the Tunisian government as well as international institutions viewed these subsidies as responsible for the worsening of inequalities because they applied to all equally and not equitably. In addition, the government believed that by freeing itself from this expenditure, it would be able to create a fund for the most deprived. It even promised the trade unions that salaries would be raised. But while the government was still discussing gradual implementation, the president decided that the doubling of the price of bread should be announced immediately, at the end of 1983.[44]

But what exactly are we talking about? Were people starving to death in Tunisia in the early 1980s? The country seemed to be "making progress in the fight against underdevelopment", with special attention being paid to social programmes, as indicated in a 1980 IBRD restricted report entitled "Tunisia. Social Aspects of Development".[45] Yet, the report pointed out that "by focusing social services mainly on those who can pay for them through taxes, the benefits to the poor remain small, though by no means insignificant".[46] This was precisely one of the major problems in the implementation of social policy in the liberal Nouira and then the neoliberal Mzali frameworks. The same report stated that absolute poverty affected "no less than one Tunisian in ten".[47] The social problems, which were already massive and highly visible in the big cities with regard to housing and sanitation, inevitably became more acute with the liberalization policies.

The key to resolving this problem of aid distribution therefore seemed, for both international experts and the Tunisian government, to lie in an economic orthodoxy whose aim became specifically to combat poverty, but not necessarily inequality, by acting on employment and on prices. The consensus was that the compensation funds mainly benefit the rich. On the issue of prices, it was stated that "[t]he available information indicates that, in relative and absolute terms, the price support programme applied by the Compensation Fund benefits middle and upper income groups over the poor population and the urban population over the rural population".[48] In order to achieve adjustments, "transfers and subsidies must eventually be replaced by self-help and productive activities".[49] The report therefore recommended that a number of redistributive tools should be abandoned because

44. Most of the accounts concur in explaining the decision to use force through "corridor plots" between Prime Minister Mohamed Mzali and Interior Minister Driss Guiga. These episodes are recounted in Mohamed Mzali, *Un premier ministre de Bourguiba témoigne* (Tunis, 2010), pp. 287–309.
45. IBRD, "Tunisie. Aspects sociaux du développement", Archives nationales tunisiennes [ANT], Fonds Morched Chabbi. ANT–106 /RDE 113.
46. *Ibid.*, Introduction, p. ii.
47. *Ibid.*
48. *Ibid.*, p. viii.
49. *Ibid.*, p. iii.

they were obstacles to achieving the objectives: "housing subsidies, pricing policies, indiscriminate student subsidies, investment incentives that favour high-intensity technologies" were all considered to be obstructive.[50] New priorities were suggested, including a special effort on housing, but also other programmes that were subsequently set up, aimed at small farmers or small businesses (in particular through the Fonds de Promotion et de Décentralisation Industrielles, a fund for industrial promotion and decentralization that was set up in 1974).[51]

It was on this basis that the negotiations that preceded the price increase were conducted. The trade unions were content to negotiate compensation for low wages, seemingly ignoring the huge proportion of poor people without wages.

The material and moral expectations of the population and their perception of the political situation as they may be read in the revolt focus on the issue of "true prices". But the government and the World Bank probably did not share the same understanding. For the government, it was a matter of assessing what the compensation funds cost the state and therefore the citizens, then reducing that cost. For the working classes, it was a matter of assessing the fair value of bread and what one gives in return for the right to bread; in other words, the value of one's work and the terms of the unequal exchange between vulnerable workers and a welfare state. In fact, bread did not cost the same for everyone. It became relatively common – at least in the aftermath of the revolt – to note this structural inequality, which cruelly highlighted the main flaws of the liberal policy, which was geared towards the profits of the richest and the consolidation of the middle class in a country where workers' poverty was still endemic, as was unemployment.

An initial comment must be made about the increase in food prices. It was more significant for large loaves, the basis of the diet of the humblest, than it was for the baguettes of the urban middle classes. It was also very high for the semolina that was used to garnish ordinary dishes, especially in rural areas. To understand the impact of this sharp rise, one must look at the proportion of the budget of the poorest households that was devoted to food expenditure. Statistical studies on household expenditure and a comprehensive survey that was published in 1978 provide a measure of the inequality.[52] Overall, far from being a country where bread was wasted, at the beginning of the 1980s Tunisia was a country where malnutrition was still predominant, with strong vitamin deficiencies.

Housing was an important part of the state's social policy, but the programmes so far had been mainly property access programmes for the middle

---

50. *Ibid.*, p. vi.
51. Art. 45, law 73–82 (31 December 1973).
52. "La consommation et les dépenses des ménages en Tunisie, 1965–68" and "Enquête nationale sur le budget et la consommation des ménages 1975" (Tunis, 1978).

classes, carried out by the Société Nationale Immobilière de Tunisie (SNIT),[53] through lease-purchase programmes.[54] From 1977 onwards, the state embarked on a policy of integrating informal settlements. After having renounced the violent destruction of shanty towns, which had been a source of tension, it was then necessary, within the framework of the "contract of progress", to ensure social peace in these long-neglected districts. These operations were carried out within the framework of an urban project agreement that was concluded between the Tunisian Government and the World Bank, ratified on 24 October 1979. Preliminary studies of the development of informal settlements provide crucial information in this regard. We have focused mainly on those concerning part of Greater Tunis, and two areas in particular: the Saïda Manoubia neighbourhood, named after the Sufi saint whose mausoleum is located nearby, on the slopes that descend from the Kasbah towards the Great Sebkha, and the Jebel Lahmar ("The Red Mountain", now Ezzaïatin) neighbourhood, located between the Belvedere, the Bardo barracks, the El Manar university campus, and new residential areas (see Figure 2).[55]

All these informal settlements were subject to massive development plans in the years 1979–1980, supported by the World Bank at enormous cost.[56] The brutal implementation of these plans was at the heart of the Bread Revolt. The preliminary rehabilitation studies realized by the urban planners are valuable sources for understanding the lifestyles and tensions at work in these areas. The targeted neighbourhoods were made up of unplanned housing, self-constructions that ranged from rough "solid" housing on agricultural land that had been bought from intermediaries, to shanty towns or precarious constructions that were installed on more or less insalubrious spaces on the edge of *Sebkha* (see Figure 2),[57] or on agricultural land. It is indeed in these peripheral urban areas that the effects of the end of subsidy were most felt, as well as in certain rural areas in the north and south of the country. Between 1973 and

---

53. This was founded in 1957 (law 57–19, 10 September 1957), and was consolidated by the creation of regional directions in the 1970s. The SNIT was complemented by the Agence Foncière d'Habitat in 1974 and the Société de Promotion de logements sociaux in 1977. Sami Ben Fguira et Mongi Belarem, "Quel avenir pour le logement social en Tunisie ?". Available at: http://journals.openedition.org/confins/13450; last accessed 2 May 2019.

54. See Morched Chabbi, "État, politiques urbaines et habitat spontané"; Amor Belhedi, "Différenciation et recomposition de l'espace urbain en Tunisie", *Cahiers du GREMAMO*, 18 (2005), pp. 21–46.

55. ANT, Fonds Morched Chabbi, Fo. 235/RHA 716 – "Réhabilitation des quartiers de Djebel Lahmar et de Saïda Manoubia"; Fo. 223/RHA 720 – "Suivi socio-économique des projets de réhabilitation des quartiers de Saïda Manoubia et Jebel Lahmar" (August 1983).

56. The cost of the operations in Jebel Lahmar is valued at around 15 million dinars in 1978. See Béchir Chebab Tekari, "Habitat et dépassement du droit en Tunisie. Les constructions spontanées", in Baduel, *Habitat, État, Société*, p. 167.

57. A *Sebkha* is a saline area that is below sea level. Humid throughout the year, it is flooded in winter.

1984, out of 3,550 ha of urbanized land, 2,560 ha was occupied by housing, almost half of which was illegal housing.[58]

A number of observations can be made regarding the development plans for these neighbourhoods, and in particular the preparatory documentation that supported them.

The question of settlement density does not seem to have been a determining factor, unless one compares the density of these neighbourhoods with the middle-class neighbourhoods they adjoin.[59] Jebel Lahmar is located on the edge of one of the most affluent districts of Tunis, Mutuelleville, where ambassadors' residences and villas with gardens are located. The hill of Mutuelleville is dominated by the modernist silhouette of a Hilton hotel, which borders the Jebel Lahmar district. This district has seen much large-scale construction, such as the Taoufik Private Clinic (the first private clinic in Tunisia, inaugurated in 1979) and the building site (in the 1980s) for the headquarters of the Arab League.[60] On the other side of Jebel Lahmar, on the road to Bab Saadoun, a housing estate called Rommana provides a perfect example of the policy of access to property designed by the SNIT for the middle classes. Made up of small individual villas, it was being offered in the form of rent-sales[61] to employees of the national education ministry.

The popular district's footprint in the early 1980s contrasted sharply with the massive villas in leafy neighbourhoods. Nevertheless, the density within neighbourhoods varied greatly; for example, the Jebel Lahmar neighbourhood ranged from 200 to 1,200 inhabitants per km^2. This can be explained by the fact that there were some areas here in which housing was not yet abundant, and that more organized and less dense residential areas could be found at the edge of these districts, particularly to the north and along the Belvedere garden.

Another indicator relates to the distribution of household expenditure. It shows the considerable proportion taken up by food expenses, as well as the low level of expenditure on housing and other consumption items. The first

---

58. Morched Chabbi, "Pratiques et logiques en matière de planification urbaine. Le cas du plan de restructuration du quartier Ettadhamen à Tunis", in Nicole Haumont and Alain Marie (eds), *Politiques et pratiques urbaines dans les pays en voie de développement* (Paris, 1987), pp. 83–101.
59. According to surveyors, in 1982, the Jebel Lahmar district had a population of 41,620 people, divided into 7,710 households and 4,660 dwellings. The density of occupation of the dwellings is more indicative, since it can be observed that in sixty-eight per cent of the houses there were three to six people per room. *Projet de réhabilitation dans le centre de Tunis, Jebel Lahmar*, "Tableau 31. Répartition des logements selon le nombre de personnes /pièce (1982)", ANT, Fonds Morched Chabbi, Fo. 235/RHA 716.
60. This was relocated to Tunis between 1979 and 1990. A contest for the building's design was launched in 1983 but this was not pursued. The site became the headquarters of the Ministry of Information, then the Ministry of Foreign Affairs.
61. The rent-sale system (location-vente) was a way to ensure access to property for those who has no capital. They were just renting the house until they reached the proper sum enabling them to become the owners.

step in cleaning up required that the population of these neighbourhoods be connected to the sewerage system and to municipal drinking water. Electricity, gas, roads, and street lighting also had to be installed, and public transportation had to be created or existing lines extended. Connections to all networks had so far been made on an ad hoc basis, with the help of a client-based system in which the "omda",[62] and the bigger land vendors,[63] played an important role.

Far from being completely insalubrious areas, these urban neighbourhoods did not wait for massive state intervention before organizing themselves and allowing more or less legal connection of their dwellings to the public road networks. The same is true for the commercial businesses that set up there, since both districts had many shops and markets. The lack of other facilities was much more obvious, because it was hard to organize them outside the central state. As a result, all these districts were poorly equipped in terms of schools and nurseries, healthcare centres, sports facilities, and other public services.

The consequences of this relative overcrowding and the difficulty of access, as well as the lack of healthcare facilities, can be seen in the figures on diseases, especially among children.[64] This situation was much more critical in the case of Saïda Manoubia, which can be explained by the fact that the district was built on the edge of semi-marshland, often infested with mosquitoes. In addition, while most of the inhabitants were working people, many were manual labourers, often hired on a daily basis, and there was a very high unemployment rate, especially among young people.[65]

These different elements were at the core of the policy of rehabilitation of already old informal settlements: most of them had begun to be built as early as the 1950s. One can observe the journeys of entire families who moved from impoverished rural areas to these outlying areas,[66] attracted by the potential of the capital, or in search of better opportunities for their

62. The "omda" is the state representative at local level.

63. Usually, the land is sold to the people who settle there; but it is often sold by people who do not really own it but farm it, or just took over a piece of land. See Chabbi about the reinforcement of the local powers through planification, "Pratiques et logiques", p. 101.

64. *Projet de réhabilitation dans le centre de Tunis, Saïda Manoubia*, ANT, Fonds Morched Chabbi, Fo. 235/RHA 716.

65. In 1982, fifty-two per cent of young men were unemployed in Saïda Manoubia. The overall unemployment rate was twenty per cent compared with 8.7 per cent in the country as a whole. Jebel Lahmar had a lower overall unemployment rate (fifteen per cent) but an even higher unemployment rate for young men, at fifty-five per cent. ANT, Fonds Morched Chabbi, Fo. 235/RHA 716.

66. Fredj Stambouli, "Populations néo-citadines et besoins humains fondamentaux. Le cas de Djebel Lahmar en Tunisie", *Dritte Welt*, 7 (Enda/PNUD, Austria, 1979), pp. 302–324.

children.[67] The management of these populations, and in particular the nomads, did not go smoothly or without the implementation of repressive methods, especially in the last days of the French Protectorate.[68]

This rural exodus continued unabated during the decades following independence, in addition to more distant emigration to Europe, the Gulf, or neighbouring Libya. But it sometimes also involved the settlement of Tunisians, who moved from cramped apartments in the city centre to have a piece of land of their own and build a home, which they expected to be a villa,[69] apparently the aspiration of Tunisian families in the 1980s. Most of the inhabitants interviewed in the early 1980s intended to stay in these neighbourhoods and were slowly building a more sustainable living environment. They wanted to take advantage of the city's services and infrastructure, and they entered the job market (be it formal or informal). These expectations can be read in the replies to the surveyors' questionnaires. The inhabitants of Saïda Manoubia were at the time primarily worried about connecting to the drinking water system and accessing facilities, rather than land tenure regularization.

Although the housing issue did not seem to produce any specific social movements, it can be assumed from reading the urban planning reports that the neighbourhoods were nevertheless organized to defend their interests. Claude Liauzu observed in 1986 that riots were part of the repertoire of communication that these spaces had established with the authorities. While he deplored the fact that "these practices did not lead to directly political forms, and the local level did not become the basis of an associative life comparable to that born in other regions",[70] it is possible to read the events of 1984 as one of the modalities of this political structuring of marginalized spaces. These spaces were socially marginal, made up of the working poor, the vast majority of whom were self-employed; but they participated in the urban and local economy. Over the previous few decades, they had also been developing their own modes of organization and relationships with the authorities in order to provide for the basic needs of the population and to protect the "illegal" activities (relating to the informal economy) that were taking place there. The revolt of January 1984 was perhaps one of the forms that these social

67. This was the case for the author's grandparents, for example. In the mid-1940s, having left the island of Djerba, where he had a bit of land and a few olive trees, my grandfather chose to entrust them to a cousin and go to sell olives in town. He settled in the area of Saïda Manoubia and little by little built his house, which had a small window used for the sale of olives.

68. Zeïneb Mejri, "'Les indésirables' bédouins dans la région de Tunis entre 1930 et 1956", *Cahiers de la Méditerranée*, 69 (2004), pp. 77–101. A first report on the settlement of populations deemed undesirable in Djebel Lahmar had been written in 1955: J-B. Dardel and C. Klibi, "Un faubourg clandestin de Tunis. Le Djebel Lahmar", *Cahiers de Tunisie*, 10 (1955), pp. 211–224.

69. Single-family house.

70. Claude Liauzu, "Crises urbaines, crises de l'État, mouvements sociaux", in Brown *et al.*, *Urban Crisis*, pp. 23–41, 27.

movements took, and it is noteworthy that they also occurred in areas that were not abandoned, but were the object of state intervention. What Liauzu failed to see at the time, and becomes clear from the witness accounts already quoted, is that what he called "collective bargaining through riot" was not necessarily based on the absence of law. Rather, it was generated by the accentuation of injustice within the framework of an implicit but established contract with the state.

The implementation of restructuring plans increased financial burdens on families. We do not have any direct data, but it seems clear that connecting to electricity, water, or sewerage increased housing costs. It was specified in the agreements with international organizations that these operations should be entirely financed by the inhabitants (this being a condition of cost recovery). Similarly, the absence or lack of public facilities and services in areas where youth unemployment was endemic determined the perception by young people of their social "value" and whether or not they belonged to the national community.

The government's move towards the "truth of prices", which had been under way since the summer of 1983, was based in a culture of social negotiation that it was thought had been restored after the social crisis of 1978. It was also based on the feeling that the state had done a great deal for the most modest. The government calculated that it would be able to save money by putting an end to subsidy funds, and that part of the saving (20 million dinars) could be spent directly on the most disadvantaged. This also explains why the UGTT, having negotiated a wage increase, was unable to foresee what was going to explode in December 1983. In this calculation, the place of the weakest, if not completely neglected, was greatly underestimated in terms of the relationship that had been established between them and a state that exercised its authority in different ways in these areas and over these populations – alternating aid plans and strong forms of coercion (especially on the youth, who were accused of banditry or being pro-Islamist). Confronted with this, the forms of resistance developed specific strategies. While children lent a hand to state repression on occasion, in return for payment, in early 1984 they took to the streets to protect the few possessions their families had, or simply to set fires.

In the interplay of relations between society and the Bourguibian government, these fluctuations took place almost systemically, sometimes leading to situations of great violence and revealing the complex relationships that had been established. In this landscape, revolts can be interpreted as political statements made by the people and directed at a dominant elite, as can be clearly recognized through the symbols used.

THE VIOLENCE OF REPRESSION AND
THE CONSTRUCTION OF ISLAMISM

The end of the social welfare experiment led by Ahmed Ben Salah was accompanied by two complementary movements: the alignment of Tunisia with the model of a liberal Western economy and the strengthening of an authoritarian and repressive state. The student movements of 1967–1972 were witnesses and victims of this harsher regime. The struggles that marked these years showed the new place of educated youth in the political life of independent Tunisia.[71] Other forms of protest continued, particularly in the southern part of the country, including border incidents and tensions in working-class towns. These threatened the sovereignty of the country, and also perpetuated internal struggles: at stake was the Bourguibian state and the supposed national consensus.

The "coup of Gafsa" in January 1980 combined all these elements. Nationalists of the Youssefist branch organized a putsch from Libya and stormed the military barracks in the southern industrial city of Gafsa. The demonstrators promoted this botched action on 26 January 1980 as a chance to recall the massacre perpetrated by the Tunisian army two years earlier during "Black Thursday", bloodshed perpetrated against the workers and students who had mobilized within the framework of the general strike. The Gafsa Coup was described by the authorities as an externally led attempt to destabilize the regime. This episode continued the struggles for power that had shaken the National Movement.[72] It was also quickly described as a manipulation by Islamists, the regime's new bête noire. These scenarios were echoed in most of the ministries and embassies, which began to see the Islamists' hand behind every social movement. This rhetoric can be found both in French consular papers and in IMF reports that underlined the risk.

The insurrectional period of 1983–1984 could have ended with the announcement of price restoration, when everyone would have gone home. This is partly what happened after a moment of popular jubilation when people came out of their homes to greet the return to normality. But in reality, although the protests stopped, the repression continued. The scale of the repression makes it possible to recall what was at stake: the true value of bread. In the testimonies heard at the IVD, what is most striking is the violence

---

71. See, among others, Dhifallah, "Bourguiba et les étudiants"; Salem Labyadh and Mohamed Dhifallah, الطلبة العرب التقدميون الوحدويون (The Arab unionist students) (Tunis, 2017); Michael Ayari, *Le Prix de l'engagement politique dans la Tunisie autoritaire. Gauchistes et islamistes sous Bourguiba et Ben Ali (1957–2011)* (Paris, 2017).
72. The National Movement designed the national struggle for liberation against the French colonizer. The movement fractured, with competition between the Arab nationalists (usually called Youssefist because of their leader Salah Ben Youssef, assassinated in 1961) and the Destourians (Constitutionalists), who believed in stricter Tunisian nationalism and had Habib Bourguiba as their leader. Both groups considered themselves to be "modernists".

and the length of the repression that pursued the victims long afterwards – after their release, after the physical torture ended. Many of them never managed to find a job again, and their families were subjected to humiliation and rituals of submission. Jamel Sassi recounts that, every week, his father had to go and sign a paper certifying that his son had not been murdered by the forces of law and order. Repression still persisted in homes and workplaces. The ban on access to a civil service position, or indeed to any kind of job, was sometimes aimed at entire families. The figures vary. According to the League for Human Rights, the riots left 123 people dead and 1,500 injured. The IVD gave significantly lower figures: eighty-nine dead and 938 wounded (including 348 police). The repression did not stop after the riots, nor after the presidential pardon; that did not affect everyone, and was only carried out by Ben Ali after his 1987 coup d'état (amnesty law of 18 August 1988).

The established dialogue between the demonstrators and the authorities resulted in a provisional victory for the demonstrators. Subsequently, a lengthy repressive response was put in place, which went beyond simply bringing the actors of the revolt to their knees. This violence was legitimized through the diagnosis of an Islamist conspiracy and its rhetoric. Mohamed Mzali expresses it bluntly from the outset. The people who were on the street in January 1984 were "the underworld". His social contempt is unvarnished in his interview with *Jeune Afrique*, conducted after the events. He describes the participants as "those excluded from society, the unemployed, those who have escaped justice". Responding to *Le Monde* on 7 January, he admits that the police were overwhelmed – and claims that the country was not a police state; but states that the slogans heard in the streets were "disturbing";[73] "we were certainly expecting some commotion but not real commando operations". Later, he laments: "Alas! There were also several children pushed into the front ranks of the rioters, using the technique of martyrdom." Here, Mzali calls up an imaginary that is fuelled by images of children pushed to the front lines in the Islamic Republic of Iran's fight against Iraq.

He stands firm on the background of the "riots": "Of course, we had to start with the bread; I did it. You have to have the courage to tell the truth to the people. We had it. But there was this political manipulation [...]."[74] In short, he acknowledges a few mistakes in the maintenance of order, and indeed sacked the Minister of the Interior, but he salutes the position of a government that he considers democratic and balanced in the face of the savagery deployed by organized gangs rather than the people. The commission of enquiry he sent out issued its report on 15 March and confirmed this diagnosis.

---

73. One can conclude that he is referring to the slogan "Mzali is the enemy of God", noted by the French Embassy. This is a classic slogan of the Islamists, the other side of the coin to "There is no God but God and Mohammad is the beloved of God".

74. Paul Balta and Michel Deuré, "Le chef de l'État tunisien a annoncé qu'il reportait de trois mois toute augmentation des produits céréaliers", *Le Monde* (7 January 1984).

But the continuation of repression against the actors of January 1984, the worsening of difficulties for the most vulnerable, the decay of a power that was more than ever focused on the "Supreme Combatant", who was now no more than a puppet agitated by many "courtiers", determined the management of social problems in the country for a long time. In order to maintain the reign and credibility of the postcolonial power, the fiction of a united nation was kept alive, as witnessed by the scenes of jubilation on 6 January. However, many fractures openly appeared during those few days:

> The division of Tunisia into two worlds that ignore each other and now confront each other, the conjunction of two miseries – it would be better to say two "frustrations" – that of the underprivileged countryside and that of the suburbs where the unemployed and idle young people are piled up, has brutally brought about an unknown Tunisia. It is a hard, violent country, which finds its slogans in the class struggle as much as in Khomeinism, which rejects the Tunisia of Bourguiba, humanist and tolerant but also forgetful of social justice, and which believed that the solution to its problems lay in the increase of the gross national product. "Enrich yourself" was the regime's unspoken watchword. "God is great" resounded against him.[75]

The two antithetical slogans seemed to simplify the upcoming confrontation. It can be read differently. January 1984 certainly highlighted the flaws in the Open Door Policy initiated in 1981. The few tolerated parties – and among them the Communist Party – were not represented in the streets, and thus formed a bloc that could be described as bourgeois in the face of the Islamists and the far-left parties, who, while taking care not to claim authorship of the revolt, expressed their support for it. On the political stage, liberalization and democratization appeared for what they were: the mask of a political landscape where real opposition is muzzled and/or repressed.

In the face of this, the consensus of the "advanced" classes (the political and economic elite, but also a large part of the middle class that bought into the state) was constructed as a façade of democracy. On the social level, the revolt attacked the symbols of the state and the goods of the wealthy class as much as those of the middle class: January 1984 was, in the words of Paul Balta, "the great fear of the wealthy".[76] But the wealthy were not only the class that had become considerably richer over the past decade: all property owners were designated as the privileged. The authorities wanted to seize power by maintaining pressure and reinforcing repression against the "bad poor". The middle class, which was initially indignant and subsequently afraid, had to continue to support the government. Social fear transformed into political fear, while social anger was disguised as an attack on the values and identity

---

75. Ministère des Affaires Etrangères, encrypted telegram from the Tunis Office, no. 100, Note of 19 January 1984 "Situation en Tunisie", signed by Perol.
76. Paul Balta, "La grande peur des nantis", *Le Monde*, 1 February 1984.

of modern Tunisia, the country that had built and carried this middle class. The impasses in the educational model and in spatial and generational inequalities were not put at the centre of the debate. Employees, including the most modest, have found themselves increasingly attached to the world of the wealthy, and to the security projected by the state.

The few days of the Bread Revolt were much more than an ephemeral food riot. They were one of those episodes in which we see the disappearance of an implicit social order, alongside promises of progress, hope, and a certain capacity to imagine a society as being open and fluid, or at least allowing forms of meritocracy, whether offered by schools, factories, or small informal trades. The value of bread is less measured by hunger than by the gap, transformed into a divide within a few days, between those who can "be part of it" and those who remain on the sidelines, who build other registers of belonging, other systems of recognition, whether through recourse to violence, religion, or emigration.

I would like to return to Partha Chatterjee's notion of "political society".[77] We can ask ourselves, as he does with regard to a certain number of social movements in India, whether what is at stake here is not precisely those who are too often considered to be on the margins, and constitute most of the populated modern world. To say this is not simply to say that those who took to the streets of Tunisia at the end of 1983 were a "silent majority." Rather, as Chatterjee suggests, they constitute a political force that belongs to a non-continuous and heterogeneous modernity, a political force whose social mainsprings are shifting and cannot be explained solely by the rationality of the state and its economy. Their dialogue with those who govern is undertaken through different modalities: one of these is revolt, but the most frequent is negotiation and the game of clientelism, which, in short, allows the greatest number to live their lives in the "system", even if they are most often operating outside the law. As he writes, "political society [is] a site of negotiation and contestation".[78]

When this fragile and always violent link – expressed so well by Jamel's testimony – breaks down, what Chatterjee calls "popular political art" brings into play techniques, new or tried and tested, to recover lost ground.

In the face of this, the state will play its part. It will break with its usual policy of integrating dissident elements to make people believe in change. Another strategy has to be pursued, first in the streets and then more silently in the jails, the neighbourhoods, and the whole territory. The most ferocious repression seen in Tunisia has been connected to designating particular categories as pariahs and dangerous (here, the young rioters or the Islamists) in combination with (re-) building spaces for negotiation and surveillance at

77. Chatterjee, *The Politics of the Governed.*
78. *Ibid.*, Part 3.

the neighbourhood level and showcasing the state's capacity for integration and rehabilitation, especially for the representatives of the middle classes.

There is little doubt that the revolution of 2011 can be read as another such crisis. Its very trigger puts the question of breach of contract back at the centre. Mohamed Bouazizi illegally set up his cart to sell his goods, as usual, on 17 December 2010, but was prevented from ensuring his subsistence in the interstices between the tolerated and the illegal. It was in this gap, and in the humiliation it produced, that the revolution broke out. As with bread, it was not simply a confrontation, or a discussion about a corrupt system (although this was also a central issue), but a political statement, from the working classes, on the meaning of social justice. The dignity that was demanded included possible access to the spaces between the legal and the (politically and economically) represented, in the very place where many of the world's people live. The revolt of 1983–1984 was not a revolution, but it played out a scenario that could have led to very deep changes in society and politics. Instead, the Tunisian authorities of the time, while playing the game of liberalism for a few years, were reinforcing their complex populist and authoritarian strategies to prevent another expression of the politics of the oppressed.

IRSH 66 (2021), pp. 69–91 doi:10.1017/S0020859021000158
© The Author(s), 2021. Published by Cambridge University Press on behalf of
Internationaal Instituut voor Sociale Geschiedenis

"We Cannot Please Everyone": Contentions over Adjustment in EPRDF Ethiopia (1991–2018)

Mehdi Labzaé

Centre français des études éthiopiennes (CFEE), Addis Ababa, Ethiopia
École Normale Supérieure, Paris, France

E-mail: mlabzae@protonmail.com

Sabine Planel

Institut des mondes Africains, Paris, France
Institut de recherche pour le développement (IRD), Marseille, France

E-mail: sabine.planel@ird.fr

ABSTRACT: This article looks at how rural inhabitants navigated state power under a regime led by a former socialist party that negotiated its conversion to a market economy while keeping tight control on the whole society. In that regard, it addresses adjustment in a very specific context, by analysing a distinctive chronology, raising the ruling party's ability to negotiate with the international financial institutions, and considering popular reactions from a rural point of view. The regime led by the Ethiopian Peoples' Revolutionary Democratic Front (EPRDF) managed to delay measures of structural adjustment during the 1990s and 2000s while deepening structures of state control it partly inherited from the former military junta. Brutal structural adjustment plans were refused, while international financial institutions were kept away from the Ethiopian government's policy mix, by way of elaborate ideological and institutional arrangements. The EPRDF coined its own version of the "developmental state" and renewed state control of the economy while deepening its articulation to global markets. Under the EPRDF, all sectors of society and especially peasantries were closely monitored and mobilized in the name of development. But although the open expression of dissent remained rare, peasants resorted to many strategies to cope with political control and to some extent divert it. By taking agricultural policies as a case study, the article describes peasant practices and questions differences between resistance, false compliance, and diversion, underlining how blurred such labels can actually be.

In May 2012, Ethiopia's Prime Minister Meles Zenawi spoke at the African session of the World Economic Forum in Addis Ababa. On stage, he lectured to an audience of economists, journalists, and politicians about the need to keep some sectors of the economy under state control. Telecommunications was cited as among the sectors that should not be privatized, as well as roads and infrastructure. Likewise, the banking sector should remain out of the reach of foreign investors. Meles calmly concluded: "we cannot please everyone".[1] This was enough to shock people not used to the Ethiopian government's parlance, but it was not a surprise to observers familiar with the man and his regime. This speech was among his last public appearances; Meles died three months later.

Meles was the leader of a party that had fought its way to power over seventeen years of guerrilla warfare. Before toppling the Marxist military regime known as the *derg* in May 1991, Meles and his comrades led an ethno-nationalist party with a strong Marxist–Leninist stance, the Tigray People's Liberation Front (TPLF). Fighting their way from their Northern province to the capital city, they created a pan-ethnic coalition known as the Ethiopian Peoples' Revolutionary Democratic Front (EPRDF). The EPRDF led the country from 1991 to 2019, when it was rebranded by Meles's most famous successor, Abiy Ahmed. The latter made substantial promises to liberalize political life and economic activity.

By the time they took power, EPRDF cadres were still calling themselves Marxists, following the Albanian model.[2] In subsequent years, they had to temper their leftist stance and negotiate a long and rather jerky process of adaptation to the market economy. Compared with most other post-socialist countries, however, the opening and liberalization of the economy proceeded slowly.[3] The ruling party followed its own version of the "developmental state", inspired by neo-Keynesian models of the Asian "tigers".[4] This implied a slow opening of the economy to foreign capital under tight and growing control by the party elites, who continued to publicly denounce the international financial institutions as Trojan horses aiming at importing their Western neo-liberal ideology into Ethiopia.

Unlike several West African countries, the slow adoption of free-market policies in Ethiopia took place without substantial political liberalization. Ethiopia had no place in any of the successive "waves of democratization", as the EPRDF took command of the *derg*'s control apparatus and expanded

1. See the video "Africa 2012 – Africa's Leadership and Social Entrepreneurs Award for Africa 2012", YouTube. Available at: https://www.youtube.com/watch?v=-qwgI62M6bc; last accessed 27 April 2020. The above-mentioned quotation is at 3:20.
2. See, e.g., Jean-Nicolas Bach, "*Abyotawi Democracy*: Neither Revolutionary nor Democratic, a Critical Review of EPRDF's Conception of Revolutionary Democracy in post-1991 Ethiopia", *Journal of Eastern African Studies*, 5 (2011), pp. 641–663; and John Young, *Peasant Revolution in Ethiopia: The Tigray People's Liberation Front, 1975–1991* (Cambridge, 2006).
3. For a different chronology, see *The China Journal*, "Special Issue: Transforming Asian Socialism; China and Vietnam Compared", 40 (1998); London Jonathan, "Viet Nam and the Making of Market-Leninism", *Pacific Review*, 22:3 (2009), pp. 375–399.
4. See Elsje Fourie, "China's Example for Meles' Ethiopia: When Development 'Models' Land", *Journal of Modern African Studies*, 53:3 (2015), pp. 289–316.

it even further.[5] Successive elections saw EPRDF landslide victories. In court, opposition leaders and journalists were facing "terrorism" charges, especially after the 2009 Anti-Terrorism Proclamation considerably extended the definition of this crime.[6] In rural areas, where until the mid-2010s around eighty per cent of the population lived, government programmes aimed first and foremost at controlling the peasantry through party and state structures, in the name of development.[7] Chronic humanitarian emergencies and persistent food insecurity legitimized growing state control, embedded within the policies of the developmental state.[8]

Although Ethiopia saw massive unrest in 2005, 2012, and again from 2014 onwards, there were no "adjustment riots" similar to those described in other pieces published in this volume. Repression, coupled with regular state interventions to control prices and the distribution of food and energy, prevented urban populations from rising up. But the absence of a nationwide social movement does not amount to the absence of small-scale opposition and day-to-day resistance. Under the EPRDF, rural dwellers found ways to subvert state policies and managed to address growing inequalities driven by liberalization and its effect on their livelihoods. Food riots and social movements opposing neoliberal policies in Africa remained largely urban-based, often led by trade unions, unemployed youth, and student activists.[9] However, rural inhabitants did not stay away from political settlements.

Given that the Ethiopian regime's adoption of neoliberalism differs from global patterns of neoliberalization, this article analyses processes of neoliberalization at various scales. It considers neoliberalization of government action as a scalar structuration process that frames power relations and access to state resources by delimiting scales.[10] For the sake of clarity, we will nevertheless focus on two opposing scales: elite politics and field-level peasant voices. Although in-between situations are not directly addressed, considering adjustment through its scalar dimensions nevertheless allows us to take them into account.

5. See, e.g., Wendy James, Donald Donham, Eisei Kurimoto, and Alessandro Triulzi (eds), *Remapping Ethiopia: Socialism and After* (Oxford, 2002).

6. See Proclamation no. 652, 2009, most notably its Article 6 introducing ten- to twenty-year prison terms for the widely defined crime of "encouragement of terrorism".

7. See René Lefort, "Powers – *Mengist* – and Peasants in Rural Ethiopia: The May 2005 Elections", *Journal of Modern African Studies*, 45:2 (2007), pp. 253–273; *idem*, "Powers – *Mengist* – and Peasants in Rural Ethiopia: The post-2005 Interlude", *Journal of Modern African Studies*, 48:3 (2010), pp. 435–460; Sarah Vaughan, "Revolutionary Democratic State-building: Party, State and People in EPRDF's Ethiopia", *Journal of Eastern African Studies*, 5 (2011), pp. 619–640.

8. See Sabine Planel, "A View of a *Bureaucratic* Developmental State: Local Governance and Agricultural Extension in Rural Ethiopia", *Journal of Eastern African Studies*, 8 (2014), pp. 420–437.

9. See John Walton and David Seddon (eds), *Free Markets and Food Riots* (Oxford, 1994).

10. See Neil Brenner, "The Limits to Scale? Methodological Reflections on Scalar Structuration", *Progress in Human Geography*, 25 (2001), pp. 591–614.

We question how peasant attitudes of apparent conformism can actually challenge authority.[11] Various swathes of the population engage in criticism of the government, displaying different strategies depending on their social status and the roles they play in their communities and in the state apparatus. The capacity to politicize material issues and social practices is not granted equally to all social groups; peasants are mostly denied such ability.[12] Civil servants who have daily contact with peasants often claim that the latter do not understand what is at stake in state policies. Farmers elected as local representatives also define social and farming good practices based on their understanding of the EPRDF motto. On the one hand, small acts of defiance such as foot dragging or absenteeism are interpreted as laziness, not as political practices. On the other hand, any open expression of grievances is taken as political, if not partisan, opposition, and is met with harsh repression. Accordingly, the ability of state agents or representatives to frame the limits of politics means they play a part in the manufacturing of consent in a constantly evolving authoritarian context.[13]

As a consequence, the article is divided into two parts. The first part describes how EPRDF elites coined their own ideology of a "developmental state" and how they subverted international injunctions to pursue privatization and liberalization. This jerky process of economic liberalization is analysed through written production by party cadres. The article shows the evolutions in the practical translation of this doctrine that was adapted in party crises and purges. The second part of the article focuses on the rural level and offers a more embedded vision of power relations in the local, highly politicized context. Based on enquiries regarding agricultural policies conducted during repeated stays in the countryside between 2010 and 2018 (Figure 1), the text shows how rural inhabitants reacted to government policies.[14] Though structural adjustment was not high on the developmental agenda, ethnographical data shows how increasingly selective economic policies, marking more and more market-oriented tendencies, were met with popular resistance.

---

11. See James Scott, *Domination and the Arts of Resistance: Hidden Transcripts* (New Haven, CT, 1992); and Alf Lüdtke, "La domination comme pratique sociale", *Sociétés contemporaines*, 99–100:3 (2015), pp. 17–63.
12. On the social distribution of political competency and on how to grasp it in social science, see Olivier Schwartz, "Sur le rapport des ouvriers du Nord à la politique. Matériaux lacunaires" *Politix*, 13:1 (1991), pp. 79–86.
13. See, e.g., Béatrice Hibou, *Anatomie politique de la domination* (Paris, 2011).
14. The authors worked together and separately on land registration and fertilizer distribution in six Ethiopian regions (weeks-long stays in Tigray in 2012 and 2017; weeks-long stays in Amhara in 2011 and 2016; repeated weeks-long stays in the Southern Region each year from 2010 to 2018; months-long stays in Benishangul-Gumuz and Gambella from 2013 to 2018; and weeks-long stays in Afar in 2012 and 2016). We crossed different qualitative methodologies, based on ethnography of state practices in rural villages and series of interviews with farmers and civil servants. We both paid specific attention to farmers' and civil servants' political behaviours and perceptions.

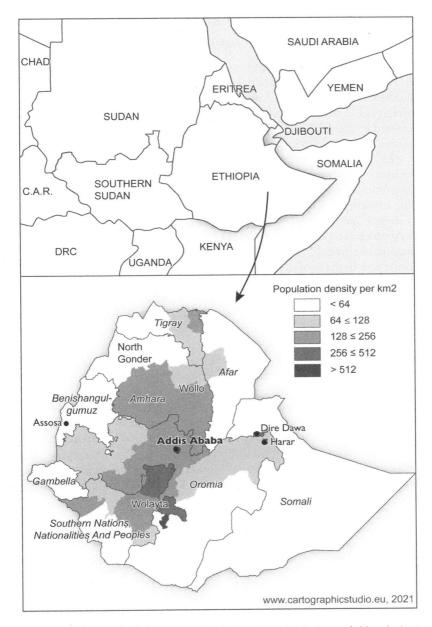

Figure 1. Map of the Federal Democratic Republic of Ethiopia displaying fieldwork sites and population densities.

THE DEFERRED EPRDF ADJUSTMENT

The EPRDF way of adapting reforms, 1991–2001

The year 1991 was an awkward moment for a socialist movement to reach state power. After seventeen years of civil war and state predation, the TPLF had to rebuild the national economy. And this could hardly be done without substantial foreign aid,[15] at a time when donors had no taste for the Marxist concepts put forward by the EPRDF coalition. New rulers had to craft a new economic policy, one that would satisfy both foreign donors and the rank and file of the party who had hitherto been fighting in the name of a socialist ideal. The party's inner circle forged its way out of Marxist–Leninism through practical and theoretical arrangements. Himself a TPLF sympathizer before breaking with the movement, Medhane Tadesse writes: "TPLF leaders who had venerated Enver Hoxha of Albania only months before triumphantly entering Addis Ababa had to show a great deal of pragmatism and adapt to the changing international context."[16]

In order to win the confidence of, and loans from, the Bretton Woods pair, the new regime had to adopt adjustment plans. However, the timing and scope of the adjustment differed from those in other sub-Saharan countries:[17] it was more about negotiating a smooth exit from the socialist economy than it was about liberalizing markets and organizing the rolling back of the state. The government adopted its first structural adjustment programme (SAP) in 1993. This first step essentially consisted of the privatization of formerly non-profitable state enterprises, including many state farms created by the previous regime. Accounting for less than ten per cent of GDP, industry was very weak and highly concentrated in Addis Ababa and to a lesser extent Dire Dawa.[18] The economy remained agrarian, and most of the workforce was engaged in household agriculture. The state owned almost ninety per cent of industrial enterprises, and the entire banking sector.[19] Attempts to control prices and agricultural production through quotas set by the Agricultural Marketing Corporation led to losses in agricultural productivity over the *derg* period, while industry remained

---

15. See, e.g., Dereje Feyissa, "Aid Negotiation: The Uneasy 'Partnership' between the EPRDF and the Donors", *Journal of Eastern African Studies*, 5 (2011), pp. 788–817.

16. See Medhane Tadesse, "The Tigray People's Liberation Front (TPLF)", in Gérard Prunier and Éloi Ficquet (eds), *Understanding Contemporary Ethiopia: Monarchy, Revolution and the Legacy of Meles Zenawi* (London, 2015), pp. 257–282, quotation on p. 276.

17. Philippe Hugon, *L'économie de l'Afrique* (Paris, 2010).

18. According to the World Bank data, industry accounted for six per cent of the Ethiopian GDP in 1992, reaching 11.5 per cent in 2000 and nine per cent in 2012. Industrial take-off took place afterwards, with 27.2 per cent of GDP in 2018. See https://data.worldbank.org/indicator/NV. IND.TOTL.ZS?locations=ET; last accessed 25 October 2019.

19. See René Lefort, "The Ethiopian Economy: The Developmental State vs. the Free Market", in Gérard Prunier and Éloi Ficquet (eds), *Understanding Contemporary Ethiopia: Monarchy, Revolution and the Legacy of Meles Zenawi* (London, 2015), pp. 357–394, quotation on p. 359.

nascent.[20] State farms were found suitable for privatization, since they could not be kept afloat without a high degree of coercion and forced labour. Dismantling them was more of a relief for the new regime. In 1996, a second SAP was declared, but a clash with the International Monetary Fund (IMF) in subsequent years brought it to an end. The 1998–2000 war with Eritrea slowed negotiations with the international financial institutions. In the late 1990s, Meles Zenawi had several arguments with the Fund's economists, who were (unsuccessfully) pushing for opening up the banking sector to foreign capital.[21] In the 1990s, tariffs were lowered and foreign exchange offices were opened within the private banking system.

Instituting and controlling the private sector

In terms of structural reform, getting rid of unprofitable units of production was not enough to satisfy international organizations; more needed to be done in order to secure donors' support. Former guerrilla fighters then crafted their own model to bring privatization to a higher level. State enterprises were sold to "endowment funds" created for this very purpose. Legally speaking, these funds consisted of private holdings. However, they were completely controlled by the central committees of EPRDF branches. From its creation in 1989, the EPRDF had been a coalition of parties closely affiliated to the TPLF. Each branch of the party administrated one of the newly created regional states, within a federal framework. Each endowment fund's board membership largely overlapped with each regional party's central committee. What the state had to sell was bought by the party.

Gebru Asrat, a long-time member of the TPLF central committee and President of the Tigray region from 1991 to 2001, describes the process as follows:

> [A]t governmental level, we had agreed to work with imperialist institutions such as the International Monetary Fund and the World Bank. This is why we had to accept the practical policy ameliorations at each level. When these institutions gave us directives calling for structural adjustment, we accepted it without debate. [...] These programmes framed by foreign influences were contrary to the revolutionary democracy we pretended to follow, it didn't fail to create confusion. [...] To the question "but then, doesn't this process destroy the pillars of our programme?", we had prepared an answer stating than in order not to lose benefits expected from international institutions and the World Bank, we should accept to implement their policies. We stated that to realise the programme whereby

---

20. See Christopher Clapham, *Transformation and Continuity in Revolutionary Ethiopia* (Cambridge, 1990), pp. 157–174.
21. The argument was made public by the economist Joseph Stiglitz in *Globalization and Its Discontents* (New York, 2002), pp. 27–33.

the state plays a huge role in the economy, that we were following hitherto, we would operate through development institutes kept under the parties' control. We also stated that to avoid opposition from the IMF and the World Bank, these economic enterprises controlled by the parties should be registered as foundations involved in charity works.[22]

Behind closed doors and towards their party members, TPLF cadres were crystal clear about the fool's game they were playing with the Bretton Woods institutions. The latter eventually accepted it. They designed a complex para-statal economy made up of investment funds, state enterprises, and private companies, and restricted to national investors supporting the EPRDF only.

Breweries, transportation and shipping companies, cement factories, and public works companies were sold off to these funds. The biggest among them was the Endowment Fund for the Rehabilitation of Tigray (EFFORT), created in 1995 and affiliated to the TPLF. In 1995, some enterprises were simply given to EFFORT.[23] EFFORT's original capital was made up of what the Front had gathered from its administration of the liberated regions during the civil war, added to a 320-USD-investment operated by each of the twenty-five Tigrayan businessmen, including sixteen members of the party's central committee.[24] Subsequent presidents of the funds were all prominent TPLF members, including a Minister of Defence (Siye Abraha), Meles's special counsellor (Sebhat Nega), a regional Vice-President (Abadi Zemo), and eventually Meles's own wife, Azeb Mesfin.[25]

Other companies were used to keep control of the national economy. In June 2010, major state companies were brought together in a new military corporation called Metal and Engineering Corporation (Metec). With an original capital amount of 10 billion birrs, the conglomerate gathered ninety-eight companies. Metec soon became the state's and the army's main business partner.

Party-controlled endowment funds were not the only beneficiaries of privatization. Some enterprises were genuinely sold to private entrepreneurs. But here again, EPRDF planners managed to keep control over potential newcomers to the Ethiopian market. As a former mayor of Addis Ababa and long-time economic special advisor to the Prime Minister wrote, eighty-five per cent of the privatized enterprises were sold to national investors: of the 295 state companies sold over the 1991–2011 period, 264 found Ethiopian

---

22. Gebru Asrat, *Lu'alawinetna démokrasi beityop'ya [Sovereignty and democracy in Ethiopia]* (Addis Ababa, 2015), pp. 156–158. Translation: Mehdi Labzaé.
23. Sarah Vaughan and Mesfin Gebremichael, *Rethinking Business and Politics in Ethiopia: The Role of EFFORT, the Endowment Fund for the Rehabilitation of Tigray* (London, 2011), p. 36.
24. *Ibid.*
25. The succession of EFFORT's directors remains unclear but Gebru Asrat gives some insights in his book. See Asrat, *Lu'alawinetna démokrasi beityop'ya*, p. 160.

acquirers.[26] But one man, in particular, took the biggest share in the clean-out of state assets: Mohamed Al Amoudi, the Ethio-Saudi billionaire running the Mohamed International Development Research and Organization Company (MIDROC).

MIDROC bought the most profitable enterprises, with the blessing of the TPLF. In 2008, worried US diplomats wrote that the Sheikh's acquisitions accounted for fifty-five per cent of the total number of privatized companies. They specified: "Al Almoudi is known to have close ties to the ruling TPLF/ EPRDF regime, and rumours persist of favourable treatment."[27] Born to a Yemeni father and an Ethiopian mother in the Ethiopian province of Wollo, Al Amoudi built his fortune in Jeddah before taking advantage of the privatization of refineries in Morocco and Sweden, where he became one of the biggest foreign investors. When the TPLF came to power, Al Amoudi owned millions of petrodollars to invest in a market under reconstruction following years of civil war. He soon took an oligopolistic position in his homeland.

Links between the ruling elite and the Sheikh are not obvious. However, the Sheikh repeatedly brought his support to the ruling coalition. He wore the usual EPRDF T-shirt flocked with a bee for each electoral campaign. He announced a million-dollar gift for the funding of the Grand Ethiopian Renaissance Dam.[28] When Meles Zenawi died, the Sheikh appeared on public television to express his sympathy.[29] Many government contracts were granted to the Sheikh's conglomerate, most often cloaked with great opacity. In 2017, the conglomerate owned the country's biggest gold mine, the majority of the country's public works and construction enterprises (Dil Paints, Vision Aluminium, Kombocha Steel Products, etc.), the first private university (Unity), real estate groups (Huda, Modern Building Industries), flower and tea farms (Jittu, Wushwush), drink retailers (Moha), giant farms (Saudi Star), hotels, and so forth.

EFFORT and MIDROC exemplify how the new ruling class profited from its accession to power to secure its economic accumulations following the classical "straddling" pattern.[30] The whole process can be described as what Jean-François Bayart called a "Thermidorian situation", in which a small revolutionary elite abandons its radicalism when securing its political position through economic reforms that in turn open up unprecedented business opportunities for them. Cambodia and Iran followed similar trajectories, as did the

26. See Arkebe Oqubay, *Made in Africa: Industrial Policy in Ethiopia* (Oxford, 2016), p. 109.
27. See the diplomatic cable dated 11 January 2008, leaked by WikiLeaks. Available at: https:// wikileaks.org/plusd/cables/08ADDISABABA82_a.html; last accessed 21 December 2018.
28. See Daniel Berhane, "Al Amoudi Pledges 1.5 Billion Birr for Renaissance Dam", *Horn Affairs*, 12 September 2011.
29. Published on YouTube on 29 August 2012. Available at https://www.youtube.com/watch? v=Yo8hwvYdtoA; last accessed 25 October 2019.
30. See Jean-François Bayart, *L'État en Afrique. La politique du ventre* (Paris, 2006).

Indian state of West Bengal throughout the 1990s and 2000s.[31] Former guerrilla fighters did not become businessmen overnight, and for a long time the enrichment of a small Tigrayan elite remained hidden. But the political crisis that occurred in Ethiopia after 2015 led to the public exposure of many scandals.[32]

The eventual acceptance of capitalism and the birth of the developmental state

Throughout the 1990s, selling public enterprises to party holdings and to a tycoon did not amount to full acceptance of capitalism by TPLF elites. The recognition of the ineluctability of capitalism by Meles Zenawi himself occurred in 2001. This had more to do with internal party struggles than with debates and negotiation with foreign donors.

In 1998–2000, members of the TPLF central committee were highly divided in their positions on the war with Eritrea. The conflict started with skirmishes on the border in a remote village but soon escalated. Most TPLF leaders, including Defence Minister Siyé Abraha, Tigray President Gebru Asrat, and Army Chief of Staff Tsadqan Gebretensae, positioned themselves as hardliners and wanted to invade Eritrea in order to remind their northern neighbour that its success in guerrilla warfare was long over. These hardliners were both strongly nationalist and leftist. Meles, Arkebe Oqubay, and Abay Tsehaye were more concerned about the reaction of the international community and less eager to punish the Eritrean regime militarily.[33] After a ceasefire was negotiated in Algiers, conflicts between Meles and most of his party continued in inner-circle meetings.

The quarrel ended in late 2001, when Meles managed to rally most of the EPRDF members – and especially its Amhara branch – to his side.[34] Internal debates focused more on political economy than on national interests. Meles managed to marginalize the leftist group by denouncing their "Bonapartist tendencies".[35] Debates were framed in the old-fashioned Marxist idiom that TPLF insiders had mastered perfectly, although the ideological content of the argument differed from its terminology.[36] The quality and complexity of

---

31. About Iran, see Fariba Adelkhah, Jean-François Bayart, and Olivier Roy, *Thermidor en Iran* (Brussels, 1993). About Cambodia, see Evan Gottesman, *Cambodia After the Khmer Rouge: Inside the Politics of Nation Building* (New Haven, CT, 2003). About West Bengal, see Ritanjan Das, "Producing Local Neoliberalism in a Leftist Regime: Neoliberal Governmentality and Populist Transition in West Bengal, India", *Contemporary South Asia*, 27:3 (2019), pp. 373–391.

32. See Samuel Bogale, "Analysis: The Sour Taste of Sugar in Ethiopia. Corruption, Incompetence and Empty Hope", *Addis Standard*, 21 November 2017.

33. See Medhane Tadesse and John Young, "TPLF: Reform or Decline?", *Review of African Political Economy*, 30 (2003), pp. 389–403; Asrat, *Lu'alawinetna démokrasi beityop'ya*, pp. 283–289.

34. See Paulos Milkias, "Ethiopia, TPLF and the Roots of the 2001 Political Tremor", *International Conference on African Development Archive*, 8 (2001), pp. 1–31.

35. See Asrat, *Lu'alawinetna démokrasi beityop'ya*, p. 284.

36. As is often the case in instrumental ideological debates. See Negash Gebregziabher Tefera, "Ideology and Power in TPLF's Ethiopia: A Historic Reversal in the Making?", *African Affairs*, 118 (2019), pp. 463–484.

these arguments certainly played a role in the delay of the Ethiopian adjustment. Meles depicted the leftists as too radical and persuaded his comrades that an official acceptance of capitalism was a sine qua non for foreign capital and international aid to flow in.[37] He won a slim majority of the votes in an internal party evaluation in December 2001. His opponents were purged. Corruption accusations were crafted to send the then Defence Minister Siye Abraha to jail.

Making amends to capitalism did not amount to an outright acceptance of the free market. Ideologically, the TPLF then promoted the "developmental state", according to which state investment was to lead industrialization.[38] In the name of the fight against "neoliberal forces", it advocated for strong control of the state over the economy. In this framework, economic expansion and (the absence of) political opening up were closely linked. A market economy could be adopted only after the economy was sufficiently industrialized. Until then, agriculture had to remain the engine driving economic growth.[39] The rural population, amounting to more than eighty percent of the population up until the late 2000s, had to be enrolled in public works and in political "participation" through government activities. Large state-funded industrial projects were launched with much governmental fanfare: the Great Ethiopian Renaissance Dam on the Blue Nile, sugar factories, industrial parks – all were built with Metec's involvement.

The party's hegemony was seen as a *sine qua non* for development, even at the cost of successive unfair electoral campaigns and clampdowns on opposition parties. According to TPLF elites, Ethiopia could not yet afford democracy, for democracy and the free market would only profit "rent-seeking forces"[40] and worsen inequalities. In short, the EPRDF had to drive the country towards development, and both the total adoption of a market economy and the opening up of the political field could only occur once the peasantry was lifted out of poverty.

37. See Assefa Fiseha, "Development with or without Freedom?", in Dessalegn Rahmato, Meheret Ayenew, Asnake Kefale, and Birgit Habermann (eds), *Reflections on Development in Ethiopia: New Trends, Sustainability and Challenges* (Addis Ababa, 2014), pp. 67–129.

38. Christopher Clapham, "The Ethiopian Developmental State", *Third World Quarterly*, 39 (2017), pp. 1151–1165.

39. Meles Zenawi was among the main thinkers behind the Ethiopian version of the "developmental state". His notes and thoughts were published after his death in the volume *Ityopia. Yehidasé guzo: Yelimatna yedémokrasi ginbata dersetoch keMeles Zénawi* [*Ethiopia: the Renaissance travel. Meles Zenawi's notes on development and democracy building*] (Addis Ababa, 2017).

40. The accusation of "rent-seeking" was, according to Sarah Vaughan and Mesfin Gebremichael, the TPLF's "most common condemnatory political insult" (*Rethinking Business and Politics in Ethiopia*, p. 14). The notion of "rent-seeking" also counts among "neoliberal" concepts that found their way into the TPLF's parlance, for it was first coined by Bretton Woods economist Anne Krueger.

Rural policies of the developmental state

As tools intended to drive industrialization over the long run, agrarian policies were the pillars of EPRDF thought. Until the mid-2000s, agriculture was conceived as the engine of economic growth. Through learning and mobilization, smallholders would make productivity gains, ensure food security, and eventually drive industrialization.[41] Echoing the party's socialist origins, land and agricultural policies were deemed "pro-poor policies".

The privatization of land was continuously rejected in the name of protecting smallholders.[42] Land sales were officially forbidden and the right to ownership of land "is exclusively vested in the State and in the Peoples of Ethiopia".[43] In EPRDF thought, privatization of land could only foster land concentration and eventually amount to the re-formation of a feudal class that the 1975 land reform and subsequent redistributions had eradicated. This credo was maintained despite continuous urging by foreign donors and "progressive" party members to establish a land market. That was partly done through land registration programmes fostering land rentals.

But after the 2001 internal crisis, noticeable shifts occurred in land policies. With the assistance of donors, access to land was reorganized. In towns, urban land leases were promoted, with strong state control over subsequent construction activities. In rural areas, georeferenced cadastral maps were drawn, containing information about landholders. Although prepared with donor assistance, these programmes greatly increased state control in rural areas. With the introduction of landholding books, rental land markets became a major means to access land. Distributing certificates also prepared peasants for a deeper inclusion in the banking system, by accessing credit through using land as collateral. Large estates were leased to foreign and national investors, mainly in the lowland peripheries.

By adopting the Growth and Transformation Plan (GTP) in 2010, the government implicitly acknowledged the failure of the egalitarian "pro-poor policies".[44] Agrarian policies then shifted towards a more selective development model that still aimed at food sufficiency but counted on investors rather than

41. See Atakilte Beyene (ed.), *Agricultural Transformation in Ethiopia: State Policy and Smallholder Farming* (London, 2018).
42. See Svein Ege (ed.), *Land Tenure Security: State–Peasant Relations in the Amhara Highlands, Ethiopia* (Rochester, NY, 2019); and Tom Lavers, "Food Security and Social Protection in Highland Ethiopia: Linking the Productive Safety Net to the Land Question", *Journal of Modern African Studies*, 51:3 (2013), pp. 459–485.
43. Article 40–3 of the Constitution of the Federal Democratic Republic of Ethiopia.
44. See Meheret Ayenew, "The Growth and Transformation Plan: Opportunities, Challenges and Lessons", in Dessalegn Rahmato, Meheret Ayenew, Asnake Kefale, and Birgit Habermann (eds), *Reflections on Development in Ethiopia: New Trends, Sustainability and Challenges* (Addis Ababa, 2014), pp. 3–30; and René Lefort, "Free Market Economy, 'Developmental State' and Party-State Hegemony in Ethiopia: The Case of the 'Model Farmers'", *Journal of Modern African Studies*, 50:4 (2012), pp. 681–706.

Figure 2. Farmer carrying a bag of fertiliser he has just collected from the local authorities in Tigray (2012). Photograph by the authors.

on smallholders. Non-competitive farmers were consequently relegated to social protection.[45] Before the adoption of such reforms, each farmer was supposed to equally invest in agricultural inputs and, above all, to buy selected seeds and fertilizer on credit (Figure 2). Rural authorities closely and rigorously

45. See Lavers, "Food Security and Social Protection in Highland Ethiopia".

monitored the implementation of agricultural modernization programmes, paying more and more attention to the recovery of the "fertilizer debt".[46] The supply and management of agricultural inputs entailed a great deal of political control, through the routinized and bureaucratized exercise of state domination.

In the name of development, forcing farmers to buy fertilizer regardless of their specific needs was the norm. Such a non-liberal articulation to the market properly reflects the jerky adjustment of Ethiopia to global capitalism. Forcing farmers to buy fertilizer offered an unprecedented opportunity to strengthen the banking sector while developing party-affiliated regional microfinance institutions. It promoted the financial inclusion of the poorest, in a surprising level of understanding of egalitarian and free access to finance. Before the adoption of the most selective GTP programmes, social distinction in rural areas largely mirrored state action.

Rural policies constitute the main vehicle through which local populations are integrated into a lower level of state administration and into a market economy. They are the means through which local society encounters the state. Ethiopian "street-level bureaucrats" were first and foremost agents of the Ministry of Agriculture, the Development Agents (DA) tasked with the setting up of various farmers' lists, the teaching of improved farming techniques, and the distribution of agricultural inputs.[47]

Like land redistribution a few decades ago, agricultural policies contributed to state formation at the local level by giving state power its concrete and most local embodiments and by giving content to local political fields.[48] Elites, though small, had to support the party-state, at least publicly. Although officially elected by fellow peasants, farmers were called to act as local militiamen enforcing law and order, as leaders of the many working groups active at village level, as secretaries of local assemblies for the most literate, or as judges for communal affairs in the case of the oldest ones. Some productive and compliant people were awarded the status of "model farmers",[49] and hence they were invited to become more active in party mobilization. Partially as a result of the very implementation of the regime's development policies, this small elite was expected to be numerous and under constant renewal, so that ideally the EPRDF could reach every single house, if not every single individual.[50] Unlike the high-level national cadres

46. See Sabine Planel, "Le *developmental state* éthiopien et les paysans pauvres. Économie politique du développement rural en Éthiopie", *Politique africaine*, 142 (2016), pp. 57–76.
47. See Michael Lipsky, *Street-Level Bureaucracy: Dilemmas of the Individual in Public Services* (New York, 1980).
48. See Bruce Berman and John Lonsdale, *Unhappy Valley: Conflict in Kenya & Africa* (London, 1992).
49. See Lefort, "Free Market Economy".
50. See Sarah Vaughan, "Federalism, Revolutionary Democracy and the Developmental State, 1991–2012", in Gérard Prunier and Éloi Ficquet (eds), *Understanding Contemporary Ethiopia* (London, 2015), pp. 283–311.

discussed above, these men had limited resources to contest the party's hegemony. As a result, hierarchies among rural societies echoed state action.

POPULAR ADJUSTMENTS: PEASANT WAYS OF ADAPTING TO REFORMS

Satisfaction or repression? On the demobilizing role of state structures

Adaptations by party elites to "lefticize" injunctions towards free-market policies were made in the name of protecting the peasantry, whether the latter agreed or not. But from 1991 to 2014, rural Ethiopia saw very little large-scale opposition to the regime. Was the economic content of the developmental state sufficient to prevent the rural masses from contesting it? For a long time the party claimed there was a strong economic dimension to its redistribution policies. But although party elites held a paternalistic view of the rural masses, local authorities took a much more authoritarian approach to the people they governed. Social and political mobilization was deterred more by repression than by unfair redistributive policies. As James Scott wrote, "agrarian peace […] may well be the peace of repression (remembered or anticipated) rather than the peace of consent and complicity".[51] The ability of the regime to meet popular expectations and provide necessities for the survival of the poorest was not total, and it was insufficient to explain the absence of outright rebellion.[52]

Furthermore, elaborate state domination discouraged farmers from openly expressing their opinions. Political mobilization and control were routinized and ubiquitous in everyday lives, occasional episodes of repression were brutal, and street-level bureaucrats often resorted to coercion with those they considered as reluctant. Farmers not willing to accept land registration, opposed to their expropriation for "development" purposes, or unable to repay their fertilizer debt could then be jailed. Similarly, civil servants were subjected to harsh evaluations by party cadres, where their careers could be severely damaged.[53] Surveillance was ubiquitous. In towns, shopkeepers and hotel owners could be asked to make daily reports at the *kebele* – the smallest administrative unit. In rural villages, such reports were made by members of the *kebele* cabinet, who could also denounce civil servants to the next level of administration, called

---

51. See James C. Scott, *Weapons of the Weak: Everyday Forms of Peasant Resistance* (New Haven, CT, 1987), p.40.
52. See James C. Scott, *The Moral Economy of the Peasant: Rebellion and Subsistence in Southeast Asia* (New Haven, CT, 1977); Edward Thompson, "The Moral Economy of the English Crowd in the Eighteenth Century", *Past & Present*, 50 (1971), pp. 76–136; Johanna Siméant, "Three Bodies of Moral Economy: The Diffusion of a Concept", *Journal of Global Ethics*, 11:2 (2015), pp. 163–175.
53. See Mehdi Labzaé, "Les travailleurs du gouvernement. Encadrement partisan et formes du travail administratif dans l'administration éthiopienne", *Genèses*, 98 (2015), pp. 89–109.

wereda. From 2011 onwards, a system of surveillance and propaganda called "one-to-five" was put in force. For every five households, a man was in charge of gathering his neighbours to teach them about the latest government programmes, advise them how to use the right agricultural techniques, or prompt them to attend meetings. He also made regular reports to the *kebele*.

Before 2014, the absence of riots or large-scale peasant revolt did not amount to the absence of critical opinions about the regime and its developmental policies.[54] The next section describes how rural people voiced criticisms of a regime that promoted development while leaving the poorest behind.[55] For peasants, any comment not in line with the party's credo could be interpreted as an act of organized opposition and met with repression. But as always in such power-laden relations, subordinates were not passively subjected to power, and their compliance could hide forms of discontent. Voicing criticism or opposition required some acting,[56] but mundane gestures can also be understood as a form of protest.

Low-scale criticisms of the adjusted developmental state

Whether or not they expressed resentment regarding their growing inclusion in market-oriented policies, rural dwellers resorted to many different ways of criticizing the EPRDF regime. The poorest focused on the deprivation resulting from government policies. Peasants tried to escape debts, missed as many meetings as they could, adapted to land registration by keeping parcels hidden from the surveyors, and more generally avoided top-down mobilization state structures.

Public reproaches were tolerated from highly marginalized farmers, isolated elders, or people deemed insane, but never from poor people, who accounted for the majority of the population and whose willingness and capacity to cooperate with the government was commonly praised by local civil servants.[57] Criticisms and reproaches most often came from older farmers, who could rely on their relative social status and refer to local cultural practices such as poetry.[58] These peasants were not necessarily the richest, but they had land and enough cattle to plough without borrowing oxen from their

54. See Getie Gelay, "Peasant Poetics and State Discourse in Ethiopia: Amharic Oral Poetry as a Response to the 1996–97 Land Redistribution Policy", *Northeast African Studies*, 6:1–2 (1999), pp. 171–206; Assefa Tefera Dibaba, "'God Speak to Us': Performing Power and Authority in Salale, Ethiopia", *Journal of African Cultural Studies*, 26:3 (2014), pp. 287–302; Tsegaye Moreda, "Listening to their Silence? The Political Reaction of Affected Communities to Large-Scale Land Acquisitions: Insights from Ethiopia", *Journal of Peasant Studies*, 42 (2015), pp. 517–539.
55. See Planel, "Le *developmental state éthiopien et les paysans pauvres*".
56. See Scott, *Domination and the Arts of Resistance*.
57. See Planel, "Le *developmental state éthiopien et les paysans pauvres*".
58. See Gelay, "Peasant Poetics and State Discourse in Ethiopia", p. 6.

neighbours, sometimes had children working in town and bringing them some cash money, and enjoyed relative social respectability in their neighbourhood. For them, there were routinized ways of expressing dissent that were tolerated by the authorities.

Playing the old, surly man. In the presence of state agents (Figure 3), these old men would generally cultivate an image of old grouchy farmers, continually grumbling against the government. Drunkenness – real, exaggerated, or entirely performed – could help them make reproaches sound less aggressive. Civil servants would usually listen to them, often with a wry smile, not being entirely sure about the seriousness of the accusations made by the old fellow:

> February 2013, in a remote Gumuz village. Sisay, a land administration agent, talks to an old farmer, Hailu, whose land is to be expropriated: "That's what the law says, only 5 hectares per person!"
> Empty calabashes at Hailu's feet suggest that he has already drunk a lot. Sipping his homemade beer, he answers: "This is YOUR law!" While civil servants threaten the arrival of high-ranking party officials to settle the dispute, Hailu continues, laughing: "Bah! No work, they're not working! They couldn't care less! They're just party members; apart from that, they don't do anything!"
> Sisay: "That's enough, Mister Hailu, that's enough!"
> Hailu: "You, land administration, shut up!"[59]

Comparing the EPRDF with the former socialist regime constitutes another very common way to question the EPRDF's so-called pro-poor policies. Since the mid-2000s, such policies were turned towards greater promotion of new development entrepreneurs. This was rightly perceived by many elders as covert acceptance of inequalities by the regime. Most elders would acknowledge the EPRDF's success in bringing a more peaceful life and the end of forced conscription, whereas the *derg*'s repression and military campaigns fuelled civil war for seventeen years. But farmers questioned the EPRDF's official condemnation of the socialist regime, arguing that by that time, equality was not only a slogan. Strategies of this kind were mostly used when land issues were concerned, echoing the 1975 land reform. Elders might embellish their recollections of life under socialism. But romanticizing the good old days remains a means to voice strong criticism of the current regime, as shown in this abstract:

> March 2013, in one of the villages surrounding Assosa. Zerihun, a land administration agent advises Alemayehu, an old farmer, to invest more in his parcel: "You could ask the state to have a pump and a generator that would allow you to irrigate. From the river to the road, you could irrigate all this! [...]" His colleague insists: "Come on, move on, use the generator! [...] You could become an investor, you could ask new parcels, if you have the capacity, you'll get it!"

59. Field notes, Benishangul-Gumuz, 16 February 2013. Translation: Mehdi Labzaé.

Figure 3. A visit of land administration civil servants to rural parcels for survey in Benishangul-Gumuz (2015). Photograph by the authors.

Alemayehu answers: "Our land is narrow! What capital do we have to buy these machines?"

Zerihun: "If you show the government that you have the capacity, you could become investors, and you'll get new parcels. There's a Development Agent in your *kebelé* who teaches you how to do it, right?"

Alemayehu: "Yes, there is one! And we are the ones teaching him! [...] The government, me, I never saw him! It's been 21 years that this regime is in place, but it didn't even complete what the *Derg* had started! By the time of the *Derg*, we were working and we were sure of getting something to eat. We were sure to get the harvest, everything was in common!"

Civil servants looked at each other with a sickly grin and went to the next parcel. They are too young to remember what life under the *Derg* looked like, and had nothing to answer to Alemayehu.[60]

Peasant utilitarianism as political gesture

Peasant utilitarianism results from their relegation to a subaltern position in power relations and reflects their restricted capacity to enrich themselves, to get better livelihoods, and to gain assets. This structural position narrows their ability to confront the local government administration. The required

60. Field notes, Benishangul-Gumuz, 12 March 2013. Translation: Mehdi Labzaé.

participation in government policies left them little room for manoeuvre, but peasants managed to deviate somewhat from the rules and thus express their dissatisfaction. Peasants were familiar with the EPRDF propaganda that had reached every village; they collectively experienced state repression when dismissing government advice: they had learned the political meaning of their gestures. Such strategies, although mostly silent, individual, and usually relegated as quasi-folkloric traditional behaviours by analysts, can truly be political.[61]

Farmers' mobilization for the sake of government objectives varied, often depending on the benefits they expected from participation in state programmes. As a matter of consequence, it might evolve quickly. To this regard, the case of Haïle, a relatively wealthy farmer, is of particular interest:

> I've been serving the government and the country for 24 years [as local agricultural trainer], I was committed to the people and worked for the others for 24 years. But I've resigned now. The government didn't even assist me when I asked the agricultural office for a generator. I will manage on my own, I won't ask anything. I fell down the mountain within a day, when they chose not to assist me. Now, I don't want to participate anymore, I quit. Now, I don't want to owe them anything.[62]

Being enrolled in party-state structures and hence acting as a state representative was a collective responsibility that might concern every farmer – regardless of his material and social position. Control was tight, close, and highly embodied. Individuals had to continuously adjust their positions towards the state, and moreover towards the party. Expressions of discontent were very discreet and often blurred, so as to allow the one who protested to publicly change his mind and show compliance in case his turn came to integrate state structures. Be it actual or simply potential, the enrolment into party-state structures concerns every farmer and consequently prevents farming communities from mobilizing against the government.

Obvious signs of disobedience were not favoured, but incomplete obedience constituted a day-to-day answer to top-down incentives, as shown by Abeba's rhetoric in the following abstract. Married to an old and idle man, she was raising five children still living in the family house and ran the farm by herself. Full of enthusiasm, she had hopes for her future and wanted to start a dairy farm with one of the new cow breeds that the DA had advised her to buy:

> I've taken 1 quintal of fertilizer, they forced me to take 1 quintal for half a parcel of land [...] they warned me: "if you don't take the whole amount of fertiliser, a

---

61. See Jim Handy, "'Almost Idiotic Wretchedness': A Long History of Blaming Peasants", *Journal of Peasant Studies*, 36:2 (2009), pp. 325–344.
62. Field notes, Eastern Tigray, 26 October 2017. Translation: Alexander Asmelash.

quintal, we will drop you from the Safety Net and from every other support provided by the government".[63] Me, I want fertilizer, but not a quintal. So, last summer I took only half a quintal. It's the same situation every season, they tell us to
use 1 quintal but me I've taken only 50 kg. They don't have any evidence to remove
me from the programme, they just want to threaten me. And if they finally do so,
then they would only take one or two persons off the beneficiaries list […]
Nowadays, if you experience a conflict with people from the village administration, then you receive only half of your share, the remaining part disappears
and never goes back to the district [*wereda*].[64]

Mobilization and political control concerned both men and women,
although in different policy sectors.[65] Abeba's response exemplifies a quite
common way of dealing with threats. Farmers often pretended to consent,
dragging their feet, responding late, and thus balancing between governmental
requests and their awareness of their rights. They resorted to partial forms of
obedience, fully endorsing and exposing an image of the simple, ignorant, and
reluctant farmer, very similar to what Alf Lüdtke described among working-
class groups.[66] Commonly acknowledged, especially by civil servants, peasant
backwardness was relatively tolerated, and farmers often mobilized it to resist
daily state domination:

When civil servants ask peasants to take part in the drawing of a "land use map" of
their *kebele*, with chalk powder on the bare ground, one of the farmers answers:
"But what is the peasant's thought? What is it? The peasant's thought is not
right! Haven't you already drawn this map? You already went everywhere with
your devices. […] What are we useful for?"[67]

Nevertheless, in trying to adjust unreachable government expectations to
their own plans and capacities, farmers might place themselves in a very delicate position, reinforcing their dependence on government agents – be they
civil servants or farmers, powerful or not, rich or poor. For most of them,
but especially for the poorest, coping with policies in an authoritarian context

---

63. Funded by a pool of foreign donors, the Productive Safety Net Programme provides cash
money or food aid in exchange for public work done by local communities. It targets food insecure
villages and households and is perceived as one of the major governmental aid programmes in rural
Ethiopia.
64. Field notes, Eastern Tigray, 25 October 2017. Translation: Alexander Asmelash.
65. Agricultural policies mostly concerned men, since most households remained male-headed,
and women ploughing by themselves without resorting to sharecropping arrangements were
rare. Health, and more recently education programmes, tended to be more oriented towards
women. See, e.g., Alessia Villanucci and Emanuele Fantini, "Santé publique, participation commu-
nautaire et mobilisation politique en Éthiopie: la *Womens' Development Army*", *Politique africaine*, 142 (2016), pp. 77–99.
66. See Alf Lüdtke, "La domination comme pratique sociale", *Sociétés contemporaines*, 99–100:3
(2015), pp. 17–63.
67. Field notes, Benishangul-Gumuz, 29 January 2015. Translation: Mehdi Labzaé.

represented such a risky strategy. This was particularly true when farmers were trying to engage with micro-credit programmes:

> Speaking freely and joking around, Kidane catches his neighbours' attention. Aged 55, he owns a small plot of land and raises 4 children. He knows how to request governmental support, and was engaged in several programmes when we met. Registered as a vulnerable farmer, he is an early member of the Safety Net programme but had multiple uses of micro-credit in the past, although micro-credit loans are officially earmarked for small income generating projects. When we raised this point, he answered: "Dedebit [the regional micro-credit institution in his region] always asks for the reason we have to borrow money, but we cannot answer that it is to refund a neighbour. I never say so. Mentioning the true motive would be an insult [all farmers gathered around busted out with laughter as he had used a slightly irreverent term]. It can't be done. Dedebit people come here to check how properly we use the money. If it's not the case, they won't provide us anymore. So, we have to pretend."[68]

Farmers regularly diverted the so-called development tools from their formal and politicized uses, adapting them for their own benefit. Since the latter are partially seasonally based and quickly evolve (especially for the poorest households), such strategies constitute a sensitive and delicate exercise. People who play such games remain discreet, since it can lead to harsh punishment. Confinement remains in use in rural administration as a tool to improve the implementation of public policies and to politically control rural populations.

Reselling fertilizer on the black market constituted one of these strategies. Fertilizer distribution officially counted among state monopolies and represented a flagship point in the EPRDF development strategy. The political content of fertilizer distribution was well known to peasants and local civil servants. Thus, the resale of fertilizer on the black market, which emerged and grew steadily from the turn of the 2010s,[69] constitutes a strategy to cope with and adapt government programmes to individual views and needs. Although it was common knowledge that peasants resold some of their fertilizer, transactions were carried out with the utmost discretion.[70] As an old peasant explained: "It is done secretly, using spoken agreement, not on the market and not with traders – otherwise you get caught and sent to prison."[71]

On this specific point, we need to tone down the acknowledgement of vulnerable peasant agency – and its empowering effects. In this context, labelling such practices as "farmers' agency" and granting them empowering effects might be something of an overinterpretation. When farmers engage in dangerous, illegal strategies, as seen in the above case, they expose themselves to risky

---

68. Field notes, Eastern Tigray, 27 October 2017. Translation: Alexander Asmelash.
69. See Jan Nyssen *et al*, "Geographic Determinants of Inorganic Fertilizer Sales and of Resale Prices in North Ethiopia", *Agriculture, Ecosystem and Environment*, 249 (2017), pp. 256–268.
70. See Planel, "A View of a *Bureaucratic* Developmental State".
71. Field notes, Eastern Tigray, 27 October 2017.

situations that often accelerate their dispossession. True, it may be considered at an individual level as a resisting strategy – the only way to escape the fertilizer debt circle while offering access to the input. But at a collective level, it mainly exposes vulnerable farmers and increases inequalities by including wealthy farmers in adjusted policies and denying social protection to "non-competitive agents".[72] The eventual result is an increased role of the market in regulating public life within communities.

CONCLUSION

In July 2019, Prime Minister Abiy Ahmed gave a speech at the World Economic Forum in Davos. It appeared that his views could not be more different from Meles's lessons. Inviting investors to his country, he presented Ethiopia as "a large market of over 100 million people", while endlessly repeating that his government was now entirely committed to installing a functioning free-market economy.[73] A new round of privatization was announced, the banking and telecom sectors would be open to foreign capital, and Ethiopia was about to resume its World Trade Organization membership negotiations. Discursively at least, the EPRDF *aggiornamento* had reached its end.

Interestingly, Abiy's rise to power in 2018 was the result of more than two years of demonstrations, riots, repression, and internal party negotiations. The trigger for the movement was the planned extension of the federal capital Addis Ababa into the surrounding Oromia region, the largest in Ethiopia. Students took to the streets first and were soon followed by large swathes of the population. Claims were first oriented towards social justice: jobs for youngsters, better prices for average peasants, removal of corrupted elites. It seemed that although SAPs were adapted to the party's views, these liberal measures were eventually met with opposition.

However, the peasants' behaviours demonstrate that they did not remain idle and passive in the twenty-three years preceding the movement that toppled the regime. Rural inhabitants resorted to myriad ways of adapting to political control. Listening to farmers, we heard multiple grievances, expressions of anger towards the government, complaints about the way food aid was or was not delivered, denunciations of the capture of resources by party elites (be they local or not), and rebukes of the misbehaviour of field-level bureaucrats and fellow peasants perceived as vehicles of state power.

72. See Tom Lavers, "Social Protection in an Aspiring "Developmental State": The Political Drivers of Ethiopia's PSNP", *WIDER Working Paper*, 130 (2016).
73. See the video "Abiy Ahmed: A Conversation with the Prime Minister of Ethiopia (Davos 2019)", posted by the World Economic Forum on YouTube on 10 February 2019. Available at: https://www.youtube.com/watch?v=x2l7KscqRro; last accessed 28 April 2020. The above-mentioned quotation is at 8:30.

When faced with such elaborate ways of diverting state power, we need to question the categories by which we differentiate resistance from compliance. Actions such as taking out credit to divert its use from the original purpose, reporting a neighbour for this misbehaviour, or being elected to a land administration committee only to secure better repartition of land holdings are all coping strategies that involve taking part in control structures. By doing so and by getting involved in political activities, peasants give substance to structures of control while they divert it, to some extent, for their own purposes. Control and diversion are two sides of the same coin, but their political effects differ significantly at the individual and the collective level.

The routinized state-party embodiment in rural society prevents the scaling up of individual protests. This unnoticed fact undercuts peasants' political voices, with three main consequences. Firstly, it prevents individual actions from scaling up to collective mobilization. Secondly, it prevents these individual tactics from producing tangible results, even at the local level and for mundane purposes. By remaining individual, resisting strategies are easily circumcised by local authorities and communities. Thirdly and for the worst, it has a de-politicizing effect on peasant voices, by denying them any legitimacy to take part in political settlements outside of state-party structures. Although their participation is constantly required, peasants are assigned to the margins of politics. In turn, they act as if they were actually convinced that "the peasant's thought" has no value. As social scientists, our work is first and foremost to document and unravel such practices and reflections.[74]

---

74. See Schwartz, "Sur le rapport des ouvriers du Nord à la politique".

IRSH 66 (2021), pp. 93–112 doi:10.1017/S0020859021000122
© The Author(s), 2021. Published by Cambridge University Press on behalf of the
Internationaal Instituut voor Sociale Geschiedenis
Peasant Resistance in Burkina Faso's Cotton Sector

BETTINA ENGELS[*]

Freie Universität Berlin
Otto Suhr Institute for Political Sciences
Ihnestr.22
14195 Berlin, Germany

E-mail: bettina.engels@fu-berlin.de

ABSTRACT: This article examines how and why smallholder peasants mobilize for collective action to put forward their claims. Taking the resistance by cotton farmers in Burkina Faso as a case study, it demonstrates that institutions of neoliberal governance – which are presented by their proponents as making governance more "effective" by improving the participation of various public and private stakeholders in different degrees – nevertheless fail to represent the interests of the large population of agrarian poor. In the 2010s, the cotton sector in Burkina Faso became a field of contention, with smallholder cotton producers mobilizing on a massive scale to take collective action. It is argued that the mobilization of cotton farmers can be explained through the effects of the sector's liberalization. Economic liberalization, which has been promoted by the World Bank since the mid-1990s, has changed the institutional setting of the sector and has significantly impacted the ways and means of collective claim-making available to farmers. Building on primary data (qualitative interviews, focus group discussions, observations) collected during several months of field research between 2018 and 2020, and analyses of press reports and a variety of documents, recent protests by cotton farmers are examined and related to these liberalization policies.

At the mention of protests and uprisings against structural adjustment and liberalization policies, we might think of protests by students and public sector

* I am very grateful to all the people in Burkina Faso who shared their knowledge and experience on cotton production with me. In particular, Mohamed Dagano, Brahima Diabaté, Hermann Moussa Konkobo, and Ouiry Sanou supported me with tremendous patience and confidence. Feedback by the participants of the workshop "When 'adjusted' people rebel" in Amsterdam on 29–30 January 2020 is highly appreciated. Leyla Dakhli-Mital and Vincent Bonnecase in particular did a great job of preparing the workshop and providing thorough feedback on the manuscript. Huge thanks also go to Hannah Cross, Kristina Dietz, Elisa Greco, Clare Smedley, and Leo Zeilig.

employees, of the anti-globalization movement and demonstrations against international summits, or of riots related to high food and fuel prices.[1] In this article, by contrast, I look at resistance by smallholder peasants, a group often assumed to be less likely to engage in protest. Many scholars suppose that conditions are more favourable for social mobilization and contentious collective action in cities than in rural areas. Consequently, smallholder peasants are, when compared with urban "middle-class" groups and workers, rarely considered as central figures with respect to protests against structural adjustment. This does not mean that peasant resistance against liberalization does not exist; but it seldom features in academic debates, especially in political sciences and sociology, and in many parts of the world it is largely neglected by politicians and social movements. Of course, this does not hold true universally: vibrant rural movements that engage in struggles against liberalization, for example in India,[2] Mexico, and Brazil,[3] have become globally famous. Peasants and farmers were a central force in the N30 anti-World Trade Organization (WTO) protests in Seattle 1999.[4] But also beyond these outstanding examples, smallholder peasants in general are by no means mere victims of liberalization and structural adjustment policies. They react in multiple ways: adapting to the conditions and politics; wriggling through them; trying to escape them; or resisting them both individually and collectively. Some even hold "that many of the most visible alternatives to capitalism in the countryside stem from [...] agrarian struggles against neoliberalism".[5] It is argued that the rise of peasant movements in the late twentieth century is not a game of mortal combat played by a doomed-to-die peasantry, but

---

1. See, for instance, Javier Auyero, "Glocal Riots", *International Sociology*, 16:1 (2001), pp. 33–53; Silvia Federici and Goerge Caffentzis, "Chronology of African University Students' Struggles: 1985–1998", in Silvia Federici, George Caffetzis, and Ousseina Alidou (eds), *A Thousand Flowers: Social Struggles Against Structural Adjustment in African Universities* (Asmara, 2000), pp. 115–150; Amory Starr, "'(Excepting Barricades Erected to Prevent Us from Peacefully Assembling)': So-called 'Violence' in the Global North Alterglobalization Movement", *Social Movement Studies*, 5:1 (2006), pp. 61–81; John Walton and David Seddon, *Free Markets and Food Riots: The Politics of Global Adjustment* (Oxford, 1994).
2. Krishna Murari, "Farmers' Movements in Independent India", *Indian Journal of Public Administration*, 61:3 (2015), pp. 457–479.
3. Leandro Vergara-Camus, *Land and Freedom: The MST, the Zapatistas and Peasant Alternatives to Neoliberalism* (London, 2014).
4. Marc Edelman, "Peasant–Farmer Movements, Third World Peoples, and the Seattle Protests Against the World Trade Organization, 1999", *Dialectical Anthropology*, 33:2 (2009), pp. 109–128.
5. Kristina Dietz and Bettina Engels, "Radical Transformation: Creating Alternatives to Capitalism in the Countryside", in Haroon Akram-Lodhi, Kristina Dietz, Bettina Engels, and Ben McKay (eds), *Handbook on Critical Agrarian Studies* (Cheltenham, forthcoming); see Marc Edelman and Wendy Wolford, "Introduction: Critical Agrarian Studies in Theory and Practice", *Antipode*, 49:4 (2017), pp. 959–976; and Philip McMichael, "Reframing Development: Global Peasant Movements and the New Agrarian Question", *Canadian Journal of Development Studies/Revue canadienne d'études du développement*, 27:4 (2006), pp. 471–483.

an indication "of the incompleteness of the transition to capitalism in agriculture".[6]

In this article, I examine how and why peasants mobilize for collective action to raise their claims. Taking various forms of resistance by cotton farmers in Burkina Faso as a case study, I demonstrate that institutions of neoliberal governance – presented by their proponents as making governance more "effective" by improving the participation of various public and private stakeholders to multiple scales – nevertheless fail to represent the interests of the large population of agrarian poor.

In the 2010s, the cotton sector in Burkina Faso became a field of contention, with smallholder cotton producers mobilizing on a massive scale to take collective action. A boycott campaign by cotton farmers – with farmers either refusing to produce cotton or significantly reducing the area they use for cotton cultivation – resulted in an almost thirty per cent decrease in production in 2018–2019 compared to the previous season. I seek to demonstrate that the mobilization of cotton farmers can be explained through the effects of the sector's liberalization. Liberalization has changed the institutional setting of the sector, and has significantly impacted the ways and means of collective claim-making available to farmers. A core element for such claim-making was the creation in 1998 of a national association of cotton producing cooperatives (Union Nationale des Producteurs de Coton du Burkina Faso or UNPCB). The UNPCB is a typical corporatist institution created according to the logic of liberal, corporate, multi-stakeholder governance. It aims to rationalize production, though ultimately it functions more to tame and control farmers rather than to represent their interests and help them raise their claims. Consequently, the union itself has become a major point of conflict. It was established in a top-down way by state authorities, hand in hand with the state-owned cotton company SOFITEX and an elite of relatively wealthy farmers, and therefore advances their interests. Such an institution, created in the context of neoliberal policies and economic restructuring, fails to integrate the interests of the majority of cotton producers, who are smallholders; the latter, as a consequence, have had to organize themselves by creating parallel organizations or aligning themselves with other organizations, and they draw on non-institutionalized means of collective action in order to put forward their claims.

The article begins with an explanation of the methodology and data used. This is followed by an outline of the development of the Burkinabé cotton sector, focusing on its institutional framework. This framework changed significantly due to the policies of economic liberalization that have been promoted by the World Bank since the mid-1990s. Subsequently, protests by cotton farmers since the early 2010s are presented, including a focus on the role of

---

6. Marc Edelman and Jun Borras, *Political Dynamics of Transnational Agrarian Movements* (Winnipeg, 2016), p. 3.

the UNPCB. I then explain why the current protests are taking place, and relate them to the liberalization policies.

METHODOLOGY AND DATA

The empirical material for this case study was collected during five research stays in Burkina Faso, in February–March 2018, February–March and September–October 2019, and February–March and December 2020. In total, I carried out around thirty semi-structured interviews and focus group discussions (FGDs) in Bobo-Dioulasso, Dédougou, Houndé, Ouagadougou, and a few villages in the provinces of Mouhoun (Boucle du Mouhoun region, central-west) and Tuy (Haut-Bassins region, southwest). Interviewees included cotton farmers, workers at the SOFITEX cotton plant, and representatives from labour unions, civil society organizations, cotton companies and the UNPCB. Interviewees were selected to represent a wide range of perspectives on the protests taking place in the cotton sector, including wealthier and poorer farmers, those who have participated in the protests and those who have not. Interviews and FGDs were conducted in French, Mooré, and Dioula (mostly with translation to French). In addition, I had numerous informal conversations, visited the cotton fields, and attended the meetings and mobilization events of the social movements and labour unions.

Secondary sources include reports, mainly from the Burkinabé press, and documents from international organizations (such as the World Bank and the Organisation for Economic Co-operation and Development or OECD), development agencies, state authorities, the cotton industry, trade unions, and non-governmental organizations (NGOs).

Data were analysed through an open coding system, focusing on the various actors' experiences with and perspectives on the effects of the liberalization process, particularly institutional restructuring; the ways in which various interests in the sector are articulated and negotiated; and conflicts and protests, especially the recent boycott campaign.

BURKINA FASO'S COTTON SECTOR

Cotton production in the former state of Upper Volta (created under colonial rule in 1919), nowadays Burkina Faso (as the country has been named since 1984), has a long history, going back to the pre-colonial period. In pre-colonial times, cotton was cultivated on a small scale, alongside other crops, for household consumption (to make clothes and blankets) and as a cash crop.[7]

---

7. Jean Capron, *Communautés villageoises bwa, Mali-Haute-Volte* (Paris, 1973).

Production increased under colonial rule, as the colonial authorities aimed to supply their armies and the workers in the factories of industrializing Europe with cotton clothes. The expansion of African cotton production did not, however, work out as smoothly as planned. The colonial powers did not provide sufficient inputs and infrastructure, nor did they offer attractive purchase prices.[8] Their efforts to compel farmers to cultivate cotton likewise failed almost completely.[9]

Since the 1950s, the sector was developed by the French state-owned cotton company Compagnie Française pour le Développement des Fibres Textiles (CFDT, created in 1949), which went on to take charge of the entire West African CFA franc zone's supply of cotton to the French textile industry.

Nationalization of the cotton sector after decolonialization

Burkina Faso gained formal independence from French colonial rule in 1960. In 1979, the Burkinabé government nationalized the cotton sector and created the monopolistic company Société Burkinabé des Fibres Textiles (SOFITEX), a joint venture of the government and the CFDT. The sector was (and remains) organized according to a highly vertically integrated *filière* model. The *filière* system was set up by CFDT in the 1950s and is typical of cotton production in former French colonies in West Africa. It is characterized by state-controlled monopolistic companies such as SOFITEX that organize cotton production.[10] SOFITEX is in charge of the proliferation and distribution of seeds, fertilizer, and pesticides; it guarantees credits for agricultural inputs for producers; it provides agricultural extensions (i.e. providing education and consultancy services to facilitate the application of research and specialized knowledge to agricultural practices); and it organizes the purchase, transport, ginning, and sale of the grains and fibres. The purchase price is fixed before the season begins so that farmers have some security.

Cultivation itself is done by smallholder peasants, mainly on a family or household basis. Most smallholders own a few hectares; those who are better off may own up to fifty hectares. A small minority of wealthy producers own over 100 hectares, and some even hold over 300 hectares. This does not mean, however, that farmers cultivate cotton on the whole area they hold; most produce cotton (Figure 1) on a part of their land and cultivate other crops (such as

8. Thomas J. Bassett, *The Peasant Cotton Revolution in West Africa: Côte d'Ivoire, 1880–1995* (Cambridge, 2001); Allen Isaacman and Richard Robertson, "Cotton, Colonialism, and Social History in Sub-Saharan Africa: Introduction", in Allen Isaacman and Richard Robertson (eds), *Cotton, Colonialism, and Social History in Sub-Saharan Africa* (Portsmouth, NH, 1995), pp. 1–39.
9. Leslie C. Gray, "Cotton Production in Burkina Faso: International Rhetoric versus Local Realities", in William G. Moseley and Leslie Gray (eds), *Hanging by a Thread: Cotton, Globalization, and Poverty in Africa* (Athens, OH, 2008), pp. 65–82, p. 69.
10. Gray, "Cotton Production in Burkina Faso", pp. 833–834.

Fig. 1 Cotton plant. Photograph by the author.

cereals, groundnuts, beans, sesame, and cashew) on other parts. They also do not usually cultivate all their land at the same time, but may leave some areas fallow so the soil can regenerate. Additionally, they may not have the assets and labour at their disposal to cultivate all their land at once. Farmers decide what they will cultivate in view of the soil quality, their household consumption, market factors, and the available assets and labour. Labour is mostly unpaid family labour, such as farmers' wives and children; producers who have some cash and who cultivate larger areas also hire labour on a daily or weekly basis. The main motivation for cotton cultivation is that the *filière* system provides farmers with access to fertilizer, pesticide, and guaranteed purchase. Yet, farmers have no choice regarding whom they can buy agricultural inputs from and to whom they can sell the cotton: SOFITEX holds the monopoly for both input supply and purchase.

Contract farming does not exist for cotton in Burkina Faso; farmers cultivate land they hold tenure rights for or own. Access to land and land rights in Burkina Faso are negotiated and regulated through various formal and informal institutions that may overlap, be complementary, or be concurrent. Traditional institutions vary among regions, localities, and ethnic groups; however, traditional chiefs (*chefferie traditionnelle*) always play a central role. Peasants either have ownership rights defined by traditional institutions and/or codified by formal land titles, or they have tenure rights through traditional institutions.[11]

Since the 1960s, farmers have been encouraged by the state to organize themselves into village-level cooperatives (*groupements villageois*, GVs), "which, however, seldom became genuine cooperatives although this was the state's ambition. Peasants joined forces, but rarely resources. The GVs are to a large extent a structure facilitating the work of various extension services."[12] The cooperatives were in charge of administering credits to the cotton farmers. In order to have access to input supplies and to be able to sell the cotton, every farmer had to be a member of a cooperative (though, as a rule, only male farmers were members; women could only become members in exceptional cases, such as when the husband dies). At the beginning of the season, SOFITEX would sell inputs to the cooperatives on credit (with interest), and after the harvest, it would purchase the cotton at the fixed price. When the cotton was collected at the end of the season, producers would be paid the basic price minus the cost of the inputs they had received on credit at the beginning of the season. At the end of the season, they could potentially get a premium in case the effective export price for cotton at the time exceeded the basic price. If the export price was below the basic price, this deficit was topped up from a fund (*fond de lissage*) so that the farmers would still be paid the guaranteed price. The fund was topped up in years of high world market prices for cotton.[13]

11. For more details, see Luigi Arnaldi di Balme and Peter Hochet, *Aperçu du cadre juridique et institutionnel de la gestion des ressources naturelles et foncières au Burkina Faso* (Ouagadougou and Paris, 2010); Leslie C. Gray, "Environmental Policy, Land Rights, and Conflict: Rethinking Community Natural Resource Management Programs in Burkina Faso", *Environment and Planning D: Society and Space*, 20:2 (2002), pp. 167–182; Quentin Gausset, "Le foncier et les arbres dans le sud-ouest du Burkina Faso. Présentation de l'approche contractuelle de PETREA", in Anette Reenberg and Henrik Secher Marcussen (eds), *Etablir le lien entre la recherche et la politique: Bridging Research and Policy – Proceedings of the Workshop, 2–3 December 2004* (Ouagadougou, Burkina Faso, 2004); Quentin Gausset, "L'aspect foncier dans les conflits entre autochtones et migrants au sud-ouest du Burkina Faso", *Politique africaine*, 4 (2008), pp. 52–66.
12. Lars Engberg Pedersen, "Politics, Development and Custom: People's Struggle for Evasion in Yatenga, Burkina Faso", in Tor Benjaminsen and Christian Lund (eds), *Politics, Property and Production in the West African Sahel: Understanding Natural Resources Management* (Uppsala, 2001), pp. 75–100, p. 83.
13. Cornelia Staritz, Susan Newman, Bernhard Tröster, and Leonhard Plank, "Financialization and Global Commodity Chains: Distributional Implications for Cotton in Sub-Saharan Africa", *Development and Change*, 49:3 (2018), pp. 815–842, p. 13.

More than ninety-five per cent of Burkina Faso's cotton fibre is exported; hence there is very little value created in the country itself. During the "revolutionary" period of Thomas Sankara's presidency (1984–1987), local production – i.e. spinning, weaving, and further processing – was promoted. A national textile factory, Faso Dan Fani, operated in the town of Koudougou. Sankara was well-known for wearing Dan Fani cloth himself and for encouraging members of the government and public servants to do likewise.[14] However, under pressure from the World Bank to privatize state-owned companies, the governments of Blaise Compaoré, who succeeded Sankara as president (1987–2014), and Prime Minister Kadre Désiré Ouédraogo agreed in 1997 to sell Faso Dan Fani, which was eventually closed in 2001.[15]

Liberalization from the mid-1990s onwards

From the mid-1990s onwards, the World Bank pushed the liberalization of the cotton sector in Burkina Faso, as it urged economic liberalization in developing countries in general. The first measure taken to restructure the *filière* was the reorganization of the GV cooperatives into *groupements des producteurs de coton* (GPCs) in 1996. Until then, the GVs had been organized strictly at the village level, so all agricultural producers from one village formed one cooperative and had to share credits and inputs. In many cases, farmers complained that they could not rely on others – that others took seeds, fertilizer, and pesticides on credit, charging them to the cooperative's account, but then failed to produce, and those who worked hard ended up having to pay off the debts of others. The GPCs, in contrast, were established on a voluntary basis by cotton producers who trust each other. Often, farmers from the same village are members of different GPCs. Members might be removed from the GPC if they do not follow the rules, and potential members might not even be accepted if they have a bad record.[16] In general, as compared to former GV cooperatives, the GPCs have far fewer members and are less diverse.[17] In

---

14. Ernest Harsch, "The Legacies of Thomas Sankara: A Revolutionary Experience in Retrospect", *Review of African Political Economy*, 40:137 (2013), pp. 358–374, p. 371; Rémy Herrera and Laurent Ilboudo, "Les défis de l'agriculture paysanne. Le cas du Burkina Faso", *L'Homme & la Société*, 183–184 (2012), pp. 83–95, p. 88.
15. Ernest Harsch, "Burkina Faso in the Winds of Liberalisation", *Review of African Political Economy*, 25:78 (1998), pp. 625–641, p. 631; Mathieu Hilgers, *Une ethnographie à l'échelle de la ville. Urbanité, histoire et reconnaissance à Koudougou (Burkina Faso)* (Paris, 2009), p. 123.
16. Jonathan Kaminski, Derek Headey, and Tanguy Bernard, "The Burkinabè Cotton Story 1992–2007: Sustainable Success or Sub-Saharan Mirage?", *World Development*, 39:8 (2011), pp. 1460–1475, p. 1463.
17. Brian Dowd-Uribe, "Liberalisation Failed: Understanding Persistent State Power in the Burkinabè Cotton Sector from 1990 to 2004", *Development Policy Review*, 32:5 (2014), pp. 545–566, p. 558.

many cases, more well-off farmers join together in one cooperative, while poorer farmers make up another. Many of the problems that the GVs faced continue to exist after the restructuring, such as problems of internal management, producers ordering more seeds (on credit) than they are able to sow, and difficulties of debt repayment.[18]

In 1998, the UNPCB was created to be the national organization of cotton farmers. This was not a process initiated "from below" by a broad movement of the cotton farmers themselves. Rather, its creation was, at least partly, a reaction of the authorities to some peasants' attempts to independently organize the cooperatives into an umbrella body (the Fédération Nationale des Organisations Paysannes, or FENOP, created in 1996) meant to represent their interests.[19] Subsequently, some wealthier producers, together with SOFITEX and the government, pushed the creation of the UNPCB as a more "peaceful", corporatist organization, with the intention of taming the farmers' movement.[20] The UNPCB is hierarchically structured, with the GPCs being the smallest unit at the local level. The GPCs elect a board at the department level (*union départementale*) and the departmental boards vote for representatives at the provincial level (*union provinciale*). Currently, more than 9,000 cooperatives (now formally called the Coopératives simplifiées de production de coton, SCOOPS-PC) exist and are represented by 177 departmental unions and twenty-eight provincial unions. The provincial unions delegate three representatives each to the general assembly at the national level. The UNPCB's operational bodies at the national level are the administrative council, consisting of twelve members elected by the General Assembly; the Surveillance Council (five members elected by the General Assembly); and technical staff (190 employees). The UNPCB is in charge of supporting the producers and providing technical advice to them; representing them in negotiations with the cotton companies and the state authorities; and facilitating the credit system for agricultural inputs, that is, supporting the collection of credits and assuming liability cooperatively. Financially, the UNPCB depends heavily on external donors (such as the French Development Agency and the European Union).

In 1999, the government made the UNPCB become a SOFITEX shareholder, with the aim of increasing "ownership" of the producers in the sector. Initially, the share was thirty per cent, but this was later cut to five per cent.

18. Brian Dowd-Uribe, "Engineering Yields and Inequality? How Institutions and Agro-Ecology Shape Cotton Outcomes in Burkina Faso", *Geoforum*, 53 (2014), pp. 161–171, pp. 164–165.
19. Dowd-Uribe, "Liberalisation Failed", p. 557.
20. *Ibid.*, p. 558; Kaminski, Headey, and Tanguy "The Burkinabè Cotton Story 1992–2007", p. 1462.

In 2004, the government authorized the creation of two fully private cotton companies: Société Cotonnière du Gourma (SOCOMA) and Faso Coton. SOFITEX thus no longer holds the monopoly in the sector; however, the two private companies are much smaller and relatively less important, and more than eighty per cent of production remains under SOFITEX control. The three cotton companies do not compete with each other; rather, the total cotton producing zone is divided among them. SOFITEX controls the west, Faso Coton the centre, and SOCOMA the east. The *filière* system functions in the same way in all zones, with the UNPCB representing the producer cooperatives and the respective cotton company in charge of supplying seeds, fertilizer, and pesticides on credit to the cooperatives, providing agriculture extensions, and taking care of the purchase, transport, ginning, and sale of the cotton (Figure 2).

In 2006, the Association Interprofessionnelle du Coton du Burkina Faso (AICB) was established as a corporatist agency of the cotton companies, the government, and the UNPCB. Most importantly, it is in charge of fixing the purchase price before the beginning of the season.

COTTON FARMERS' DISCONTENT AND PROTESTS

Protests by cotton farmers have occurred frequently since the late 2000s, especially in the SOFITEX zone. It is by far the largest company, and part of the farmers' discontent concerns SOFITEX specifically. The purchase price is a major issue of contention. In addition to demanding higher purchase prices, farmers complain about the poor quality of the seeds, fertilizer, and pesticides they are supplied. Many producers are continuously in debt, and though cotton cultivation does come with risks and challenges, farmers stick to it because it is their only chance to access agricultural assets (input supply, credit, technical support, access to the market).[21] Many farmers state that they would actually prefer to cultivate maize or other cereals if they could obtain credit to do so.[22] Cotton farmers can at least get some fertilizer for maize cultivation on credit from the cotton companies if they produce a certain amount of cotton. Farmers also point to problems such as delayed payments after the harvest has been collected and widespread corruption, especially related to the transport and quality classification of the cotton.[23]

---

21. Dolores Koenig, "Rural Development Is More Than Commodity Production: Cotton in the Farming System of Kita, Mali", in Moseley and Leslie, *Hanging by a Thread*, pp. 177–206, p. 188.
22. Dowd-Uribe, "Engineering yields and inequality?"; FGDs with cotton farmers, Tuy province, 9 February 2019 and 25 September 2019.
23. Dowd-Uribe, "Engineering Yields and Inequality?", pp. 165–166; Gray, "Cotton Production in Burkina Faso", p. 75; Leslie C. Gray and Brian Dowd-Uribe, "A Political Ecology of Socio-Economic Differentiation: Debt, Inputs and Liberalization Reforms in Southwestern Burkina Faso", *The Journal of Peasant Studies*, 40:4 (2013), pp. 683–702, p. 696; interview with cotton farmers, Dédougou, 26 February 2019.

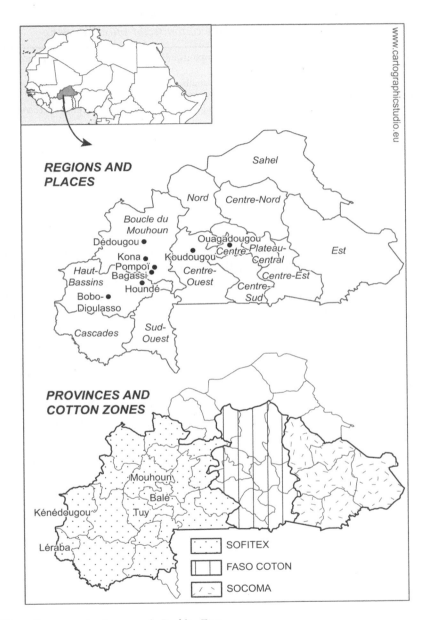

Fig. 2 Cotton production zones in Burkina Faso.

Farmers' protests and conflict over UNPCB leadership in 2011

Protests by cotton producers first occurred in April 2011, the time of year when, after the harvest has been completed, prices for the next season are

Table 1 *Institutional development of the cotton sector since the 1950s.*

1950s	Development of the sector by the Compagnie Française pour le Développement des Fibres Textiles (CFDT)
1979	Nationalization of the cotton sector: creation of SOFITEX
1980s	Organization of the producers into *groupements villageoises* (GVs)
1996	Reorganization of the producers into *groupements des producteurs de coton* (GPCs)
1998	Creation of the Union Nationale des Producteurs du Coton du Burkina (UNPCB)
1999	UNPCB becomes a shareholder in SOFITEX
2004	Authorization for private cotton companies Faso Coton and SOCOMA
2006	Establishment of the Association Interprofessionnelle du Coton du Burkina Faso (AICB)

set.[24] On 6 April 2011, a group of cotton farmers in the province of Léraba, in the Cascades region in South West Burkina Faso, marched to the provincial authority (the *haut-commissariat*) and claimed a balance report covering the last four years and the removal of the agricultural extension service team.[25] On 27 April, after attending a meeting with the UNPCB and the management of SOFITEX, cotton farmers marched in Bobo-Dioulasso, Burkina Faso's second largest city and the capital of the cotton-producing zone in the south-west. Farmers demanded that the purchase price be raised from 245 CFA francs (€ 0.32) to 500 CFA francs (€ 0.76) per kilo, that the price of fertilizer be reduced to 15,000 CFA francs (€ 22.87) per kilogram, and that there be fundamental reforms in SOFITEX management, including the dismissal of the company's general director. The protesters declared that they would stage a boycott, refraining from cotton production, if their claims were not met.[26]

The 2011 conflict was entangled with leadership rivalry within the UNPCB. In March 2010, Karim Traoré succeeded François Traoré,[27] who had been in office since the body was created in 1998, as the head of the UNPCB. Karim accused his predecessor of striving to remain in office

24. I am particularly grateful to Ernest Harsch for sharing documentation on the 2011 protests with me.
25. Mamoudou Traoré, "Plaine aménagée de Douna. Les producteurs mécontents menacent de troubler l'ordre public", *Le Pays*, 6–8 May 2011.
26. Une lettre pour Laye, *Observateur Paalga*, 29 April–1 May 2011; UNPCB aux marcheurs de Bobo et de Dédougou, "Abandonnez la rue pour vos champs", *Le Pays*, 17 May 2011.
27. Traoré is a common patronym in Dioula-speaking areas of Western Africa, including Burkina Faso, Mali, and Côte d'Ivoire. Thus, the fact that both Karim and François are named Traoré does not imply that they are related.

illegitimately; François accused Karim of having been installed by SOFITEX.[28] According to the local press, François Traoré and a couple of other former members of the UNPCB's national board were among those who mobilized the meetings, marches, and petitions in 2011.[29] Karim Traoré reacted by publicly stating that the demand for a purchase price of 500 CFA francs was "utopian" and "illogical".[30] This enraged many farmers and spurred marches in Bobo-Dioulasso and Dédougou, another important town in the SOFITEX zone, on 12 May.[31] Protesters reiterated their determination to boycott if the government and SOFITEX did not respond to their claims.[32] In a declaration on 17 May 2011, the UNPCB condemned the marches and declared itself the "only legal frame of struggle" in the cotton sector.[33] The UNPCB leadership argued that the farmers were allowing themselves to be made instruments of the members of the former national board. "Leave the streets and go back to your fields", Karim Traoré urged them.[34]

In response, a number of peasants boycotted cotton production in the 2011–2012 season.[35] In the province of Kénédougou in the southwest (Haut-Bassins region, bordering Mali), peasants refused to grow cotton and, in July 2011, even partly damaged the fields of others who were not participating in the boycott. State security forces intervened violently and arrested "rebel" peasants. Several peasants fled their villages to escape arrest.[36] One person was killed and numerous others were injured by the security forces; altogether, 225 hectares of cotton crop in the region were destroyed.[37] On 12 July, cotton producers from the rural municipalities of Safané, Bagassi, and Pompoi in the province of Balé, and Kona, in the province of Mouhoun (both located in the Boucle du Mouhoun region in North West Burkina Faso) furiously rushed to the city of Bankuy, armed with machetes, catapults,

28. Ousséni Bance, "Karim Traoré, Président de l'UNPCB. 'Je reconnais avoir milité dans le CDP mais François est dans les instances du MPP'", *lefaso.net*, 29 December 2014. Available at: https://lefaso.net/spip.php?article62517; last accessed 18 January 2021.
29. *Une lettre pour Laye, Observateur Paalga*, 29 April–1 May 2011.
30. UNPCB, "Revendiquer 500f cfa par kg de coton graine est utopique", *Le Pays*, 5 May 2011.
31. UNPCB aux marcheurs de Bobo et de Dédougou, "Abandonnez la rue pour vos champs", *Le Pays*, 17 May 2011.
32. Abdoul Razac Napon, "Crise du coton. Psychose et frustrations dans les zones cotonnières", *L'Evènement*, 10 August 2011.
33. Karim Traoré, "UNPCB aux marcheurs de Bobo et de Dédougou. 'Abandonnez la rue pour vos champs'. Déclaration de l'UNPCB, Bobo-Dioulasso 13 May 2011", *Le Pays*, 17 May 2011.
34. *Ibid.*, my translation.
35. Abdoulaye Tao, "Guerre entre cotonculteurs. Péril sur l'or blanc", *Le Pays*, 12 July, 2011.
36. Apollinaire Kam, "Boycott de la campagne cotonnière à N'Dorola. Affrontements entre forces de l'ordre et cotonculteurs", *lefaso.net*, 15 July 2011. Available at: https://lefaso.net/spip.php?article43013; last accessed 18 January 2021.
37. Thomas J. Bassett, "Capturing the Margins: World Market Prices and Cotton Farmer Incomes in West Africa", *World Development*, 59 (2014), pp. 408–421, p. 409.

and other traditional (non-gun) arms, to demand the release of a protester who had been arrested.[38]

The leadership struggle created a severe crisis for the UNPCB. Many farmers felt cheated by the UNPCB and considered Karim Traoré's board a "machine" of SOFITEX.[39] Traoré managed to temporarily calm tempers by back-pedalling, meeting with the farmers, and declaring their demands were justified.[40] In 2015, however, a year in which Burkina Faso underwent a political transition after the fall of long-time President Blaise Compaoré, the cotton farmers' discontent broke out on a large scale once again. They accused Karim Traoré of having supported Compaoré's regime, of abusing the UNPCB's funds to finance activities of the ruling party – Congrès pour la démocratie et le progress (CDP), of which Compaoré was an active member – and of misappropriating funds for other private purposes. Again, farmers threatened boycotts.[41] On 30 October 2015, Traoré was arrested and officially accused of the misappropriation of 84 million CFA francs (€ 127,000).[42] He was convicted and spent six months in prison. On 27–28 February 2017, Bambou Bihoun, a wealthy cotton farmer from Tuy province, was elected president of the UNPCB.[43] Once again, the association is being headed by a moderate president who seeks collaboration with the cotton companies and the government rather than confrontation and conflict.

"Zero cotton": The 2018–2019 boycott campaign

In recent years, to put forth their demands, farmers from various cooperatives in the SOFITEX zone have set up a network, the Collectif des Paysans, and have begun to organize into a nationwide youth association,[44] the Organisation Démocratique de la Jeunesse du Burkina Faso (Democratic Youth Organization of Burkina Faso or ODJ). It is not by chance that mobilization has increased in recent years, and cotton production is by no means

---

38. Serge Coulibaly, "Arrestation d'un Anti-coton", *Le Pays*, 15–17 July, 2011.
39. Napon, "Crise du Coton"; *Observateur Paalga*, 25 July 2011.
40. Tielmè Innocent Kambiré, "Union nationale des producteurs de coton du Burkina. Les cotonculteurs du Kénédougou fument le calumet de la paix", *Sidwaya*, 3 October 2011; Josias Zounzaola Dabiré, "Mesententes entre cotonculteurs. Le calumet de la paix fumé à Kourouma", *Le Pays*, 5 October 2011.
41. Jessie K. Luna, "The Chain of Exploitation: Intersectional Inequalities, Capital Accumulation, and Resistance in Burkina Faso's Cotton Sector", *The Journal of Peasant Studies*, 46:7 (2018), pp. 1–22, p. 11.
42. Rahamatou Sanon, "Arrestation de Karim Traoré. Le conseil de gestion de l'UNPCB mécontent", *Le Pays*, 3 November 2015.
43. Romuald Dofini, "Producteurs de coton. Bihoun Bambou est le nouveau président de l'UNPCB", *lefaso.net*, 28 February 2017. Available at: https://lefaso.net/spip.php?article71892; last accessed 18 February 2021.
44. "Youth" in terms of a social category, not necessarily age.

the only sphere in Burkina Faso that is currently being shaped by intense social mobilization. On 30–31 October 2014, long-time President Blaise Compaoré was overthrown by a popular insurrection after twenty-seven years in power. The regime change has favoured social mobilization in various social and political fields in the country. The successful mass protests in the capital that led to Compaoré's ouster also had a mobilizing effect in the rural provinces. The general mood of "nothing will be as before" gave significant impetus to the mobilizations and has contributed to further strengthening Burkina Faso's vibrant civil society organizations. The ODJ is one of the organizations that was strongly involved in the struggles that eventually resulted in the overthrow of Compaoré.[45]

While the leadership contest within the UNPCB seems, for now, to have been settled, farmers' discontent with the association endures. This was expressed in particular in the hitherto most widespread boycott campaign by Burkinabé cotton farmers in the 2018–2019 season. In the previous season (2017–2018), yields were poor due to unfavourable weather conditions (insufficient rainfall in particular), and – according to the farmers – also due to poor-quality fertilizer. In January 2018, smallholder cotton producers represented by the ODJ held a press conference to complain about the poor quality of fertilizer delivered to them in the SOFITEX zone. They pointed out that the fertilizer contained stones, which, according to them, resulted in significantly lower yields (the cotton harvest starts in December, so by the end of January farmers are able to assess the season's yield). They demanded that farmers who had received inferior quality fertilizer should be compensated. "As the benefits are shared, losses have to be shared, too", a spokesperson of ODJ in Tuy province stated, "The cotton producing farmers must not be left alone to deal with the catastrophic consequence of the season. All actors of the *filière* have to bear the costs. Thus, simply cancel the total debts of the cotton season 2017–2018 due to *force majeure*."[46]

They demanded, moreover, that the quality of the harvested cotton be assessed by independent experts – with neither the UNPCB, nor SOFITEX being involved – and urged farmers to refuse to pay back their credit for the season until the assessment was complete. They accused the UNPCB of not representing the interests of the farmers: "They [the persons responsible at the UNPCB] let us know that they would not put pressure on SOFITEX",

45. For more details, see Bettina Engels, "Political Transition in Burkina Faso", in Hans J. Giessmann and Roger Mac Ginty (eds), *How Regimes Change: Post-Conflict Transitions Revisited* (Cheltenham, 2018), pp. 223–237; Bettina Engels, "A Stolen Revolution: Popular Class Mobilisation in Burkina Faso", *Labor History*, 60:2 (2019), pp. 110–125.
46. Irmine Kinda, "Campagne cotonnière. L'ODJ incrimine l'engrais", *Burkina24*, 30 January 2018. Available at: https://www.burkina24.com/2018/01/30/campagne-cotonniere-lodj-incrimine-lengrais/; last accessed 18 February 2021; my translation.

the spokesperson of the protestors reported.[47] Suspecting the UNPCB of corruption, the protesters announced that they would address the anti-corruption state authority and the civil society network Réseau national de lutte anti-corruption (National Network for the Fight Against Corruption, or REN-LAC).

On 30 April 2018, cotton farmers represented by the ODJ presented their demands to the regional state authority (*Gouverneur*) of the Haut-Bassins region, complaining that the government had supported SOFITEX and its subcontractors with 14 billion CFA francs (about € 21 million) but had not compensated the farmers. To back up their demands, the farmers launched a boycott of cotton cultivation.[48] The initiative to boycott spread rapidly, particularly within the SOFITEX zone, and went beyond the organized groups. The province of Kénédougou was a case in point; in the 2018–2019 season, almost all the farmers there joined the boycott. Even the initial organizers of the boycott campaign were surprised by this.[49]

Boycotts mean that farmers decide not to cultivate cotton at all, or to significantly reduce the area used for cotton cultivation and instead grow cereals (such as maize, millet, and sorghum), beans or cash crops (such as sesame, groundnuts, and cashew). In principle, farmers who decide not to grow cotton are not supposed to take inputs for the season on credit from the respective cotton company. However, as for most farmers cotton cultivation is virtually the only means to gain access to fertilizer, some might have taken fertilizer from the cotton companies and then used it to grow maize or other crops instead. This became a particular problem in cases where there was no consensus within a GPC on whether and to what extent to boycott cotton, as debts are collectivized and at the end of the season the members who have grown cotton will also be held accountable for the credits of those who boycotted it. In most cases, however, farmers within the GPCs did discuss this issue among themselves until they came to an agreement; and if some individuals decided to reduce the surface area they would cultivate, they announced it in advance and thus ordered fewer inputs on credit.

Consent for the boycott campaign varied among farmers, not only regionally – with some provinces showing a higher degree of participation than others – but also within villages, GPCs, and even families. But regardless of whether they supported the boycott in principle, cotton producers widely agreed that a full boycott would be challenging in view of the absence of cash-

---

47. Herman Frédéric Bassolé, "Campagne cotonnière 2017–2018. Des producteurs dénoncent la mauvaise qualité des engrais", *lefaso.net*, 31 January 2018. Available at: https://lefaso.net/spip.php?article81703; last accessed 18 February 2021; my translation.
48. ODJ, Conférence de presse des militants paysans de l'ODJ des zones cotonnières (SOFITEX, FASO-COTON et SOCOMA) du Burkina Faso, 28 May 2019. Déclaration liminaire (Ouagadougou, 2019).
49. Informal conversation, Bobo-Dioulasso, 26 September 2019.

generating alternatives, and because refusing cotton cultivation is particularly difficult for poor farmers who cannot afford fertilizer to grow other crops. Systematic data are lacking on who participated to what extent in the boycott, but it can be assumed that the poorer farmers are, the greater the obstacles to engaging in the boycott – namely the difficulty of refusing to take any inputs at all on credit from the cotton company at the beginning of the season.

Why do farmers boycott cotton cultivation, given that they risk losing a substantial part of their livelihoods? The assumption behind the boycott campaign is, as one of its leaders explained in an interview,[50] that "if all farmers would produce 'zero cotton', SOFITEX would have to shut down and its managers would lose their salaries". The call to boycott was passed on from person to person, from village to village, promoted by the Collectif des Paysans and local activists within the ODJ. Representatives from the cotton industry confirmed that they were indeed following the spreading calls for a boycott "with concern".[51] In any case, the campaign resulted in a significant decrease in cotton production in the 2018–2019 season: while the Burkinabé cotton companies had set a target output of 800,000 tons, only 436,000 tons were produced, a twenty-nine per cent decrease from the previous season. This led to Burkina Faso going from being Africa's largest cotton producing country to fourth-largest, after Benin, Mali, and Côte d'Ivoire. Though weather conditions and the unstable security situation in Burkina Faso also negatively impacted cotton production, all actors involved consider the boycott to be a major cause.[52]

The main demands that farmers raise in their protests include the increase of the purchase price to 500 CFA francs; lower prices for and greater quality control of agricultural inputs; changes to the allocation mechanism for these inputs; and relief of farmers' internal and external debts for the 2017–2018 and 2018–2019 seasons. Key claims also concern the UNPCB: the dissolution of the national and departmental boards; an independent audit of all its offices at the national, departmental and provincial levels; and examination of cases of possible misuse of UNPCB funds and the conviction of all found responsible for it.[53] A year after they had first presented their claims, protesting farmers went to see the Governor of the Haut-Bassins region again. Stating that the conflict was beyond his authority, he advised the farmers to address the government at the national level. Thus, cotton farmers from the three cotton-producing zones covered by SOFITEX, SOCOMA, and Faso Coton joined

50. Houndé, 14 February 2019; my translation.
51. Interview, Bobo-Dioulasso, 8 February 2019; my translation.
52. Nadoun Coulibaly, "Burkina Faso. La production cotonnière chute de 30% et dégringole à 436 000 tonnes", *Jeunes Afrique*, 16 April 2019.
53. Issoufou Ouédraogo, "ODJ. Des producteurs menacent de boycotter la culture du coton", *lefaso.net*, 28 May 2019. Available at: https://lefaso.net/spip.php?article89937; last accessed 18 February 2021.

forces and held a workshop in Ouagadougou on 16–17 March 2019. They agreed on some major demands, which they submitted on 27 May to the Ministry of Agriculture and Water.[54]

Farmers also expressed their dissatisfaction with the UNPCB by withholding their union dues, which add up to 750 CFA francs (€ 1.14) per ton of cotton that a cooperative sells: of which 250 CFA francs each goes to the departmental, provincial, and national levels. "These guys don't do their work", the farmers explained, "We refuse the payment of the contributions because the union does not represent our interests. [...] And we do not understand what happens with the money."[55] Moreover, farmers stayed away from meetings, disregarded recommendations by SOFITEX agents, and bought or sold inputs on the local markets, thus sidestepping SOFITEX altogether.[56]

The UNPCB as an issue of discontent

Many studies, primarily by the World Bank, portray the integration of producers – in this case, of the UNPCB – into the governance institutions of the cotton sector as a success of liberalization policies. This largely reflects the idea of "participation" that has been introduced as an integral element of "new" modes of liberal economic governance since the 1990s. Participation of various stakeholders is created in a top-down model that determines and limits, a priori, precisely who is supposed to participate in what ways and in which arenas, with the aim of making governance more effective. However, who the stakeholders actually are, and whose interests can and should be represented by whom and in which way are matters that can be contested. The UNPCB, since its creation, has been substantially influenced by SOFITEX and the government, and both have steadily and successfully hindered more critical or radical farmers from gaining influence or taking up any responsibilities or posts within the union. From the local to the national level, the UNPCB is entangled with the authorities and political parties: with the CDP, Compaoré's ruling party, until he was overthrown in 2014, and since then with its successor, the Movement pour le Peuple et le Progrès (MPP). The links between the authorities and the UNPCB became particularly obvious in 2013 and 2014, when, related to the fall of Compaoré, then-president of the UNPCB Karim Traoré, who was close to the ruling elite, was also overthrown.

Moreover, posts within the UNPCB are mostly occupied by wealthy producers (rich and middle-class farmers) who have significant amounts of land, equipment, and access to (often unpaid family) labour. The current president

---

54. ODJ, "Conférence de presse des militants paysans".
55. FGD with cotton farmers, village in Tuy province, 25 September 2019, my translation.
56. Luna, "The chain of exploitation", p. 11.

of the union is one of the richest cotton farmers in the country, cultivating a very large area relative to the vast majority of the smallholders and even most middle-class farmers in the sector. Karim Traoré is likewise among the richest cotton farmers in the country. By contrast, the majority of cotton producers have rather small land holdings and insufficient access to the necessary means of production and labour. These farmers produce a maximum of one ton of cotton per hectare each season, often less, and struggle to repay their debts.[57] Those who benefit substantially from cotton production are a minority of larger farmers and "actors employed higher up the cotton commodity chain [...] including cotton company employees, state actors, agribusiness, banks, textile manufacturers, and end consumers of cotton products".[58]

It would be misleading to consider the UNPCB a genuine representative of cotton farmers as a whole. A significant share of the producers feel substantially unsatisfied with the UNPCB.[59] Many farmers feel the UNPCB is hindering them in putting their demands forward rather than representing them. They complain that they cannot raise claims directly with the respective cotton companies or the authorities, but must address them to the UNPCB, since the companies and the authorities negotiate exclusively with the UNPCB.

CONCLUSION

The policies of economic liberalization, as promoted by the World Bank since the mid-1990s, have affected Burkinabé cotton farmers with regard to how they are organized: there was a shift in the cooperative system from the GVs to the GPCs, which are required to be incorporated into the hierarchical structure of the UNPCB. This change in the institutional setting also implies a change in the modalities of wielding power in the sector: the state authorities and SOFITEX remain the principal powerful actors, but since the creation of the UNPCB they now exercise even more control over the sector indirectly through the union.

The way liberalization was implemented strengthened rather than weakened the control and influence of the state in the sector. So, instead of a relative loss of state control over the economy, there has rather been a shift towards a mode of indirect private governance, where the state exercises control through

---

57. Alain Bonnassieux, "Filière cotton, emergence des organisations de producteurs et transformations territoriales au Mali et au Burkina Faso", *Les Cahiers d'Outre-Mer*, 55:220 (2002), pp. 421–434; FGD with cotton farmers, Tuy Province, 7 February 2019.
58. Jessie K. Luna, "Getting Out of the Dirt: Racialized Modernity and Environmental Inequality in the Cotton Sector of Burkina Faso", *Environmental Sociology*, 4:2 (2018), pp. 221–234, p. 221.
59. Dowd-Uribe, "Engineering yields and inequality?", p. 166; FGDs with cotton farmers, Tuy province, 9 February 2019, 25 September 2019, 26 September 2019, and 3 October 2019, and Mouhoun province, 26 February 2019; interview with cotton farmer, Houndé, 14 February 2019.

allegedly private actors (SOFITEX) – which may result in the modes of control becoming more difficult to see through for some actors, such as smallholders. Liberalization implies a shift in power, from labour – and, with respect to agriculture, from smallholder producers – to the merchants. In the case of the cotton sector, this means more power has gone to SOFITEX. As SOFITEX is state-owned, liberalization thus led to a higher degree of centralization of power in the cotton sector. For the farmers, the maintenance of the *filière* system implies that they are less exposed to the vagaries of the global market, as well as to instabilities in the price and availability of inputs, and to fluctuations in the purchase price.

The creation of the UNPCB was a core element of the reform of the sector, that is, the way in which the Burkinabé state implemented the demand for liberalization by external actors. Policymakers, representatives of state authorities, the World Bank and other donor agencies, the cotton industry, and the UNPCB itself all claim that the union was created to strengthen the position of farmers and to include them in the governance of the sector. However, from the perspective of many smallholder producers (particularly the poorer ones), the UNPCB weakens their position and instead sustains the interests of SOFITEX, the rich producers, and the state. Therefore, while the farmers' discontent is now, as before, directed at the authorities and SOFITEX, the UNPCB leadership has become an additional target of anger.

The UNPCB was intentionally created as a corporatist institution whose interaction with the authorities and the cotton companies is supposed to be collaborative and highly institutionalized. In this sense, it serves more to tame and control the farmers than to represent their interests in potential confrontations with the cotton companies and the state. Indeed, SOFITEX has been, and probably still is, strongly involved in ousting more radical farmers from the UNPCB and replacing them with moderate ones in positions of responsibility in the union.

It is worth noting that liberalization and structural adjustment policies as such are not so much at the centre stage of the farmers' mobilizations; protests are rather triggered by quite concrete issues such as the purchase price and the quality of seeds and fertilizer. It can be argued, of course, that these issues result from economic liberalization. However, it remains open to interpretation whether the protests can be framed as farmer resistance to liberalization and structural adjustment. In any case, since liberalization, the producers' very means of organizing, notably the UNPCB itself, have become fields of contestation in their own right. The various resistance efforts of the cotton farmers, including their refusal to pay their dues to the UNPCB and the boycott, are related to the effects of the way the sector is structured. Economic liberalization has substantially impacted the institutional setting within the sector and changed the rules of the game, affecting the conditions and mechanisms by which interests can be articulated and negotiated. It is these rules that are centre stage in the recent conflicts.

IRSH 66 (2021), pp. 113–137 doi:10.1017/S002085902100016X

Privatizing the Commons: Protest and the Moral Economy of National Resources in Jordan*

MATTHEW LACOUTURE

Department of Political Science
Wayne State University
Detroit, MI, USA

E-mail: lacouture.matthew@wayne.edu

ABSTRACT: This article interrogates the social impact of one aspect of structural adjustment in the Hashemite Kingdom of Jordan: privatization. In the mid-2000s, King Abdullah II privatized Jordan's minerals industry as part of the regime's accelerated neoliberal project. While many of these privatizations elicited responses ranging from general approval to ambivalence, the opaque and seemingly corrupt sale of the Jordan Phosphate Mines Company (JPMC) in 2006 was understood differently, as an illegitimate appropriation of Jordan's national resources and, by extension, an abrogation of the state's (re-) distributive obligations. Based on interviews with activists, I argue that a diverse cross-section of social movement constituencies – spanning labour and non-labour movements (and factions within and across those movements) – perceived such illegitimate privatizations as a moral violation, which, in turn, informed transgressive activist practices and discourses targeting the neoliberal state. This moral violation shaped the rise and interaction of labour and non-labour social movements in Jordan's "Arab uprisings", peaking in 2011–2013. While Jordan's uprisings were largely demobilized after 2013, protests in 2018 and 2019 demonstrate the continued relevance of this discourse. In this way, the 2011–2013 wave of protests – and their current reverberations – differ qualitatively from Jordan's earlier wave of "food riots" in 1989 (and throughout the 1990s), which I characterize as primarily restorative in nature.

* The author would like to thank the Special Issue editors and participants in the 2019–2020 IISH workshop "When Adjusted People Rebel", as well as Cody Melcher, William Cotter, Sharon Lean, and internal and external reviewers for helpful comments. This research would have been impossible without MT's dedicated research assistance and friendship, Sara Ababneh's and Ahmad Awad's willingness to lend their time and expertise to my project, and the generosity and hospitality of many Jordanians along the way. All errors are my own. This research was supported by a 2018–2019 Fulbright US Student Research Grant.

> "Out, Out, Corruption! ... We want Jordan to stay free!
> No course and no alternative ... for corruption, except to leave!
> [...]
> Phosphates ... They sold it! They stole it! ...
> Potash ... They sold it! They stole it! ...
> The Electricity [Company] ... They sold it! They stole it! ...
> The Water ... They sold it! They stole it! ...
> Aqaba ... They sold it! They stole it!"
>
> Protest chant, Amman, Jordan, 2011[1]

"They stole the phosphate and did not privatize the company." This is what Salem tells me, sitting at the far end of a conference table in his offices at the Jordanian Federation of Independent Trade Unions (JFITU). His statement punctuates a list of grievances – against the Jordanian Phosphate Mines Company (JPMC), its now-exiled CEO, and even the government – which motivated his labour activism.[2] Yet, as a JPMC employee himself, he surely knew that the company had been privatized in 2006, albeit under opaque circumstances. So, what exactly did he mean that the company had been "stolen" *instead* of privatized? In my discussions with both labour and non-labour activists in Jordan – and as reflected in the protest chant reproduced above – Salem's sentiment, that some privatizations were akin to theft, was a common refrain. Yet, Salem's framing suggests that it was not that privatizations were seen as bad per se, but that the practice of privatization could be perceived as either legitimate, or illegitimate. To untangle the ambivalence undergirding perceptions of privatization as well as other dimensions of "structural adjustment" in Jordan, this article posits that certain practices of state divestment violated widely "known and accepted rules and principals" in Jordan, which constituted a *moral economy* around the just (re-) distribution of the socioeconomic benefits derived from national resources.[3] I argue that the disruption of this moral economy became a "framing discourse" for struggles, peaking in 2011 and 2013, against structural adjustment in Jordan by labour and non-labour social movements.[4]

In doing so, I also attempt to sketch out a qualitative distinction between the "food riot" and movements against privatization, through juxtaposing the

---

1. Protest chant quoted in *Ammon News*. "Demands to Open the Privatization Files [Arabic]", 16 August 2011. Available online at: http://www.ammonnews.net/article/95003; last accessed 22 February 2021.
2. Salem [pseudonym], Jordanian Federation of Independent Trade Unions (JFITU), interview with author, Amman, Jordan, 30 July 2019.
3. E.P. Thompson, "The Moral Economy of the English Crowd in the Eighteenth Century", *Past & Present*, 50:1 (1971), pp. 76–136.
4. For a discussion of moral economy as a "framing discourse", see Nicola Pratt, "Maintaining the Moral Economy: Egyptian State–Labor Relations in an Era of Economic Liberalization", *Arab Studies Journal*, 8 (2000), pp. 110–123, 112.

moral economy of *commodities* with what I conceptualize as a moral economy of *national resources*. In Jordan, mass unrest in response to austerity policies and rising prices in 1989 and 1996 exemplify the "modern" food riot, defined by Waldon and Seddon as "protest incidents [...] triggered by visible and abrupt exactions which simultaneously generate palpable hardship, a clear perception of responsible agents, and a sense of injustice grounded in the moral economy of the poor".[5] By contrast, as a modality of *adjustment*, the privatization of public assets stands as perhaps the most *structural* – systematically reconfiguring and dispossessing livelihoods and communities as much as companies.[6] Correspondingly, I want to suggest that, in the aftermath of King Abdullah II's accelerated programme of privatizations after 1999, social resistance in Jordan has become more systemically oriented and transgressive – belying the notion that the Arab uprisings "missed" Jordan.

In what follows, I trace the development of a moral economy around Jordan's national resources, specifically (but not limited to) phosphate and potash.[7] I draw primarily on data collected through interviews with activists as well as Jordanian newspaper accounts of protest events. Because my discussions were limited to those either directly or indirectly involved in activism during events that occurred nearly ten years prior to my fieldwork, my aim is not to reconstruct a "collective subject" (see Mélanie Henry's contribution) or to assert that the discourse described by my interlocutors was homogeneous, nor, indeed, to claim that it constituted a counter-hegemony. Rather, my goal here is to demonstrate that a diverse cross-section of social movement constituencies – spanning labour and non-labour movements (and fractions within and across those movements) – perceived privatizations as a moral violation, which, in turn, informed transgressive activist practices and discourses.

A MORAL ECONOMY OF NATIONAL RESOURCES

In E.P. Thompson's early and influential formulation, the grievances of working-class rioters in eighteenth-century England "operated within a popular consensus as to what were legitimate and what were illegitimate practices" in the sphere of inherently unequal market relations.[8] This focus on ground-up, popular conceptions of legitimate state, market, and social practices is central to the conception of moral economy developed in this article. We can see a slightly different perspective in James C. Scott's *The Moral*

5. John Walton and David Seddon, *Free Markets and Food Riots: The Politics of Global Adjustment* (Cambridge, MA, 1994), pp. 52–53.
6. David Harvey, *The New Imperialism* (Oxford, 2003).
7. Interviews (N=46) were conducted in English and Arabic (with the assistance of a translator in transcription) across Jordan from September 2018 to August 2019 (Wayne State University IRB Protocol #1806001528).
8. Thompson, "The Moral Economy of the English Crowd", p. 79.

Economy of the Peasant, wherein moral economy expresses the shared social understandings governing the terms of just economic distribution grounded in an "implicit moral threshold" of basic subsistence.[9] While retaining an emphasis on shared perceptions of legitimacy and redistributive ethics between unequal classes, recent scholarship has eschewed readings of Thompson and Scott that limit the applicability of moral economy primarily to pre-capitalist or transitional contexts or actors.[10] As Palomera and Vetta assert, any prevailing socio-economic order – including capitalism and its neo-liberal variant – necessarily reflects past struggles through which the institutional, material, and discursive elements of hegemony were set into motion and became embedded into daily experience.[11] Thus, moral economy in this sense serves as a way to capture the localized symbolic and material arenas in which prevailing social orders (as the product of past struggles) are legitimated, (re-) produced, and (re-) interpreted.[12]

In some conceptions, the moral economy also demarcates the outer limits of social struggle. For example, in Walton and Seddon's global study of "IMF riots" (incited by austerity programmes), the horizon of struggle often ended at a demand for prices to return to their previous levels, rarely endangering the globalized circuits of structural adjustment and free market capitalism.[13] Posusney makes a similar claim with regards to "restorative" labour protests in Egypt under the developmentalist order of President Gamal Abdel Nasser.[14] In this framing, social mobilization arising from moral economies is seen as conservative – that is, principally concerned with "resurrecting the status-quo ante" – rather than as capable of producing a "new consciousness" or raising transgressive demands against the state.[15]

By contrast, contemporary struggles against neoliberal orders, such as the "Pink Tide" in Latin America in the 2000s and, as I argue, struggles against privatization in Jordan, open up the possibility that innovative social

---

9. James C. Scott, *The Moral Economy of the Peasant: Rebellion and Subsistence in Southeast Asia* (New Haven, CT, 1977). Scott also emphasizes "reciprocity" as a pillar of moral economy, a concept which plays less of a role in Thompson's account and in the present article. See Elizabeth D. Mauritz, *Moral Economy: Claims for the Common Good* (Ph.D., Michigan State University, 2014), p. 77.

10. Thomas Clay Arnold, "Rethinking Moral Economy", *American Political Science Review,* 95:1 (2001), pp. 85–95.

11. Jaime Palomera and Theodora Vetta, "Moral Economy: Rethinking a Radical Concept", *Anthropological Theory,* 16:4 (2016), pp. 413–432.

12. *Ibid.*

13. Walton and Seddon, *Free Markets and Food Riots.*

14. Marsha Pripstein Posusney, "Irrational Workers: The Moral Economy of Labor Protest in Egypt", *World Politics,* 46:1 (1993), pp. 83–120.

15. *Ibid.,* p. 85; Joel Beinin and Marie Duboc, "A Workers' Social Movement on the Margin of the Global Neoliberal Order, Egypt 2004–2012", in Joel Beinin and Frédéric Vairel (eds), *Social Movements, Mobilization, and Contestation in the Middle East and North Africa* (Redwood City, CA, 2013), pp. 205–228.

movements, capable of articulating new and transgressive discourses, may emerge as moral economies break down.[16] Indeed, as Wood has argued, Thompson's overall intellectual project – including his work on moral economy – should be read as demonstrating how consent to rule is always partial and never entirely top-down: rather, unequal power relations are often incompletely tolerated and unevenly (re-) produced across space and time.[17] Moreover, in such moments of rupture, as Chalcraft has shown, social actors may come to question and challenge the hegemonic "common sense" that keeps subaltern consent in place.[18] In this article, I build on this conception of moral economy as reproducing hegemony while also providing openings for its dissolution. At the same time, I also move beyond a focus on specific commodities linked to subsistence (e.g., bread, rice, fuel),[19] to propose that *national resources* can underpin – both materially and symbolically – moral economies, while also forming the basis, however ambivalent, for transformative discourses of resistance.

To do this, I draw on Lyall's work on the "moral economy of oil" in Ecuador, which explains how state elites "cultivated expectations that oil resources ought to ensure for all citizens a minimum level of development (i.e. public works, employment and welfare programmes)".[20] In the process, Lyall also sketches out a key distinction between subsistence-based food riots and revolts around national resources, which "manifest not only in local settings of protest, but also on a *national* [...] scale".[21] While Lyall's focus is on the top-down manipulation of redistributive ethics, we can also expand it to incorporate the bottom-up (historical and current) struggles that are always a part of moral economy. In this sense, the moral economy of national resources serves as a prism through which the working class and the urban and rural poor alike experience what Harvey has theorized as "accumulation by dispossession", or the process through which the "corporatization and privatization of hitherto public assets [...] constitute[s] a new wave of

16. On the Pink Tide, see, for example, Eduardo Silva, "Exchange Rising? Karl Polanyi and Contentious Politics in Contemporary Latin America", *Latin American Politics and Society*, 54:3 (2012), pp. 1–32.

17. Ellen Meiksins Wood, *Democracy Against Capitalism: Renewing Historical Materialism* (New York, 2016); John Chalcraft, "Labour Protest and Hegemony in Egypt and the Arabian Peninsula", in Sara C. Motta and Alf Gunvald Nilsen (eds), *Social Movements in the Global South* (London, 2011), pp. 35–58.

18. John Chalcraft, "Egypt's 2011 Uprising, Subaltern Cultural Politics, and Revolutionary Weakness", *Social Movement Studies*, (2020), pp. 1–17.

19. For an extensive overview, see José Ciro Martínez, *The Politics of Bread: State Power, Food Subsidies and Neoliberalization in Hashemite Jordan* (Ph.D., King's College, 2018).

20. Angus Lyall, "A Moral Economy of Oil: Corruption Narratives and Oil Elites in Ecuador", *Culture, Theory and Critique*, 59:4 (2018), pp. 380–399.

21. *Ibid.*, p. 6. See also Gabriela Valdivia and Marcela Benavides, "Mobilizing for the Petro-nation: Labor and Petroleum in Ecuador", *Focaal*, 63 (2012), pp. 69–82.

'enclosing the commons'".[22] Hence, more than other aspects of structural adjustment, privatization – by commodifying national assets and, indeed, the public sector itself – precludes the possibility of a return to the status quo ante.

The argument: Moral economy and protest

To summarize, in certain cases, privatizations may be experienced as a breach of legitimate state–society practices, creating the possibility for innovative social movements and transgressive demands to emerge. In turn, I argue that through the moral economy of national resources, differently situated social movement constituencies across Jordan – workers, the urban and rural unemployed, denizens of "special economic zones", university graduates, professionals, and many others – were mobilized to challenge the hegemonic "common sense" of the state's neoliberal project.[23] This occurred, in reciprocal fashion, across two levels. Firstly, negative experiences of privatization revealed to disparate actors the contradictions between the king's neoliberal promises – for example, that state-run enterprises had failed, and privatization was the only path to prosperity – and the deleterious material consequences wrought by many privatizations. Even actors not directly affected by privatizations came to associate them with their own poor material circumstances and the highly unequal distribution of economic prosperity in Jordan. Secondly, those localized experiences of privatization were focused, articulated, and transformed by different social movement constituencies so as to include and appeal to local and trans-local movement constituencies, mass audiences, and media commentators.[24]

Denouncements of "bad" privatizations were articulated by demonstrators through accusations of pervasive corruption (*fasad*) and by vilifying those most closely associated with illegitimate privatizations as thieves (*haramiyya*). Taken together, those articulations worked to generate a mutually comprehensible discourse of resistance to the state's neoliberal project, as reflected in the images, poster slogans, and chants of demonstrators between 2011 and 2013, and as expressed to me in interviews with activists. It should be noted that this discourse had significant limitations. Specifically, while between 2011 and 2013 some protesters became increasingly daring in their calls for the "overthrow of the regime" (*isqat al-nizam*), popular consensus generally remained limited to demands for the "reform of the regime"

22. David Harvey, "The 'New' Imperialism: Accumulation by Dispossession", *Socialist Register*, 40 (2009), pp. 63–87, 75.
23. Chalcraft, "Subaltern Cultural Politics", pp. 3–4.
24. David A. Snow, "Framing Processes, Ideology, and Discursive Fields", in David A. Snow, Sarah A. Soule, and Hanspeter Kriesi (eds), *The Blackwell Companion to Social Movements* (Hoboken, NJ, 2007), pp. 380–412.

(*islah al-nizam*).[25] Nevertheless, the fact that an anti-neoliberal discourse continues to pervade mass demonstrations and strikes (most recently in 2018 and 2019) warrants further inquiry into its origins – to which I now turn.

TWO MORAL ECONOMIES

Prior to 1989, state hegemony in Jordan was maintained through welfare institutions, employment inducements, price subsidies, and a developmentalist discourse premising the state as the buffer between Jordan and the vicissitudes of global capitalism.[26] As summarized by Greenwood, Jordan's social "bargain" – dating back to the nation's colonial founding under Emir Abdullah (r. 1921–1951) in the 1920s – "offered citizens economic security in exchange for their political loyalty (or at least acquiescence) to the Hashemite monarchy".[27] The material inducements provided by the state, in order to mobilize society to productive ends and stave off social unrest, constituted two distinct, but related, moral economies. The first revolved around the provision and pricing of commodities – such as bread and fuel – while the second functioned through the intervention of the state as the most important conduit of national development and employment. Both of these moral economies were disrupted in the wake of neoliberal reforms beginning in 1989 and accelerating after King Abdullah's ascension in 1999.

The moral economy of commodities

Born out of the struggles between the British-controlled colonial state under Emir Abdullah and the pre-existing tribal communities of Transjordan, the moral economy of commodities became fully realized in the 1970s under King Hussein (r. 1952–1999).[28] As Martínez has demonstrated, the critical moment came with the establishment of the Ministry of Supply (MoS) in 1974, which did much more than centralize the "pricing and distribution" of basic goods (its raison d'être) but also embodied an "image of a managerial state that could intervene to combat the instabilities of capitalism".[29] Almost overnight, the king began to reinforce this image by publicly articulating a "middle way somewhere between the nationalization of the means of

---

25. See Ziad Abu-Rish. "Protests, Regime Stability, and State Formation in Jordan", in Mehran Kamrava (ed.), *Beyond the Arab Spring: The Evolving Ruling Bargain in the Middle East* (Oxford, 2014), pp. 277–313.
26. Marie Baylouny, "Militarizing Welfare: Neo-Liberalism and Jordanian Policy", *Middle East Journal*, 62:2 (2008), pp. 277–303; Joseph A Massad, *Colonial Effects: The Making of National Identity in Jordan* (New York, 2001).
27. Scott Greenwood, "Jordan's 'New Bargain': The Political Economy of Regime Security", *Middle East Journal*, 57:2 (2003), pp. 248–268, 250.
28. Martínez, *The Politics of Bread*, ch. 2.
29. *Ibid.*, pp. 69–70.

production and the unregulated free market".[30] The cornerstone of this "middle way" was the provision and distribution of Arabic bread (*khubz 'arabi*) – along with a bundle of other basic commodities – at a reliably low price.

The moral economy of national resources

While Jordan lacks the oil reserves of its neighbours in Iraq and Saudi Arabia, natural resources – specifically phosphate and potash – nonetheless have constituted "the foundation for the enhancement of Jordanian private and public investments, modernisation of its infrastructure and the expansion of public services in health and education".[31] In economic terms, the mining industry in Jordan (also including the extraction of cement and calcium carbonates) has significantly contributed to GDP and national exports since the 1970s (see Table 1). Finally, while the mining sector represents a relatively small percentage of total national employment, the sector has been *qualitatively* vital as a major employer and trainer of two important regime constituencies: educated workers (e.g. engineers and geologists) and Jordanians living in and around the main extraction and production sites.[32]

The connection between Jordanian national interests and natural resources is enshrined in the 1952 Constitution, which stipulates that "[a]ny concession granting any right for the exploitation of mines, minerals or public utilities shall be sanctioned by law" – that is, via parliament (Article 117).[33] Originally, however, through their 1928 treaty with Emir Abdullah, it was the British who first had the power to issue mineral concession rights in Jordan.[34] Consequently, British colonial priorities determined the initial pace of mineral exploration and the timing of the first mining concessions in Jordan (1935 for phosphate and 1930 for potash).[35] Later, in the 1950s,

---

30. *Ibid.*, p. 70.

31. Rami Alrawashdeh and Salah Al-Thyabat, "Mining in Jordan: Challenges and Prospects", *International Journal of Mining and Mineral Engineering*, 4:2 (2012), pp. 116–138.

32. Claudie Fioroni, *Perplexed Employees and Powerless Managers: Neoliberal Effects in the Phosphate Kingdom of Jordan* (Ph.D., The Graduate Institute Geneva, 2017), pp. 124–125.

33. Quoted in Omar Razzaz, "Report on Privatizations" (2014), p. 5. Available at: https://jordankmportal.com/resources/privatization-assessment; last accessed 22 February 2021.

34. Anan Ameri, *Socioeconomic Development in Jordan (1950–1980): An Application of Dependency Theory* (Ph.D., Wayne State University, 1981), p. 68, n. 1.

35. Principally, British colonial priorities, limited infrastructural development, and low global demand all contributed to the late discovery and exploitation of commercial quantities of phosphate rock in Jordan. See Fioroni, *Perplexed Employees*, pp. 91–98. By contrast, colonial extraction of potash and bromine from the Dead Sea began in 1930 under a concession granted by the British Palestine Mandate. After the 1948 Arab–Israeli War, potash production was taken up on both sides of the Dead Sea and the Jordanian government granted the Arab Potash Company a concession in 1956 lasting through 2058. See Jacob Norris, *Land of Progress: Palestine in the Age of Colonial Development, 1905–1948* (Oxford, 2013), pp. 158–168.

Table 1. *Economic Significance of the Minerals Industry in Jordan.**

Year	Contribution of minerals to exports (%)	Contribution of minerals to GDP (%)
1970	26.3	1.7
1980	41.0	3.5
1990	38.4	5.4
2000	23.1	2.9
2010	14.0	3.3

*Potash and phosphate made up over two thirds of mineral exports in the 2000s, with cement making up the next largest percentage (ten per cent).
Source: Rami Alrawashdeh and Philip Maxwell, "Jordan, Minerals Extraction and the Resource Curse", *Resources Policy*, 38 (2013), p. 106.

"nationalist bureaucrats" such as Hamid al-Farhan struggled with hostile American and British donors to secure the autonomy to develop the nation's resources (see Figure 1).[36] It was not until the 1960s and 1970s that a measure of resource autonomy was achieved, though Jordan's mineral concerns have always been supported, even proudly so, by high levels of foreign involvement, "from planning and implementation to financing".[37] Following the civil war between the monarchy and the Palestinian Liberation Organization (PLO) in 1970, state-provided employment began to skew disproportionately towards East Bank Jordanians, who, since the founding of the Hashemite monarchy in the 1920s, had constituted the state's most important social base.[38]

With these internal and external struggles in mind, we can read the following statement from King Hussein, regarding the state's massive investments in the exploitation of Dead Sea minerals for potash production in the 1970s, as articulating the (top-down) terms for the moral economy:

> This project has special significance for our national growth and development. Its progress, after many years of hard efforts, delays, and difficulties, is great proof that we have assumed control over our national capabilities, and that we have set ourselves on the path of practical planning for our economy and that we are now able to mobilize qualified Jordanian youth to carry out the responsibilities

36. Paul T. Kingston, "Breaking the Patterns of Mandate: Economic Nationalism and State Formation in Jordan, 1951–57", in Eugene Rogan and Tariq Tell (eds), *Village, Steppe, and State: The Social Origins of Modern Jordan* (London, 1994), pp. 187–217.
37. Joseph A. Rowley, *Image and Image-Making: The Case of Jordan* (Ph.D., University of Richmond, 1990), p. 104.
38. The terms "East Bank" Jordanian or Transjordanian refer to a historically constructed category referencing the Bedouin tribes that pre-existed the establishment of the state of Jordan (beginning in 1921 under British colonialism) in the territories east of the Jordan River. See Yitzhak Reiter, "The Palestinian–Transjordanian Rift: Economic Might and Political Power in Jordan", *Middle East Journal*, 58:1 (2004), pp. 72–92; Massad, *Colonial Effects*.

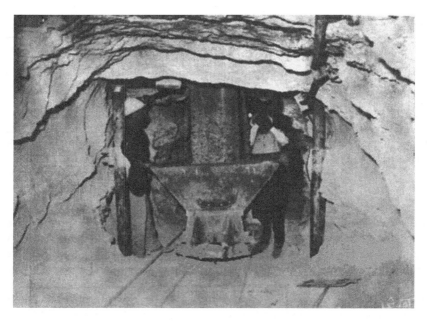

Figure 1. Underground phosphate mining in Rusaifeh, Jordan in 1953. Photograph from a 1961 booklet. Accessed at Zaman.com, on February 2, 2021.

of development [...] The Arab Potash Project is a splendid model for our strife against backwardness and stagnation. It is a courageous and ambitious attempt at the utilization of our natural resources.[39]

Given the symbolic and material importance of natural resource exploitation to state hegemony, as reflected in this statement, it becomes easier to piece together why, despite mounting domestic and international pressures in the 1980s and 1990s to privatize national resource companies, King Hussein remained reluctant until his death.[40]

Jordan's moral economy of national resources is perhaps most physically embodied by the so-called Big Five companies – including the Arab Phosphate Company (APC) and the Jordan Phosphate Mines Company (JPMC) – which were first established as private enterprises in the 1950s.[41] Yet, the "poor capacities" of the private sector necessitated heavy state

39. Timothy J. Piro, *The Political Economy of Market Reform in Jordan* (Lanham, MD, 1998), p. 107.
40. Jane Harrigan *et al.*, "The IMF and the World Bank in Jordan: A Case of Over Optimism and Elusive Growth", *Review of International Organizations*, 1:3 (2006), pp. 263–292.
41. The "Big Five" was comprised of semi-public (or shareholding) companies in the tobacco, cement, phosphates, potash, and petroleum industries.

involvement from the very beginning.[42] By the end of the 1980s, the level of state intervention in these companies was significant and included ownership of controlling stakes and the ability to appoint and displace actors from company boards. For example, prior to its privatization in 2006, the JPMC was ninety per cent state-owned and its operations were conducted in "extensive" coordination with the Ministry of Industry and Trade and the Natural Resources Authority.[43] In return, from the 1970s, the mining sector (phosphate, potash, and cement) propped up Jordan's export sector.[44]

Hence, beyond their importance to the economy, according to Piro, the phosphate and potash companies were positioned by the state as "symbol[s] of national will, development, and modernization".[45] The national symbolic nature of these resources emanated from three central dynamics related to Jordan's status as a "late developing" country.[46] Firstly, resource exploitation required massive mobilizations of foreign and domestic capital on top of substantial investments in national infrastructure. These investments, in turn, were justified in terms of the national project to "modernize" Jordan.[47] Relatedly, the state-controlled enterprises provided employment for key professional-class workers, as well as Jordanians living in the otherwise economically overlooked mining regions.[48] For example, in the southern governorate of Ma'an, the development of the Al-Shidiyah mine in 1988 was followed by consistent increases over the following two decades in education and health indicators, as well as secular decreases in the unemployment and poverty rates (Figure 2).[49] Finally, mining employees, in return for their privileged place in national development (along with an array of material benefits), were pushed to submit to state-controlled unions.[50] Consequently, similar to *khubz 'arabi*, the national resource-exploiting enterprises came to represent a material juncture through which historically constructed social pacts and multivalent understandings of legitimacy, distributive justice, and national development interfaced.[51]

42. Razzaz, "Report on Privatizations", p. 4; Timothy J. Piro, *Managers and Minerals in a Monarchy: The Political Economy of Mining in Jordan (1970–1989)* (Ph.D., George Washington University, 1992), pp. 310–311.

43. Piro, *The Political Economy of Market Reform in Jordan*, p. 48.

44. Pete Moore, *Doing Business in the Middle East: Politics and Economic Crisis in Jordan and Kuwait* (Cambridge, 2004), pp. 104–105.

45. Piro, *The Political Economy of Market Reform in Jordan*, p. 42.

46. For "late" development, see Eva Bellin, "Contingent Democrats: Industrialists, Labor, and Democratization in Late-Developing Countries", *World Politics*, 52:2 (2000), pp. 175–205.

47. Martínez, *The Politics of Bread*, ch. 2.

48. Moore, *Doing Business in the Middle East*, p. 104.

49. Rami Al Rawashdeh *et al.*, "The Socio-Economic Impacts of Mining on Local Communities: The Case of Jordan", *Extractive Industries and Society*, 3:2 (2016), pp. 494–507, 504.

50. Piro, *Managers and Minerals in a Monarchy*, p. 314.

51. José Ciro Martínez, "Leavened Apprehensions: Bread Subsidies and Moral Economies in Hashemite Jordan", *International Journal of Middle East Studies*, 50:2 (2018), pp. 173–193.

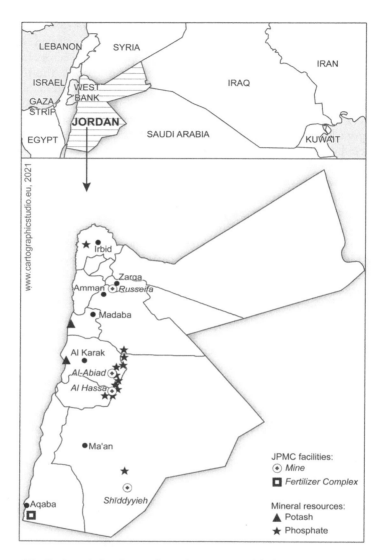

Figure 2. Distribution of phosphate and potash resources and facilities in Jordan.

FROM "BREAD RIOTS" TO PRIVATIZATION

While the moral economy of national resources remained largely sacrosanct until 1999, the economic crisis of the late 1980s marked a major disruption in the moral economy of commodities. From 1983, the global price of oil plunged and Arab foreign aid began to shift to Iraq (to aid in its war against Iran), jeopardizing the state's access to rents. Debt skyrocketed and the dinar lost thirty-five per cent of its value between November 1988 and February 1989.[52] This led Jordan to the doorstep of the International Monetary Fund (IMF), whom "policy-makers considered the only source of relief".[53] The resulting Standby Arrangement (SBA) with the IMF, signed in 1988 and implemented in 1989, was conditional upon the privatization of public sector investments, trade liberalization, cuts in state employment, and the removal of subsidies. However, for the first decade of structural adjustment, King Hussein was reluctant to go beyond modest price hikes, which were nevertheless met with widespread social unrest.

Despite the restrained nature of these reforms, "[w]ithin hours" of the 1989 IMF- mandated freeze of public wages, salaries, and hiring – coupled with increases in domestic petroleum prices – the largest protest wave in two decades erupted across Jordan.[54] Beginning in the southern city of Ma'an in April – a historical bulwark of regime support – protests quickly spread throughout the country. The social and spatial character of these "bread riots" signalled a dramatic shift in the nature of social protest in Jordan.[55] Historically, opposition to state polices sprung from the "usual suspects" of "leftist parties, Islamists, and/or Palestinian Jordanian activists".[56] However, after 1989, opposition to state policies was increasingly characterized by the predominance of East Bank Jordanians. Indeed, many of my East Bank Jordanian interlocutors viewed 1989 as their political awakening. According to one activist from the southern city of Karak, this was the moment that "changed everything": the Jordanian economy had "become naked", newly exposed to private sector interests and foreign capital.[57]

While 1989 represented a new and potentially existential threat to the prevailing order, King Hussein was able to stave off a unified national challenge to state power by quickly orchestrating a series of top-down reforms, including the lifting of martial law, in effect since 1967, and the revival, albeit limited, of electoral politics in Jordan. Additional "bread riots" erupted in 1996 and 1998, the trajectory of which largely conformed to Walton and Seddon's description of austerity protests as spreading "quickly and contagiously" and yielding "short-term successes" without disrupting processes of "long-term depredation and socioeconomic restructuring".[58] Hence, while the waves of unrest precipitated by periodic price hikes in the 1990s prefigured the social bases of the 2011–2013

52. Harrigan *et al.*, "The IMF and the World Bank in Jordan", p. 268.
53. Baylouny, "Militarizing Welfare", p. 292.
54. Harrigan *et al.*, "The IMF and the World Bank in Jordan", p. 269.
55. Lamis Andoni and Jillian Schwedler, "Bread Riots in Jordan", *Middle East Report*, 26:201 (1996), pp. 40–42.
56. Curtis Ryan, *Jordan and the Arab Uprisings: Regime Survival and Politics Beyond the State* (New York, 2018).
57. Hirak al-Karak leader, interview with author, Karak, Jordan, 22 June 2019.
58. Walton and Seddon, *Free Markets and Food Riots*, pp. 50–51.

uprisings in many ways, they also differed in important respects. The principal difference had to do with the political-economic context: according to Tariq Tell, "in contrast to 1989, *neoliberal reform was now the policy of choice for the Palace*, rather than a necessary expedient imposed by the IMF".[59]

To establish the new common sense underlying this neoliberal political economy, King Abdullah – in collaboration with Western governments and international financial institutions – began to articulate a new relationship between the state and its subjects: instead of state employees, citizens were increasingly encouraged to become "entrepreneurs".[60] Instead of a welfare and job provider, the state was in "partnership" with the private sector in creating an attractive "business environment" for domestic and international investment.[61] At the same time, the king increasingly began to place control over economic policy into his own hands – and those of a small coterie of technocratic elites – effectively circumventing parliament and simultaneously cracking down on dissent from below.[62]

The differences in the pace and scope of privatization under Abdullah II versus what came before were stark. In the 1990s, the state owned controlling shares in 109 enterprises; by the mid-2000s, the government had divested from over forty of these enterprises, including the JPMC and APC.[63] This acceleration of privatization, however, did not mean that the state had completely lost sight of its moral obligations. According to the government's own (post hoc) study of privatizations, undertaken between 2013 and 2014, privatization was not considered an unalloyed good – it was, rather, "a means and not an end in itself", the benefits of which "are numerous if the process is implemented in an environment of *transparency, competitiveness, and accountability*".[64] By these

59. Ziad Abu-rish and Tariq Tell, "Jordan's Current Political Opposition Movements and the Need for Further Research: An Interview with Tariq Tell (Part 2)", *Jadaliyya*, 24 August 2012. Available at: https://www.jadaliyya.com/Details/26936; last accessed 24 January 2021; emphasis added.

60. Nadine Kreitmeyr, "Neoliberal Co-optation and Authoritarian Renewal: Social Entrepreneurship Networks in Jordan and Morocco", *Globalizations*, 16:3 (2019), pp. 289–303.

61. Katharina Lenner and Lewis Turner, "Making Refugees Work? The Politics of Integrating Syrian Refugees into the Labor Market in Jordan", *Middle East Critique*, 28:1 (2019), pp. 65–95. See also King Abdullah II, "Speech (26 October 2011)". Available at: https://kingabdullah.jo/en/speeches/opening-second-ordinary-session-16th-parliament; last accessed 10 September 2020.

62. Jillian Schwedler, "The Political Geography of Protest in Neoliberal Jordan", *Middle East Critique*, 21:3 (2012), pp. 259–270.

63. Of the Big Five, the APC (2003) and JPMC (2006) were privatized under Abdullah II, the Cement Company was privatized under King Hussein (1998), and the National Petroleum Company remains under state control. See https://www.ase.com.jo/en/Media-Center/Library-Publications/Privatization-Jordan; last accessed 22 February 2021.

64. The Privatization Evaluation Committee was commissioned by the king through royal decree on 12 October 2012 and the commission began its evaluation in March 2013, finishing its work a year later. Razzaz, "Report on Privatizations", p. 1.

standards, the Privatization Evaluation Committee (PEC), under Omar Razzaz (who would become Prime Minister in 2018), criticized the implementation and results of a number of privatizations – in particular the 2006 privatization of the JPMC.[65]

According to the PEC, the JPMC privatization had "lacked many transparency standards and [a] commitment to best practices".[66] It is thus worth examining this privatization in more detail. The JPMC was sold under opaque circumstances, ostensibly to Brunei – via Kamil Holding Ltd – though many of my interlocutors believed this to be a smokescreen for the real buyers in the king's own circle.[67] Indeed, Walid el-Kurdi, the brother-in-law of the late King Hussein, "was personally involved in the process of the privatization" and became the head of the company in 2006.[68] Thus, for many Jordanians, the JPMC "was not privatized but rather taken over by the Hashemite monarchy".[69] By contrast, the privatization of the APC in 2003 conformed more closely to the PEC's definition of "best practices", including enhanced transparency, and was, correspondingly, viewed by many of my interlocutors in a more favourable light.[70] In order to untangle the social consequences of these different privatizations, in what follows I trace the protests as well as narratives of corruption and theft employed by differently situated activists in Jordan between 2011 and 2013.

PRIVATIZATION AND ARTICULATING RESISTANCE IN JORDAN

On a sunny May afternoon in Amman in 2012, a protester holds a sign overhead among a sea of demonstrators: sketched on one side is an outline of a map of Jordan with the word "SOLD" in English stamped over it in red; written on the other side is a list of privatized companies: "The Phosphate company, the Potash company, the Jordanian Communication, the Jordanian Cement company, the Dead Sea beaches, and Aqaba beaches, the Port of Aqaba, the Jordanian industrial city."[71] This sign (and many others like it) articulated a

---

65. *Ibid.*, p. 17.
66. *Ibid.*
67. Salem, interview with author, Amman, Jordan, 30 July 2019.
68. Claudie Fioroni, "From the Everyday to Contentious Collective Actions: The Protests of Jordan Phosphate Mines Employees Between 2011 and 2014", *Workers of the World: International Journal on Strikes and Social Conflicts*, 1:7 (2015), pp. 30–49, 33.
69. *Ibid.*, p. 33.
70. The government sold half of its 52.8 per cent stake to Canada's Potash Corp., the world's largest potash producer and Canada's largest maker of fertilizers.
71. Maria Blanco Palencia, *Al-Ḥirāk Al-Shabābī Al-'Urdunī (the Jordanian Youth Movement): Organisation, Strategies and Significance for Social and Political Change in Jordan* (Ph.D., University of Exeter, 2017), p. 141. [hereafter *The Jordanian Youth Movement*].

sense of illegitimate redistribution: privatizations are corrupt; they represent the end of the public sector as a source of livelihood in Jordan; and they are equivalent to "selling" off the country (and Jordanians' birthright). The protest chant quoted at the top of this article draws these different sentiments together: "Out, Out, Corruption! ... We want Jordan to stay free!"

Between 2011 and 2013, over 8,000 protests, marches, and strikes swept across Jordan, responding to decades of economic immiseration and stalled democratic reforms.[72] In addition to their scale, these mobilizations were unprecedented in Jordan because of the participation of groups from across the country, including the "traditional" opposition (the Muslim Brotherhood and opposition parties), as well as two new social movements: a new independent labour movement and the Hirak. The Hirak (or "movement") "encompassed nearly forty East Bank tribal youth activist groups across the kingdom, representing rural communities long thought to be unflagging supporters of the autocratic regime".[73] In this section, I demonstrate how labour and non-labour activists shared an understanding of privatizations rooted in moral economy, which served as the basis for a shared discourse of resistance to neoliberal reforms. In this way, privatization created the possibility for a broad-based and transgressive national discourse – albeit one that ultimately fell short – representing, as one activist put it, a new "genetics" of resistance in Jordan.[74]

Privatizations connected the daily experiences of immiseration and deprivation under structural adjustment to the (failed) promises of national development as symbolized, in large part, by Jordan's national resources. In the eyes of Hirak activists, public assets belonged to Jordanian citizens, and their "theft" was akin to "losing everything". As one activist from Amman put it:

> We would like to know where all that money is spent because they took that money from privatization projects. It didn't work out. I didn't sense it on my salary, I didn't sense it on my lifestyle, I didn't see it on the transportation system, the health, my education, [and] the youth are still taking loans and paying for their own salaries to the universities. [...] It didn't reflect on our lives. It was a huge mistake by the governments to do this and we didn't get any benefits [...] In the airport, the Port [of Aqaba], and our two big companies [the Port and Phosphate] unfortunately we sold more than 30% of them. This is what it feels like when you talk about the privatization. We lost everything.[75]

Whether or not Jordanians felt the outcomes of privatization "in their pockets" therefore gets to the heart of how privatizations in Jordan were

72. Tariq Tell, "Early Spring in Jordan: The Revolt of the Military Veterans", Carnegie Middle East Center, 4 November 2015, pp. 1–12, 9.
73. Sean Yom, "Tribal Politics in Contemporary Jordan: The Case of the Hirak Movement", *Middle East Journal*, 68:2 (2014), pp. 229–247, 229.
74. Hirak Hayy al-Tafaila activist, interview with author, Amman, Jordan, 29 March 2019.
75. Hirak activist, interview with author, Amman, Jordan, 1 March 2019.

experienced: as a betrayal of the state's distributive obligations and the failure of neoliberal reforms to make life better.

This shared sense that expectations of redistribution had gone unmet transcended divisions across society: from the local to the national and across labour and non-labour movement constituencies. This prompted a turn towards innovative forms of grievance articulation. As a prominent labour and Hirak activist explained:

> The [Prime Minister in 2011] Rifai government waged war on unions. Union leaders were imprisoned, fired, or relocated to distant sites for having organized strikes. These transfers made us think of *new ways to struggle for change*: using protests and echoing people's grievances about the government, such as economic policies that raised the prices of basic goods used by the poor, increased unemployment and poverty. So we founded the *Jayeen* movement. We organized demonstrations all over the country, calling for a new national unity government. *We have also demanded a special tribunal against the corrupt individuals who sold national assets such as phosphate mines, transportation, and water* [by granting foreign companies exclusive mining and management rights] at prices that didn't reflect their value.[76]

The protest movement alluded to in the above quote, Jayeen ("we are coming"), was in many ways emblematic of the "new ways to struggle for change" emerging in Jordan. Bringing labour and Hirak activists from the governorates to the capital city, Jayeen was a major participant, along with a loose confederation of other organizations, in the largest protests of Jordan's 2011–2013 uprisings under the umbrella of the "March 24 [2011] Movement".[77] As Bouziane and Lenner emphasize, 24 March represented an unprecedented attempt "to form a broad coalition for substantial political and economic reforms, transcending potential divides between different population groups" – though one that ultimately failed in the face of state repression and divisions within Jordanian society.[78] Despite the dissolution of Jayeen shortly thereafter, there were myriad other protests, strikes, sit-ins, and public demonstrations that brought Jordanians together, united around narratives of theft and

---

76. Mohammad Snayd, quoted in "Popular Protest in North Africa and the Middle East (IX): Dallying with Reform in a Divided Jordan", International Crisis Group (2012), p. 8. Available at: https://www.crisisgroup.org/middle-east-north-africa/eastern-mediterranean/jordan/popular-protest-north-africa-and-middle-east-ix-dallying-reform-divided-jordan; last accessed 24 January 2021, emphasis added.
77. Pascal Debruyne and Christopher Parker, "Reassembling the Political: Placing Contentious Politics in Jordan", in Fawaz A. Gerges (ed.), *Contentious Politics in the Middle East: Popular Resistance and Marginalized Activism Beyond the Arab Uprisings* (Basingstoke, 2016), pp. 437–465.
78. Malika Bouziane and Katharina Lenner, "Protests in Jordan: Rumblings in the Kingdom of Dialogue", in Center for Middle Eastern and North African Politics (ed.), *Protests, Revolutions and Transformations: The Arab World in a Period of Upheaval* (Working Paper No. 1, 2011), pp. 148–165, 148.

corruption. That these struggles all featured specific and emotive references to privatizations speaks to the power of national resources as a national symbol.

Ambivalence and legitimacy

Key to these narratives was a shared perception of legitimate practices of redistribution. It was not simply that state-controlled companies had changed ownership (from public to private hands), but, instead, that *illegitimate* privatizations were seen as denying to Jordanians the fruits of their national resources, for example, to national development, basic subsistence, and/or employment. These sentiments were echoed in a highly influential "economic communique" released by the National Committee for Retired Servicemen (NCRS), a dissident movement of retired East Bank military veterans. In the document, which targeted "the privatization of the public sector" and the "restructuring of the state", the NCRS accused a "small number of influential people" in the government and private sector of "sell[ing] the people's property, including companies, institutions, natural resources, capabilities, lands, [and] infrastructure".[79] While critiques of the NCRS rightly point out the East Bank nationalist undertones of the communique, I argue that, as a symbolic representation of state–society relations in neoliberal Jordan, privatizations were capacious and multivalent, and thus resist reduction to any single interpretation.[80]

Rather than simply an expression of nationalist chauvinism, the moral economy of national resources reflected a shared sense of illegitimacy in *the way many privatizations were carried out*. Indeed, accusations of theft and corruption often came from those who professed to see the value in the privatizations ("I am not against privatization" was a common refrain) – even when assets were sold to foreign entities. In the words of one Hirak activist: "I support the idea of privatization [...] the question is not about privatization or not, but how do they spend the money?"[81] In this sense, activists' perceptions of privatization mirror Jordanians' perceptions of good, tolerable, and corrupt forms of *Wasta*, or "local practices of political patronage and favouritism"; as Doughan has argued, *Wasta* "constitutes a problem only when it provides differential access to common resources managed by the state or by some other corporate entity such as a private or public corporation".[82] Though always somewhat ambivalent, what mattered, in other words, was the perception of

79. Ammon News, "NCRS Reveal Military Reveal Suspicions of Privatization corruption" [Arabic], 25 January 2011. Available at: http://ar.ammannet.net/news/90442; last accessed 19 January 2021.

80. David Assaf, "The Revolt of Jordan's Military Veterans", *Foreign Policy* (2010). Available at: https://foreignpolicy.com/2010/06/16/the-revolt-of-jordans-military-veterans/; last accessed 19 January 2021.

81. Hirak al-Tafila activist, interview with author, Amman, Jordan, 21 June 2019.

82. Yazan Doughan, "Corruption in the Middle East and the Limits of Conventional Approaches", *GIGA Focus* 5 (2017), p. 7. Available at: https://www.giga-hamburg.de/en/

legitimacy. The privatization of the JPMC is instructive in understanding this distinction.

Revolt of the workers

In 2006, when the JPMC was privatized, the brother-in-law of the late King Hussein, Walid el-Kurdi, was subsequently installed as CEO. His corrupt tenure, and its effects on JPMC workers, came to a reckoning in 2011, when el-Kurdi's son's pay stub – displaying a five-fold increase over those in similar posts – was circulated to workers.[83] The pay stub had the effect of galvanizing phosphate workers around the issue of corruption, precipitating two general strikes between 2011 and 2013. These events ultimately led workers to break away from their official trade union, The General Trade Union of Mines and Mining Employees (GTUMME) – one of the seventeen officially permitted trade unions belonging to the General Federation of Jordanian Trade Unions (GFJTU).

Fioroni's detailed ethnographic exploration of the JPMC employees demonstrates how the privatization of the JPMC created various, even conflicting grievances among the employees.[84] On the one hand, the professional-class strike organizers were motivated by their belief that the privatization had failed to produce a rationalized, meritocratic corporation. On the other hand, those in the non-professional stratum of employees were aggrieved by the newly privatized JPMC's failure – due to el-Kurdi's circumvention of long-established clientelist recruitment/advancement practices in favour of his own – to live up to its historical obligations regarding the distribution of permanent jobs to those living in the mining regions. Because the strike leaders required the participation of those living and working in the mining regions to shut down the mines, they consciously drew upon mutually comprehensible and salient aspects of the privatization – the "corruption" of employment practices, the "theft"/privatization of the company, and de facto royal family control – to rally a broad base of workers.[85]

Consequently, in April 2011, a group of about thirty JPMC employees initiated a three-day sit-in against their union, "denouncing corruption and mismanagement, asking for new [union] bylaws, a new personnel system, and the fair treatment of employees".[86] Initial responses to the sit-in came from both the GTUMME, which declared the sit-in "illegal and illegitimate"

---

publications/11567954-corruption-middle-east-limits-conventional-approaches/; last accessed 24 January 2021.

83. Fioroni, "From the Everyday".
84. *Idem, Perplexed Employees*, pp. 303–304.
85. *Ibid.*
86. Claudie Fioroni, "Bridging the Gap: Social Divides and Coalition Building in the Phosphate-Mining Industry in Jordan", *Mediterranean Politics*, 24:4 (2019), pp. 512–533, 521.

(because protesters were circumventing the union), and Walid el-Kurdi him-self.[87] At first, el-Kurdi attempted to assuage workers' concerns by signing a vague agreement with them. Instead of relenting, however, the organizers of the April sit-in proceeded to initiate two general strikes between 2011 and 2012 and, in June 2011, they established a new independent union – becoming the first workers to exit the formal GFJTU structure.[88] The first strike, in June 2011, involved a massive organizing effort and brought together "employees from all the production sites, high skilled and low skilled employ-ees, and employees from diverse tribal and local origins".[89] Notably, the strike resulted in the shutdown of all three phosphate mines. During this period, the demands of phosphate workers expanded from their specific grievances focused on the JPMC's management, remuneration, and organization follow-ing the 2006 privatization, to criticisms of the official union structure, as well as the entire Palace-led privatization project.[90]

As expressed by one of the leaders of the movement, the motivation for these actions stemmed from the illegitimate way in which the privatization had been conducted:

> Our movement it wasn't against the privatization. It's against the way Walid el-Kurdi is acting and stealing the company. […] [We were] asking for accountabil-ity, government accountability. To audit the finances of the company. […] *They stole the phosphate and did not privatize the company.*[91]

Thus, their grievances were in opposition to the state-articulated "common sense" that privatizations were a necessary step towards prosperity. At the same time, workers' demands transcended el-Kurdi as an individual by framing el-Kurdi's "theft" in terms of the corruption of the state (the *"they"* in the above excerpt).[92] In response to the first strike wave in 2011, the regime eventually stepped in:

> [After the May 2011 strike] [s]ome senators from the parliament, they contacted us, and the administration of the company, to solve the problem. And we signed an agreement with the senators – on one condition: *that the parliament would establish a committee to investigate the privatizations.* And we established our independent trade union.[93]

---

87. *Ibid.*, p. 522.
88. Workers from ten other economic sectors also followed suit in establishing new unions and, in 2013, came together to establish the Jordanian Federation of Independent Trade Unions; *Phenix Center for Economic and Informatics Studies*, "Freedom of Association Fact Sheet", p. 2. Available at: https://www.solidar.org/system/downloads/attachments/000/000/456/original/PDF2.pdf?1469200423; last accessed 24 January 2021.
89. Fioroni, "Bridging the Gap", p. 523.
90. JFITU unionist, interview with author, Amman, Jordan, 30 July 2019.
91. Salem, interview with author, Amman, Jordan, 30 July 2019.
92. *Ibid.*
93. *Ibid.*; emphasis added.

The establishment of the commission to investigate the privatizations – and the resulting 2014 report – became a point of significant pride for the leaders of the independent phosphate union.[94]

Beyond the JPMC workers' movement, the privatization of the company was articulated to, and resonated with, differently situated actors across Jordan – exemplifying the discursive power of the moral economy. Firstly, in the mining regions, the privatization had a mobilizing effect among unemployed job-seekers whose expectations of resource distribution through gaining jobs in the JPMC had been stymied by the hiring freeze. Specifically, though the hiring freeze pre-dated the privatization, it was both kept in place under el-Kurdi and compounded by el-Kurdi's periodic and conspicuous employment of his family members. Consequently, young job-seekers demonstrated in 2011 to protest the company's failure to live up to its historical obligations to distribute jobs in the regions in which it extracted mineral wealth.[95] Secondly, by bringing to light the overt corruption and nepotism on display in the JPMC privatization, the JPMC workers created common cause with the Hirak. For instance, in their own enumeration of grievances, Hirak activists frequently echoed the phosphate workers' claims that the JPMC was sold under mysterious circumstances and at an insulting price.[96] El-Kurdi's name was also commonly evoked in the demonstrations that filled the streets of Amman and across the governorates throughout the 2011–2013 period.[97]

Unravelling "illegitimate" privatizations

As previously alluded to, recent scholarship on Jordan has suggested that Jordanian's resistance to privatization was motivated by nationalism, against either "Palestinians" or foreign capital.[98] In this framing, anti-privatization sentiments by East Bank Jordanians were merely a defensive ploy to regain lost patronage benefits. Evidence for this argument includes protesters' focus on Queen Rania and her family (who are of Palestinian descent) as among the most corrupt.

94. Soon thereafter, el-Kurdi, facing corruption charges, fled to the United Kingdom.
95. Fioroni, *Perplexed Employees*, pp. 303–304.
96. Hirak activist, interview with author, Amman, Jordan, 21 June 2019; Amad Awad, interview with author, Amman, Jordan, 20 May 2019; Hirak Hayy al-Tafaila activist, interview with author, Amman, Jordan, 29 March 2019.
97. Debruyne and Parker, "Reassembling the Political", pp. 457–458; Hirak leader, interview with author, Karak, Jordan, 22 June 2019.
98. Arvid Lundberg, *Openness as Political Culture: The Arab Spring and the Jordanian Protest Movements* (Ph.D., Stockholm University, 2018), p. 64; Assaf, "The Revolt of Jordan's Military Veterans"; Sara Ababneh, "The Struggle to Re-Politicize the Political: The Discourse on Economic Rights in the Jordanian Popular Movement 2011–2012", *Youth Politics in the Middle East and North Africa*, *POMEPS Studies*, 36 (2019), pp. 54–59.

Ababneh, by contrast, has argued that resistance to privatizations was fuelled, in part, by the perceived loss of Jordan's "economic sovereignty" to international financial institutions and foreign multinational corporations.[99] However, anti-corruption slogans also targeted figures such as Omar Ma'ani, the disgraced Transjordanian former mayor of Amman and architect of the city's neoliberal transformation after 2006.[100] Moreover, if the issue were solely nationalist (either Transjordanian or Jordanian), the fact that a Canadian firm bought the APC would not have passed without much remark from many of my interlocutors.[101] Indeed, the APC privatization was often contrasted against the more negative experience of the JPMC:

> [I]n the potash company, after the Canadians came and they bought the shares from the government, the situation was completely different than the phosphate company. Why? Because [the potash privatization] worked very well. They made very good bylaws and they provided good benefits [...] And in the phosphate it's the complete opposite. I told this to Walid el-Kurdi face to face.[102]

While other activists felt both privatizations were illegitimate, these differences, in my discussions with activists, reflected ambivalence more than chauvinism.

In sum, Hirak slogans and signs frequently called for the prosecution of the "thieving corrupt ones" (*fasadeen haramiyya*), a class-based, more than an ethnicity-based, designation, which encompassed many Jordanians of Palestinian descent but also plenty of East Bank elites.[103] That some activists were willing to entertain the idea of privatizations suggests that the salient issue was not privatization per se, but whether national resources had been put towards the collective good.[104] Moreover, the consequences of these thefts were felt both materially – for instance when potash workers in Karak lost their jobs – and more symbolically and nationally, as a moral violation by the state.[105]

Beyond the "economic" and the "political"

Privatization thus served as the prism through which corruption, capitalist exploitation, unemployment, and illegitimate exploitation of national resources could be understood by activists as interconnected. This belied yet another neoliberal "common sense", namely, that economic reforms should

99. Ababneh, "The Struggle to Re-Politicize the Political", pp. 56–57.
100. Amman journalist, interview with author, Amman, Jordan, 6 August 2019.
101. Hirak activist, interview with author, Karak, Jordan, 22 June 2019.
102. Salem, interview with author, Amman, Jordan, 30 July 2019.
103. Amman journalist, interview with author, Amman, Jordan, 6 August 2019.
104. Jordanian activist, interview with author, Amman, Jordan, 6 August 2019.
105. Hirak activist, interview with author, Karak, Jordan, 22 June 2019; Hirak al-Karak activist, interview with author, Karak, Jordan, 22 June 2019.

be de-politicized and delegated to the designs of technocrats.[106] Moreover, in contrast to the moral economy of commodities, the violation of the moral economy of national resources could not be as easily resolved or deferred by, for example, rolling back prices.

Privatization was much more hardwired into the circuits of global capitalism. To roll back privatizations would mean reversing the flow of upward redistribution (and foreign capital) that neoliberalism is predicated upon. The best state actors could do was to project all of society's grievances vis-à-vis privatizations onto a few sacrificial elites, such as Walid el-Kurdi. This strategy mirrors Lyall's description of Ecuadorian elites' attempts to position themselves as "moral managers" of national resources through anti-corruption campaigns.[107] However, doing so could not turn back the clock on the articulation and spread of transgressive discourses. This was relayed quite concisely to me by a Hirak leader from a northern Amman neighbourhood: "it's all politics and economics, [they are] two faces of one coin".[108] For their part, labour activists also saw that the continuing suffering of workers was wrapped up in the policies of the state:

> In the economic path, [the] plans they are making, [...] when it's wrong, the workers will pay the price. When the political policy is not right, also the workers will pay the price. For these reasons, you can't separate things.[109]

This kind of discourse, traceable in part to the violation of the moral economy of national resources, brought diverse movement constituencies together around the realization that political and economic conditions and grievances were all intertwined – transcending place and ideology.

The work of articulation occurred reciprocally between labour and non-labour movement constituencies. Between 2011 and 2013, labour and Hirak activists, by making the "connection" between economic and political struggles, necessarily moved beyond "restorative" demands to articulate a systemic critique of the neoliberal authoritarian state. Through active efforts to merge labour and popular demands – such as the Jayeen movement (see above) – workers brought their grievances to the protest square, which were then picked up and further articulated by Hirak demonstrators. As one activist explained to me, "yes, we started with economic demands, but they realized for all those demands, the solution is politics; we started with economic demands and we find out that the solution is political and so our demands

---

106. André Bank, "Rents, Cooptation, and Economized Discourse: Three Dimensions of Political Rule in Jordan, Morocco and Syria", *Journal of Mediterranean Studies*, 14:1 (2004), pp. 155–179.
107. Lyall, "A Moral Economy of Oil", p. 6.
108. Hirak activist, interview with author, Amman, Jordan, 30 April 2019.
109. Salem, interview with author, Amman, Jordan, 30 July 2019.

became political – we want a parliament because we want a voice".[110] He further clarified the role of the Hirak: "we gave to [the worker movement] a social
aspect that is much more political; we understood privatization as a social
problem (*our* economy, *our* companies)".[111]

In making such pronouncements, activists also decried the inadequacies of
previous "political" avenues of change, such as the top-down reforms of 1989,
or of Abdullah's "economic" path – vis-à-vis promises of modernization and
economic prosperity.[112] The former had proven sufficient merely to perpetu-
ate the status quo (e.g. the moral economy of commodities), while the latter,
through neoliberal reforms such as the privatizations, had actually made life
for many in Jordan considerably worse while delimiting civil rights in the process. It was in response to the failures of both the 1990s and the 2000s that
some activists began to elaborate a systemic critique of the entire "situation"
in Jordan. As one Hirak activist summarized: "[m]ainly it is the economic system, it is the privatization that we fight so much against, the capitalist economic system in Jordan".[113] Moreover, it was in the context of the uprisings
that "neoliberalism" became a "new phrase" in activist circles.[114] In a discussion with an activist leader from Amman, he explained to me that in the 2000s,
"new faces" came into power – "the neoliberals" – who "sold everything"; he
added that "you cannot survive if they are selling off all your resources".[115]

While the societal extent of such sentiments requires further research, the
fact that they were expressed by differently situated actors – across labour/
non-labour, urban/rural, and other social divides – demonstrates that
grievances surrounding privatizations resonated with a significant cross-
section of Jordanians. In part, this was due to the fact that national resources
were inextricably tied to historical state obligations of economic redistribution
(e.g., through jobs and state welfare). Labour activists emphasized narratives of
"theft" and "corruption" in articulating resistance to privatizations in order to
win over broader worker and social support. In reciprocal fashion, Hirak activists performed the discursive work to reframe privatization as a "social issue"
impacting all Jordanians – not just those who worked at privatized companies
– because, in the view of one such activist, "the Hirak is not a political project,
it's a political experience, a political voice; Hirak, whatever it represents, it's
from the people and for the people".[116] Together, these and similar articulations reflected activists' comprehension of the structural connections between
their lived material experiences and the policies of the neoliberal state, which

110. Hirak activist, interview with author, Amman, Jordan, 29 March 2019.
111. *Ibid.*, original emphasis.
112. Hirak hai tafaileh activist, interview with author, Amman, Jordan, 29 March 2019.
113. Palencia, *The Jordanian Youth Movement*, pp. 141–142.
114. Hirak Shef al-Bedran leader, interview with author, Amman, Jordan, 30 April 2019.
115. *Ibid.*
116. Hirak activist, interview with author, Amman, Jordan, 29 March 2019.

had been made visible through the prism of illegitimate privatizations and the moral economy of national resources.

CONCLUSION

As argued in this article, privatization necessarily means more than simply a change in asset ownership from public to private. In Jordan, privatization was experienced by many activists as an instance of "accumulation by dispossession", or, in other words, the "reversion to the private domain of common property rights won through past class struggles".[117] Hence, the narratives of theft and corruption employed by my interlocutors reflected the perception that the fruits of Jordan's national resources belong to Jordanians as part of historical state–society pacts won through social struggle, the abrogation of which – through *illegitimate* (corrupt, opaque, and poorly planned) privatizations – constituted a moral violation. In this article, I have argued that the privatization of the commons in Jordan precipitated the development of a new, transgressive framing discourse of protest, which created the possibility for a national-scale movement to resist the state's neoliberal project. Yet, this discourse was only able to go so far. By 2013, the state had succeeded through the strategic use of material and political concessions and violence to demobilize and demoralize the resistance.[118] Nevertheless, through the privatization of the commons, King Abdullah II's accelerated neoliberal project has ushered in a new era of contentious politics, one that has reverberated in recent mass protests and strikes over the last two years, as many Jordanians continue to challenge the terms of neoliberalism and, by extension, authoritarianism.[119]

---

117. Harvey, "The 'New' Imperialism: Accumulation by Dispossession", p. 75.
118. Tell, "Early Spring in Jordan"; Ziad Abu-Rish, "Protests, Regime Stability, and State Formation in Jordan".
119. See, for example, Sara Ababneh, "Do You Know Who Governs Us? The Damned Monetary Fund!", *The Middle East Report Online*, 30 (2018). Available at: https://merip.org/2018/06/do-you-know-who-governs-us-the-damned-monetary-fund/; last accessed 24 January 2021; Curtis Ryan, "Resurgent Protests Confront New and Old Red Lines in Jordan", *The Middle East Report*, 292:3 (2019), pp. 30–34.

IRSH 66 (2021), pp. 139–160 doi:10.1017/S0020859021000171

"Fraudonomics": Cartooning against Structural Adjustment in Togo

Robin Frisch[*]

University of Bayreuth
D-95440 Bayreuth, Germany

E-mail: robin.frisch@uni-bayreuth.de

ABSTRACT: This article offers a sensitive reading of oppositional political cartoons in Togo in the early 1990s, during the period of structural adjustment, which was accompanied by the swift reversal of democratizing trends and the restoration of authoritarian rule. Togolese satirists perceived this moment as a moment of "fraudonomics", thus contesting rampant corruption and clientelism in politics. They poked fun at the president, local politicians, businesspeople, and bureaucrats of the international institutions. The article begins by examining the making of satirical newspapers with a focus on the biographies of the satirists. As students, they started out on the adventure of publication with their own money and learned most of their drawing and printing techniques as work progressed. Secondly, an analysis of the readership shows that, although the satirical newspapers were a crucial element of the media in the early 1990s, it was mostly an elitist and urban phenomenon. The third section analyses the changing visual repertoire of contention through in-depth analysis of four selected caricatures.

In 1982, Togo began its structural adjustment programmes (SAPs). By 1989, the country had entered its fourth round of restructuring, and the privatization and austerity measures were taking place alongside widespread street demonstrations. Student protests and strikes led to a National Conference, which enabled opposition politicians to openly criticize President Eyadéma's regime for the first time in decades. The government had stopped hiring graduated students and could hardly afford to pay workers' salaries. For this reason, students and workers were at the forefront of these mobilizations.

* I am sincerely grateful for the comments from colleagues at the African History Research Seminar at the University of Bayreuth as well as during the workshop on this Special Issue at the International Institute of Social History in Amsterdam. My special thanks go to the team of *Kpakpa Désenchanté* for authorizing the reprint of the cartoons and allowing me to delve into the world of Togolese satire.

Nonetheless, Togo's National Conference failed. Soldiers forcefully broke it apart, and Eyadéma, who had been in power since 1967, remained in office. The political and economic crises were inherently connected. Reports by the International Monetary Fund (IMF) documented the effects of this "civil unrest" as a "serious economic disruption", "virtual standstill", and "economic paralysis".[1] For the IMF, the protests signalled "political disturbances" that would harm Togo's economic performance.[2] Yet, the question is how the protesters themselves perceived the adjustment.

Research on protest in West Africa during the 1990s has focused primarily on democracy and on the effects of the structural adjustment.[3] Modernization theorists tried to explain the conditions of democratization and insisted that economic factors were key.[4] Dependency theorists took the counterposition and criticized the importation of democracy models by emphasizing external domination.[5] Both approaches offer a rather teleological and determinist vision of political change. By focusing mainly on institutions, which tends to over-emphasize the power of elites, these perspectives rarely took into consideration the political sensitivities and changing representations in the moment of political protest. Besides these two major research frameworks for African politics, more works inspired by sociology highlight the multiple forms of contention.[6] Comi Toulabor and Stephen Ellis have shown that rumour and humour were important channels of expression in the Togolese political culture.[7] Although President Eyadéma controlled the media of the one-party dictatorship, he was still ridiculed through hidden messages in songs, wax prints, or even banknotes. However, few researchers have engaged with the role of satire and contention within the context of democratization and structural adjustment in Togo.

1. Saleh Nsouli, "Structural Adjustment in Sub-Saharan Africa", *Finance and Development*, 30 (1993), pp. 20–23, 20; International Monetary Fund (hereafter IMF) "Recent Economic Developments", *Staff Country Report Togo*, 94 (Washington, DC, 1994), p. 113, 1.
2. IMF, "Recent Economic Developments", p. 5.
3. Lisa Mueller, *Political Protest in Contemporary Africa* (Cambridge, 2018), p. 263.
4. Benno Ndulu and Stephen O'Connell, "Governance and Growth in Sub-Saharan Africa", *Journal of Economic Perspectives*, 13 (1999), pp. 41–66, 42. For an excellent discussion of research on democratization, see Nicolas Van De Walle, "Démocratisation en Afrique. Bilan critique", in Céline Thiriot and Mamoudou Gazibo (eds), *Le Politique en Afrique. Etat des débats et pistes de recherche* (Paris, 2009), pp. 135–163.
5. Van De Walle, "Démocratisation en Afrique", pp. 135–163, 142–144.
6. Richard Banégas, *La démocratie à pas de caméléon. Transition et imaginaires politiques au Bénin* (Paris, 2003), pp. 8–27; Vincent Bonnecase, *Les prix de la colère* (Paris, 2019), p. 281; Achille Mbembe, *De la postcolonie. Essai sur l'imagination politique dans l'Afrique contemporaine*, (Paris, 2000), p. 256; Johanna Siméant, "Protester/mobiliser/ne pas consentir. Sur quelques avatars de la sociologie des mobilisations appliquée au continent africain", *Revue internationale de politique comparée*, 20 (2013), pp. 125–143.
7. Comi Toulabor, *Le Togo sous Eyadéma* (Paris, 1986), p. 322; Stephen Ellis, "Rumour and Power in Togo", *Africa*, 63 (1993), pp. 462–476.

The article addresses this lacuna and investigates how oppositional satirical newspapers portrayed the political and economic transformation. As the article will show, these mobilizations of the early 1990s were far from only being about structural adjustment or democracy. The satirical category of "fraudonomics" provides a useful lens through which one can examine the various representations of adjustment from the cartoonists' perspective.[8] "Fraudonomics" is a pun that was invented by cartoonists of the first Togolese satirical newspaper *La Parole*, to denounce fraud, corruption, and injustice. It allows for the criticism of fraud not only in the economic sphere, but also in the political domain, where electoral malpractices and corruption were rampant. Fraudonomics was a highly moralizing form of critique. This "repertoire of contention" contains deliberately subjective and moral perspectives, rather than neutral information.[9] For this group of journalists, who were mainly students active in the demonstrations of the early 1990s, fraudonomics was a counter-discourse to the language of the adjustment and of the regime. E.P. Thompson, in his work on the moral economy of English workers, showed that specific events and "economic stimuli" did not mechanically trigger protests.[10] Rather, protests are the expression of historic injustices or sensitivities, and representations of what is right or wrong. In line with the concept of the moral economy of protest, this article argues that the Togolese satirical newspapers opened a space for political and economic alternatives.

Political cartoons are a paradoxical form of representation. They are simplistic, yet complex. They dramatize realities, yet also de-dramatize them. Georg Simmel saw in caricatures a transgressive and boundary-searching way of being. They are distortions of reality, anti-forms, and deliberate productions of unreality.[11] Cartoons only work through exaggerated information, but they are an effective way of capturing rumours and uncovering subjective realities. In Togo, cartoons fulfilled an important need for a liberated form of criticism at a time of acute political disorientation. Furthermore, for historical research, they provide a way to break through the artificial dichotomy of

8. The original term in French was "escrocs-nomie" [Fraudonomics] and appeared as a rubric in *La Parole* (Lomé, Togo) from 1990 to 1992.
9. Charles Tilly, *Regimes and Repertoires* (Chicago, IL, 2006), p. 240. For a discussion of the concept in this review, see Marcel Van der Linden, "Charles Tilly's Historical Sociology", *International Review of Social History*, 54 (2009), pp. 237–274, 240f.
10. E.P. Thompson, "The Moral Economy of the English Crowd in the Eighteenth Century", *Past & Present*, 50 (1971), pp. 76–136. See also Vincent Bonnecase, *Les prix de la colère* (Paris, 2019), pp. 8–30.
11. Georg Simmel, *Über die Karikatur. Zur Philosophie der Kunst*, vol. 13 (Berlin, 1922), p. 248. On the role of political cartoons in Africa, see Jean-Pascal Daloz, "Les ambivalences dans la caricature des dirigeants politiques. Illustrations africaines", *Mots*, 48 (1996), pp. 74–86; Achille Mbembe "La 'chose' et ses doubles dans la caricature camerounaise", *Cahiers d'Études africaines*, 36 (1996), pp. 143–170; Marie-Soleil Frère, *Presse et démocratie en Afrique francophone. Les mots et les maux de la transition au Bénin et au Niger* (Paris, 2000), pp. 161–488.

fact and arbitrariness. They are not only a form of protest or sedition, but also a visual archive of the protest.[12] By analysing political cartoons published in Togolese satirical newspapers from 1990 to 1996, this case study provides a closer understanding of the changing moral economy of protesters during this period.

The corpus of analysis contains a sampling of three satirical newspapers that were published between 1990 and 1996. *La Parole* (1990–1993), *La Pagaille* (1991–1992), and *Kpakpa Désenchanté* (1991–1996) were published weekly in tabloid format and generally each contained about ten pages. At the height of the public debates during the period of the National Conference, *La Parole* sold 15,000 copies, while *Kpakpa Désenchanté* and *La Pagaille* usually printed around 5,000 copies.[13] As this article will show, these numbers are not representative of the entire readership, since some readers did not purchase their own newspapers but copied them or cut out individual articles. The satirical newspapers were an important part of the media that were covering the ongoing political changes. It was the first time for decades that the government had allowed the liberalization of the press. Togolese people no longer had to read or watch Eyadéma's propaganda media. While student demonstrations were taking place, reading the free press, which openly poked fun at the president, was a liberating experience.

In the aftermath of the National Conference, journalists chose not to focus only on the autocratic Eyadéma, but instead to pose wider questions regarding the foundations of the political and economic system. The cartoons depicted World Bank and IMF officials, businesspeople, and trade unionists side by side with Togolese politicians. This, in turn, offered a multilayered reading. For example, the differing contents of the speech and thought bubbles contrasted the dissonance between overt and covert intentions. Another frequent cartooning device was the animalization of persons. By turning the human characters into dogs, frogs, or gorillas, the satirists invented a world of politics that resembled George Orwell's *Animal Farm*.[14] The newspapers produced *and* reproduced protest slogans. These images, metaphors, and symbols were well-known references in the Togolese protest culture. As a highly codified way of communication, they strengthened the group identification of protesters, yet might also have excluded large parts of society who were less familiar or opposed to these messages.

12. The reflection of the role of satire, especially of humour in social protest, is inspired by an earlier discussion in this journal, see Marjolein 't Hart, "Humour and Social Protest: An Introduction", *International Review of Social History*, 52 (2007), pp. 1–20.

13. Concerning the numbers of sold copies, see Dieudonné Korolakina, "Togo. Du ludique au politique", *Africultures*, 79 (2009), pp. 62–69, 67. This research is primarily based on the volumes that are accessible at the Archives Nationales du Togo (hereafter ANT). Further information was collected through eight interviews with journalists and cartoonists at Lomé (August 2019), Cotonou (September 2019), Paris (March 2020), and Bayreuth (March 2020).

14. George Orwell, *Animal Farm: A Fairy Story* (London, 1945), p. 112.

The first section of this article examines the making of the newspapers by focusing on the biographies of the satirists. As student activists, this small group of journalists and cartoonists embarked upon the adventure of publication with their own money and learned most of the drawing and printing techniques on their own. Secondly, this article discusses the reception of the cartoons as a form of collective reading. An analysis of the readership will show that, although the satirical newspapers were a crucial part of the media at a specific moment in the early 1990s, it was mostly an elitist and urban phenomenon. The third section analyses the changing visual repertoire of contention through in-depth analysis of four selected caricatures.

THE MAKING OF THE CARTOONS

Many of the satirical journalists had similar biographies. The founders of *Kpakpa Désenchanté,* Selom Gbanou and Knock Kalao Billy, studied together through high school and university. They were politically engaged in the *Groupement de réflexion et d'action pour la démocratie,* which was a pro-democratic student organization created in 1989. They had close ties to leading opposition politicians such as Joseph Koffigoh and Yawovi Agboyibo, who both later became prime ministers. For the young students, their philosophy classes coupled with charismatic teachers were a significant source of inspiration. The *Propos scientifique,* a journal by philosophy professors at the University of Lomé that was first published in the 1980s, provided the students with their first editorial experience, albeit without the tools of humour and caricature.

A number of influences shaped the *Kpakpa Désenchanté* style. The cartoonist Hector Sonon imitated the drawings of the French newspaper *Canard Enchaîné.*[15] Publications such as *Jeune Afrique* or the *Cafard Libéré* from Senegal provided external information on the regime. Furthermore, Western cultural institutes such as the Goethe-Institut and Institut Français offered safe havens for the critical journalists. Their satirical activism created a sense of familial conviviality for the journalists, and they developed deep emotional ties to each other that exist to this day.[16] This intimacy arose not only from their shared activism, but also from their precarious work conditions. They often feared for their lives and took radical measures to protect themselves, such as the use of pseudonyms, fake identity cards, and the avoidance of public spaces.

The satirical press was an indirect result of the adjustment measures. Employment opportunities for students were reduced significantly owing to the privatization of state-owned companies, as well as the restructuring of

---

15. Interview with Hector Sonon, Cotonou, September 2019.
16. Interview with Knock Kalao Billy, Paris, March 2020.

the public administration through the suspension of recruitment.[17] The economic policies produced a new generation of politically and economically frustrated youth. The "jeunes conjoncturés", with their good university degrees but few opportunities in the disintegrating job market, were at the heart of the protests in the 1990s.[18] In this way, some of the cartoons depicting the harsh realities of Togolese citizens were not merely abstract or exaggerated discourse, but the actual lived experiences of the young journalists. In the context of punishing financial conditions, cartooning was not only an organized strategic political act, but also a pragmatic way to earn some desperately needed money. Despite the financial difficulties, it is remarkable that *Kpakpa Désenchanté* could function entirely from sales revenue, without relying on advertisements.[19]

Following their first editorial experiences at *La Parole*, the journalists regrouped and founded their own publication in 1991. According to the chief editor, Selom Gbanou, the idea to create *Kpakpa Désenchanté* came to them in 1985. The first issues were artisanal in nature, with much improvisation and hand-cutting involved. The budget was tight. Students would even participate in pro-Eyadéma demonstrations in order to receive the money that was distributed and channel it into their newspaper.[20] *Kpakpa Désenchanté* became a "lighthouse" in the Togolese press landscape.[21] Soon, other newspapers such as *Le Crocodile* and *La Pagaille* imitated its satirical style. The journalists identified themselves as the "safeguards of the opposition" and the "moles against the government". Owing to "friends on the government side", the journalists could hide when it was time to go to the *commissariat* again. Having allies in the ministries and even in the presidential office allowed them more room for manoeuvre and better access to information. Being able to operate with near autonomy was new in the Togolese context of repression, where for decades the one-party regime had controlled the media. Prior to this time, journalists mainly served the propaganda machine or were forced into exile.[22]

During the 1990s, the press became a serious watchdog of the state. Knock Kalao Billy remembered that one police officer lamented "these ducks

---

17. Komlan Kwassi Agbovi, "Les incidences sociales des programmes d'ajustement structurel et de la dévaluation sur les populations urbaines du Togo" (Ph.D., Université de Lomé, 2003), pp. 1–75.
18. Comi Toulabor, "L'énonciation du pouvoir et de la richesse chez les jeunes 'conjonctures' de Lomé (Togo)", *Revue française de science politique*, 3 (1985), pp. 446–458.
19. *L'Humanité* (Paris, France), 24 February 1993, Claude Kroes, "'Kpakpa' veut continuer de paraître". Available at https://www.humanite.fr/node/50501; last accessed 25 April 2020.
20. Interview with Knock Kalao Billy, Paris, March 2020.
21. Interview with Selom Gbanou, Bayreuth, March 2020. The following quotations are from the same interview.
22. Essohanam Batchana, *Liberté de presse et pouvoirs publics au Togo. 1946–2004* (Ph.D., Université de Lomé, 2008), pp. 250–300.

[referring to *Kpakpa Désenchanté*] leave their excrement everywhere".[23] The quality and depth of the journalism improved significantly. The first satirical newspaper, *La Parole*, reported on Togolese politics by primarily focusing on Eyadéma. *Kpakpa Désenchanté* had a much wider scope, also covering economic and cultural topics. The general style of the satirical newspapers shifted from a firmly anti-Eyadéma position to a broader investigative journalism. During the National Conference, the journalists' intention was to give voice to the unheard and oppressed opinions. Publishing a newspaper had become a way to cope with the memories of a decade-long dictatorship. In 1991, the journalists' major interest was not reconciliation, as was intended by some participants of the National Conference.[24] Above all, they wanted truth. However, watchdog journalism was still in the making, and it was difficult to uncover fraud in a system that had a high level of press censorship and state intervention.

Satire as a channel of political communication was not only new for the journalists, but also for the readers. Some cartoons had staggering emotional depth, even when all they did was make a quick and cynical joke. Although these emotions were shrouded in sarcasm, the anger, frustration, and sadness were ever present. Even so, the imagery of the cartoons was never unsubtle. The newspapers were printed on thin paper and were a much more ephemeral and low-cost medium than theatre, film, or novels. The journalists signed themselves with pseudonyms, such as "Emmerdeur" (Troublemaker), "En Mangeant" (While Eating), and "L'Enragé" (The Furious).[25] Publishing anonymously was a way to protect one's identity and lower the risk of prosecution. The cartoonists' fictitious names, such as "Catirerisq" (Satire-risk) and "Sansracune" (Without Rancour), were in line with the sarcastic style. There was not a single person behind each pseudonym, but a collective authorship. In the same way, several cartoonists worked on the same drawing.[26] Mocking the dapper-suited politicians, the "elders", and all other powerful persons created a simple but strong and protective identity, a "we" against the "they" of the dominating regime.

Cartooning emerged historically as a hybrid that drew on different forms of protest. During the 1980s, the publication of the propaganda graphic novel *Il était une fois Eyadéma* dominated the visual culture of Togolese politics. This hugely popular "bande dessinée" portrayed an invented biography of

---

23. Interview with Knock Kalao Billy, Paris, March 2020. In Èvegbe, the word *kpakpa* means "duck".
24. On the National Conference in Togo, see John Heilbrunn, "Social Origins of National Conferences in Benin and Togo", *The Journal of Modern African Studies*, 31 (1993), pp. 277–299; Kathryn Nwajiaku, "The National Conferences in Benin and Togo Revisited", *The Journal of Modern African Studies*, 32 (2014), pp. 429–447.
25. Signatures of journalists collected in *Kpakpa Désenchanté* and *La Parole*.
26. Korolakina, "Togo. Du ludique au politique", p. 66f.

Eyadéma.[27] The disenchanted cartoons of the 1990s challenged this legend and portrayed the president in every possible way as weak, untrustworthy, and even inhuman.[28] Their novelty consisted in their use as part of the repertoire of contention. Before the 1990s, cartoons never represented critical political speech. Political leaflets (or tracts), hitherto the main channel of contestation, inspired the short editorials that were published alongside the cartoons.

Because of their intellectual backgrounds, the cartoonists and journalists could be considered an avant-garde category within the Togolese protests. The newspapers were produced mainly in French by highly educated, urban groups. For this reason, the cartoons in the satirical press were far from being a subaltern story, but rather were "messages from the elite for the elite".[29]

COLLECTIVE READING

Political cartoons rapidly became one of the most persuasive tools of political communication in the 1990s. The success of this medium would not have been possible without the technological progress of printing technology and its increasing accessibility at Lomé. The official sales numbers must be taken with a pinch of salt, however, as print shops often secretly produced more in order to increase their own profits.[30] Moreover, the readership was much wider than the figures show, as "approximately ten people read one newspaper".[31] Knock Kalao Billy, the editor-in-chief, remembers that cartoons were often cut out and pasted onto walls, including those of police stations. Police officers, *gendarmes*, and ministers were frequent readers of *Kpakpa Désenchanté*. Surprisingly, regime-loyal politicians such as Colonel Damehane Yark, today's much-feared Minister of Civil Security, were enthusiastic readers of *Kpakpa Désenchanté*. President Eyadéma allegedly had four subscriptions.[32] According to the journalists, most soldiers and police officers were not opposed to the satire and were, in fact, among their most loyal readers.

27. Serge Saint-Michel, *Histoire du Togo. Il était une fois Eyadéma* (Paris, 1976), p. 48. For a critical discussion of the propaganda comic, see Selom Gbanou, "En attendant le vote des bêtes sauvages ou le roman d'un 'diseur de vérité'", *Études françaises*, 42 (2006), pp. 51–75, 55.
28. Figures 1 and 4 in this article. See also Korolakina, "Togo. Du ludique au politique", pp. 65–69, 65.
29. Frère, *Presse et démocratie*, p. 256.
30. Interview with Knock Kalao Billy, March 2020, Paris. For a discussion of the distribution of independent newspapers in Togo, see Mikaïla Saibou, "Crise de la presse imprimée en Afrique à l'ère du numérique" (Ph.D., University of Lomé), p. 41.
31. Interview with Knock Kalao Billy, March 2020, Paris.
32. *Ibid.*

Civil servants were one of the most important groups that bought the satirical press. However, in the shaky adjustment economy, their salaries were paid irregularly. Readers and vendors were therefore forced to devise new forms of distribution. Making copies or "renting" the newspapers increased the readership.[33] News and cartoons were shared by the street hawkers who were selling the newspapers "à la criée".[34] The collective reading and sharing, and the street gossip that it elicited, was an important part of political debate. The satirical press was read not only by government ministers, but also by market traders and even those who could not read the editorials but nonetheless could laugh at the humorous caricatures.[35]

It is extremely difficult to reconstruct readers' reactions as scrutiny today can hardly capture the complexities of the situation. Marie-Soleil Frère has shown, in the case of the independent press in Niger and Benin, that journalists did not express the "popular voice" they claimed to represent. In the Togolese case, the readership was also mostly urban and elite groups. The satirical press was more a "class media" than a "mass media".[36] The reasons for the shrinking readerships at the end of the 1990s were the rising frustrations with Togolese politicians as well as the people's general disappointment in the press.

The regime's answer to the critical press involved an ambiguous policy of limited liberalization and censorship. Knock Kalao Billy was imprisoned and interrogated several times at a police station. In some cases, journalists were conscripted by the regime. For example, in 1992, the editor of *La Pagaille* switched allegiance in favour of RPT (Rassemblement du Peuple Togolais), the president's party.[37] The relative liberalization of the press proved to be only a brief episode, and most newspapers soon collapsed owing to financial difficulties and physical intimidation by the regime. Repression began to take new forms, such as limiting access to printing technology and restricting access to paper.[38] The regime employed informants within the print shops, who were required to leak prospective publications to the authorities. Some of the print shops were also targeted and burned.[39]

According to Selom Gbanou, the abrupt end of most satirical newspapers was not necessarily because of repression by the regime, but the political disillusionment and personal "disenchantment" of the people. He notes that: "We tried to change the political spirit. It was a big dream to be the avant-garde

33. On the distribution in the streets, see Frère, *Presse et démocratie*, p. 444.
34. Interview with Knock Kalao Billy, March 2020, Paris.
35. Interview with Selom Gbanou, Bayreuth, March 2020.
36. Frère, *Presse et démocratie*, p. 475.
37. Saibou, "Crise de la presse imprimée", p. 179.
38. See the general discussion by Paul Nugent in *Africa Since Independence* (London, 2012), p. 391.
39. Interview with Abass Saibou, Lomé, September 2019. *Signe*, *Al-Agah*, and *Todegnon*, the most important printing houses for the opposition press, were destroyed.

of critical journalism. At the end, one can say that it was a little naïve. Maybe we had some social or intellectual impact. But politically, we did not achieve anything."[40] This finding confirms research on humour in authoritarian regimes, which uncovered the fact that satire can serve the dominating actors as a legitimizing tool. To a certain extent, criticism might stabilize a political regime. Achille Mbembe and Jean-Pascal Daloz have shown, in the case of Cameroon, that depictions of the autocratic ruler reinforced his presence in the public sphere.[41]

"NATIONAL CONFERENCE OR NATIONAL CORRUPTION?"

Eyadéma was profoundly destabilized during the National Conference, which was held between 8 July and 28 August 1991. The deputies proclaimed sovereignty and proposed a transitional government. Even though Eyadéma rejected this and did not participate in the conference, the ongoing economic crisis significantly challenged his financial sovereignty.[42] He lost control over the state's financial affairs because the party's accounts were frozen and the Public Treasury was no longer administered by the regime. For decades, these institutions had been used as mechanisms of kleptocracy.

Published just two days after the opening of the National Conference, the cartoon reproduced as Figure 1 shows a grimacing Eyadéma, his face half in shadow, distributing money into the hands of unknown people. The caption reads "National Conference of National Corruption?" Eyadéma is saying, "I am honest. I am bribing you with the cash that I stole from you!" The president is loaded with so much money that it is even pouring out of his ears. The cartoon hints at the exaggerated amounts of money that Eyadéma is holding and the perverted manner of its distribution. It also evokes his self-chosen business suit uniform. The cartoon attests to the change of his political image from military khaki to a Western double-breasted business suit.[43] This outfit was meant to counterbalance the image of the "uncivilized murderer" that was attached to his military uniform, following his boastful remarks over the killing of Silvanus Olympio.[44] The image of a business-friendly, capitalist-oriented president changed his standing in the international arena of business and donors.

---

40. Interview with Selom Gbanou, Bayreuth, March 2020.
41. Daloz, "Les ambivalences dans la caricature", pp.74–86, 85; Mbembe, "La 'chose' et ses doubles", pp. 143–170, 169.
42. See Heilbrunn, "Social Origins of National Conferences", pp. 277–299, 277; Nwajiaku, "The National Conferences", pp. 429–447, 431.
43. Ellis, "Rumour and Power", pp. 462–476, 464.
44. *Ibid.*, pp. 462–476, 465.

Figure 1. "Conférence nationale ou corruption nationale?", *La Parole* (Lomé, Togo), 10 July 1991, p. 2.

For decades, "all monies passed through Eyadéma's hands".[45] The street murmurs of the "jeunes conjuncturés" often opposed his excessive luxury. Eyadéma was known for stashing 90 billion CFA francs in Swiss bank accounts.[46] Some cartoonists surrogated the Public Treasury as "Lomé 2", which was the President's residence. Nonetheless, the "flight of Cold War monies, the fallout from the National Conference, and the effects of neo-liberalization" profoundly destabilized Eyadéma's kleptocracy.[47]

45. Charles Piot, *Nostalgia for the Future: West Africa after the Cold War* (Chicago, IL, 2010), p. 35.
46. Comi Toulabor, "L'énonciation du pouvoir", pp. 446–458, 450; Toulabor, *Le Togo sous Eyadéma*, p. 120.
47. Piot, *Nostalgia for the Future*, p. 34.

During the 1990s, the regime reinvented itself through a relentless process of regaining control over financial affairs. However, the privatization of public companies and the creation of non-governmental organizations (NGOs) made it difficult for money to be controlled centrally the way it had been done for decades in the one-party state. The capital of NGOs or the money created by relationships with foreign businesses circumvented the national treasury and went directly into the pockets of state employees, "with the result that Eyadéma and his clients skimmed less and less".[48] Cartoons of this period depicted Eyadéma standing in the shadows, referencing the shadow relations of politicians and businessmen. The international perception of Togo as "Africa's Switzerland" gained another connotation during these days.[49] Usually, this label referred to the "laissez-faire attitude" of the government and Lomé as a regional banking centre.[50] As Figure 1 metaphorically indicates, Togo became a "shadow state" under Eyadéma. James Ferguson formulates a similar diagnosis of state officials in "weak states", losing power in official politics, but gaining influence through private and illicit networks. Numerous studies on African states in this period have shown how "big men" accumulated considerable wealth and power despite institutional decay during the adjustment.[51]

After the National Conference, political assassinations became extremely frequent. Soldiers even attacked Prime Minister Koffigoh on 3 December 1991. At the beginning of 1992, it was clear to *Kpakpa Désenchanté* that Eyadéma would restore power by using physical violence. The editorial of 7 July 1992 announced that "INSECURITY is guaranteed for 200%" this year. It was in 1992 that violence became widespread and even banal. The "tiny democratization" was interrupted by various political assassinations, such as the May 1992 attack on opposition leader Gilchrist Olympio and the July 1992 murder of politician Tavio Amorin.[52] In the former attack, which was organized by Eyadéma's son Ernest Gnassingbè, twelve people were killed.[53] The satirical press covered these events extensively, depicting a

48. *Ibid.*, p. 43.
49. Colleen Lowe Morna, "Africa's Switzerland?", *Africa Report*, 9 (1990), pp. 35–38.
50. Morna, "Africa's Switzerland?", pp. 35–38, 36.
51. James Ferguson, *Global Shadows: Africa in the Neoliberal World Order* (Durham, NC, 2006), p. 15; William Reno, *Corruption and State Politics in Sierra Leone* (Cambridge, 1995); see also the outstanding analysis by Jean-Francois Bayart, *State in Africa: The Politics of the Belly* (Cambridge [etc.], 2009).
52. John Heilbrunn and Comi Toulabor, "Une si petite démocratisation pour le Togo...", *Politique africaine*, 58 (1995), pp. 85–100, 85.
53. Koffi Nutefé Tsigbé, "La presse satirique face aux assassinats politiques au Togo en 1992. Quel crédit pour l'historien? Les exemples de La parole et Kpakpa désenchanté", *Esboços. Histórias em contextos globais*, 25 (2018), pp. 68–87, 79.

martyred Amorin, or Gilchrist Olympio surviving only because of the protection offered by his father's spirit.[54]

In this context, various cartoons not only depicted political violence, but also the daily sufferings during the economic crisis. They referred to the violence of fraudonomics as a combined burden. The satire hardly distinguished between the effects of Eyadéma's violent restoration of power and the harsh economic measures. Workers, whose salaries were cut, were illustrated as floating in saucepans. Consumers were depicted as having malnourished bodies collapsing under the unbearable weight of "heavy" politicians or of symbols showing rising prices.[55] This macabre sarcasm indicates the feeling that economic reforms had "inhuman" consequences. In the late 1980s, international organizations became more aware of the social consequences of adjustment and poverty alleviation. The International Labour Organization and UNICEF advocated for an adjustment with a "human face".[56] The satirical newspapers parodied this concept by alluding to the World Bank and IMF officials as "merchants of death" or the "adjustment struct-cruel".[57]

Figure 2 shows a conversation between the US president George H.W. Bush and President of the World Bank, Jeremy Preston. Bush asks Preston about the "big decisions of the World Bank". According to him, the "biggest decision of the World Bank is to get rid of these dictators who are only investing in weapons".[58] The Togolese army was crucial to the Eyadéma's authoritarian restoration of power during the post-Cold War era. Indeed, General Eyadéma used loyal soldiers to disrupt the National Conference. Moreover, "he increased the size of the military [...] and multiplied the number and types of military units".[59] After the political assassinations and the violent repression of demonstrations, imposing the president's legitimacy through ethnic warriorhood and a martial cult seemed outdated. In contrast to the propaganda narrative of the army as a peaceful, unifying, and stabilizing force, the cartoonists perceived militarization as a serious threat. Eyadéma spoke about the army as the "backbone of the Togolese nation".[60] The satirical newspapers denounced this "military-nation" and reported that the *Forces*

---

54. See Tsigbé, "La presse satirique", pp. 68–87, 70f. Gilchrist Olympio's father, Togo's first president, Silvanus Olympio, was assassinated in 1963. Eyadéma himself claimed responsibility for it. See Kate Skinner, "West Africa's First Coup: Neo-Colonial and Pan-African Projects in Togo's 'Shadow Archives'", *African Studies Review*, 39 (2019), pp. 1–24, 2.

55. *Kpakpa Désenchanté* (Lomé, Togo), 12 December 1995, p. 3; *Kpakpa Désenchanté* (Lomé, Togo), 20 June 1995, p. 1.

56. Richard Jolly, "Adjustment with a Human Face: A UNICEF Record and Perspective on the 1980s", World Development, 19 (1991), pp. 1807–1821, 1808.

57. *Forum Hebdo* (Lomé, Togo), 1 February 1991, p. 3. [Marchands de mort], *Kpakpa Désenchanté* (Lomé, Togo), 16 November 1993, p. 1 (ajustement strut-cruel).

58. *La Parole* (Lomé, Togo), 23 December 1991, p. 6.

59. Piot, *Nostalgia for the Future*, p. 36.

60. Toulabor, *Le Togo sous Eyadéma*, pp. 95–99.

Figure 2. "Les grandes décisions de la Banque Mondiale", *La Parole* (Lomé, Togo), 23 December 1991, p. 6.

Armées Togolaises were primarily responsible for the failure of the National Conference.[61]

The cartoon also hints at the Western states' hypocrisy in the support of political change. Preston's wry smile, raised finger, and one hand hidden behind his back all imply the hatching of a ruse. The cartoon not only underscores Eyadéma's system of fraudonomics on the national level, but also hypocrisy at the international level. The cartoonists illustrate the structural adjustment as a high-level diplomatic negotiation between US politicians. In reality, Bush and Preston probably never talked about Eyadéma's arms deals. However, this invented dialogue reveals what the structural adjustment was about for the cartoonists. Instead of depicting negotiations between

61. On the "military-nation", see Tsigbé, "La presse satirique", pp. 68–87, 74.

bureaucrats, which involve reports, evaluations, and consultancy, the conversation between Bush and Preston appears to be informal. This representation of high-level decisions involving tricks and traps is an expression of fraudonomics. The cartoonists questioned the trustworthiness of all politicians and economists.

In Figure 3, Eyadéma, again in his double-breasted business suit, listens to Michel Camdessus, the managing director of the IMF, who proclaims "drastic, bitter, inhuman and devastating measures for the economic recovery". Prime Minister Koffigoh hides behind the wall as he hears the president saying he wants to fire all the "boulotteurs inutiles" [useless eaters]. The cartoon refers to the idea of the prime minister as a scapegoat for the increasingly unpopular structural adjustment. The tension between Koffigoh and Eyadéma was high since he was the first prime minister of the transitional government and one of the protagonists of the National Conference. Nevertheless, soldiers humiliated Koffigoh in an overnight coup in December 1991. He stayed in office, but lost most of his credibility. Even the journalists who worked with him during the National Conference no longer supported him. Consequently, he became a "useless eater" of public funds. Ironically, the cartoon presents IMF Director Camdessus as an ally in Eyadéma's "politics of the belly". Jean-Francois Bayart conceptualized this idiomatic expression as an unequal accumulation of power and wealth by the elite. This model draws attention to the illicit or corrupt methods that "big men" use to acquire capital.[62] In this case, the cartoonist draws Eyadéma in a typical gatekeeping role. The president choses personally, similar to the portrayal in Figure 1, how he wants to distribute the aid of the financial institutions.

Most of the cartoons published from 1990 to 1992 blamed the government but not the international institutions. This changed after the National Conference and the failing democratic transition. After a decade of adjustment, the newspapers increasingly criticized the IMF and the World Bank. In August 1993, Eyadéma won the first presidential election after the National Conference through the massive use of fraud. For most of the observers and analysts, this election was a masquerade or an "electoral embarrassment".[63]

Once more, this representation can be found in the wider context of political cultures of African countries. Bayart argues that Senegal's Abdou Diouf, Congo-Brazzaville's Sassou Nguesso, and Ivory Coast's Houphouet-Boigny used the adjustment agenda to "recover their freedom of action with regard to a political class and a bureaucracy which had cut loose financially from the

62. Bayart, *State in Africa*, pp. 10–55.
63. Trutz von Trotha, "C'est la pagaille. Quelques remarques sur l'élection présidentielle et son observation internationale au Togo, 1993", *Politique africaine*, 52 (1993), pp. 152–159, 152; Piot, *Nostalgia for the Future*, p. 33.

Figure 3. "Gnass est partant pour les plans d'ajustement strut-cruels", *Kpakpa Désenchanté* (Lomé, Togo) 16 November 1993, p. 2.

centre".[64] *Kpakpa Désenchanté* even invented a slogan for a fictive club of African dictators, the "Union syndicale des dictateurs africains".[65] The newspapers depicted "Gnass" in concert with other presidents such as Mobuto, alias "Mort Bute", or Biya as "CorBIYAr".[66] However, the cartoonists related this

---

64. Bayart, *The State in Africa*, p. 226.
65. Gbanou, "En attendant le vote", pp. 51–75, 67.
66. Roughly translated these onomatopoeic puns mean "Death Blow" [Mort Bute] and Strange Raven [CorBIYAr], cf. Gbanou, "En attendant le vote", pp. 51–75, 74.

dictator's club to French politics. The neologism "Francafrique" or "France-à-fric" ("fric" means "cash") frequently appeared in *Kpakpa Désenchanté*.[67] One cartoon, published on 7 January 1992, depicted the French president Francois Mitterrand serving money on a tray to the dictators. The caption reads, "Billions for the "demo(lish)cratie" ("démo(lir)cratie").

DEVALUATION FROM NANA BENZ TO NANA TOYOTA

On 11 January 1994, the West African Central Bank (BCEAO) devalued the regional currency, the CFA franc, by half its value. This event heightened the already acute sense of catastrophe.[68] Two days later, *La Pagaille* published a cartoon of a weeping woman – a Nana Toyota – sitting on bundles of CFA franc banknotes. In the speech bubbles, she blames the "French" and "democracy" for destroying her capital.[69] The Nana Benz were rich wax-fabric traders well known for driving expensive Mercedes-Benz cars. In the cartoon, the satirists downgrade the women's symbolic capital. They are no longer Nana Benz but Nana Toyota. These women were important economic actors and owned considerable amounts of money. Indeed, the depiction of the crying Nana Benz was a case in point, because the women suffered greatly under the devaluation.

Since the 1970s, the Nana Benz benefited from Eyadéma's "unintrusive capitalist-oriented regime".[70] During the devaluation period, the tense economic situation was further complicated by the reduction of purchasing power. The Nana Benz branded a wax fabric that depicted a dragon as the "wax of devaluation".[71] Satirical newspapers underlined the "deathly consequences" of the price explosion.[72] Moreover, the population lost trust not only in the regulatory authority of the state to provide enough money, but also in its ability to guarantee the value of money. The devaluation profoundly disrupted the belief in monetary stability.[73] In the following months, a number of public events manifested the state's powerlessness in monetary affairs: On 13 May 1994, a money transporter belonging to the BCEAO was attacked. A few days later, the head cashier of the BCEAO, who controlled the

---

67. François-Xavier Verschave, *La Françafrique. Le plus long scandale de la République* (Paris, 1998).
68. See also Piot, *Nostalgia for the Future*, p. 42.
69. *La Pagaille* (Lomé, Togo), 14 January 1994, p. 3.
70. Heilbrunn, "Social Origins of National Conferences", pp. 277–299, 282.
71. Fondation Zinsou, *Wax Stories*, Bibliothèque Nationale du Bénin (Cotonou, 2019), p. 130.
72. *Kpakpa Désenchanté* (Lomé, Togo), 8 March 1994, p. 2.
73. The governmental newspaper *Togo Presse* published wrong information concerning the level of the devaluation. First announcements said that the currency would be devalued by sixty per cent. *Togo Presse* (Lomé, Togo), 12 January 1994, p. 2.

transport, was murdered in the streets of Lomé.[74] At the end of 1994, the Central Bank introduced new banknotes, which were supposed to contain better protection against counterfeiting. However, *Kpakpa Désenchanté* reported that counterfeited 10,000 CFA franc notes appeared more than ever before.[75]

The everyday experiences with counterfeit money and the apparent incapacity of the state to manage economic affairs reflect a greater conflict in the politics of liberalization. The World Bank and the IMF perceived the French monetary policy in the franc zone as the last stronghold of state interventionism.[76] This protectionist position contradicted the liberal free-trade doctrine that dominated the international financial institutions in the 1990s. World Bank and IMF reports argued that the "overvalued" CFA franc was obstructing the adjustment.[77] For once, the cartoonists and the international financial institutions agreed in their criticism of the currency. The cartoonists perceived the CFA franc as a "fake currency" that served only French interests.[78] French Minister of Cooperation Michel Roussin was renamed "Minister of re-cooperation and devaluation". Ironically, he was the first to accuse Eyadéma of electoral fraud. Shortly after suspending French development aid for Togo, Roussin was accused of corruption himself, and had to resign. *Kpakpa Désenchanté* published a cartoon showing the "dictator's club" offering Roussin "devalued" banknotes to hide. Roussin refused "the black money" ("l'argent noir"), yet stood nakedly in front of the dictators.

After the devaluation, the new banknotes were christened "billet Koffigoh" in the streets of Lomé.[79] Criticism of Eyadéma was absent. In fact, Koffigoh was as powerless as Eyadéma in the diplomatic arena of the franc zone. However, Eyadéma could profit from the situation by blaming his unpopular prime minister.[80] The "loss of hope and of a sense of political possibility" reinstated Eyadéma's hegemony.[81]

74. The transport from Lomé to Abidjan contained the record amount of 9.5 billion CFA francs (approximately 15 million Euro), *Kpkpa Désenchanté* (Lomé, Togo), 21 June 1994, p. 2.

75. *Kpakpa Désenchanté* (Lomé, Togo), 22 November 1994, "*Affaires de faux billets*", p. 4.

76. Claude Freud, "La zone franc est-elle le bouc-émissaire de l'échec du développement?", Cahiers d'Études Africaines, 31 (1991), pp. 159–174, 170.

77. World Bank, *Un programme d'action concerte pour le développement stable de l'Afrique au sud du Sahara* (Washington, DC, 1985); International Monetary Fund, *Theoretical Aspects of the Design of Fund Supported Adjustments Programs* (Washington, DC, 1987).

78. *Kpakpa Désenchanté* (Lomé, Togo), 15 July 1994, p. 4.

79. Many thanks to Essohanam Batchana for sharing this information with me (Lomé, 2019).

80. Toulabor, *Togo sous Eyadéma*, pp. 141–158. Eyadéma had already criticized the lack of sovereignty and control in the monetary system of the CFA franc in 1972. Anti-French and anti-imperialist rhetoric was in vogue after the Sarakawa incident and the question of privatizing the phosphate company.

81. Piot, *Nostalgia for the Future*, p. 34.

GOOD GOVERNANCE" AND THE NEWSPEAK OF THE SAP

Political analysts have shown that most African rulers have managed "to adjust to adjustment". According to the argument formulated by Patrick Chabal and Jean-Pascal Daloz, the SAPs did not undermine the patrimonial foundations of the state but changed the functioning.[82]

The SAPs represented a "blessing in disguise" because the African rulers could "extract a level of foreign aid which otherwise would not be available".[83] The cartoons depicted the political elites as sharp operators who used the reform process to their own advantage. The fraudonomics of the adjustment was thus a productive form of offering "distinct financial possibilities for currency-strapped and insolvent states".[84]

The novelty of the mid-1990s was the blaming of extra-state actors in the cartoons, such as French businesspersons. The new prime minister Edem Kodjo, nicknamed "Roi Koq-Djo" or "Sa Koqueteraie", was associated with a "mafia of privatization".[85] Kodjo was governor of the IMF from 1967 to 1973 and minister of economy and foreign affairs during the 1970s under Eyadéma. His relations to the French economic and political elite meant it was thought he was in favour of the privatization of the country. Kodjo was "selling the country" by putting it into a World Bank sack. Other cartoons showed him receiving suitcases full of money from the French prime minister and the company Bouygues.[86]

Money, a constant element of the cartoons, was no longer held in Eyadéma's hands. The "patrimonial ostentation" (Figures 1 & 4) included a larger political and economic elite.[87] Neologisms such as "belly-cracy" (*ventro-cratie*), big bellies, or other symbols of wealth such as cigars and oversized chairs, referenced the unequal distribution of wealth.[88] The tensions between the rich and the poor, the powerful and the powerless, were apparent for example in a cartoon that showed a fictive conversation between Prime Minister Kodjo and a World Bank official. Kodjo asks the "Death Bank" (the *Banque Mort-diale*) what the Togolese government should do if privatization does

---

82. Patrick Chabal and Jean-Pascal Daloz, *Africa Works: The Political Instrumentalization of Disorder* (London, 1998), p. 122; Jean-Francois Bayart, Stephen Ellis, and Beatrice Hibou, *The Criminalization of the State in Africa* (Melton, 1999), p. 126.
83. See Paul Nugent, *Africa Since Independence* (London, 2012), p. 338, and Nicolas Van de Walle, *African Economies and the Politics of Permanent Crisis, 1979–1999* (Cambridge, 2001), pp. 152–172.
84. Janet Roitman, *Fiscal Disobedience: An Anthropology of Economic Regulation in Central Africa* (Princeton, NJ, 2004), p. 20.
85. These nicknames refer to Kodjo's relations to France, where he lived for many years and taught at the Sorbonne University. The "mafia of privatization" appeared in *Kpakpa Désenchanté*, 24 April 1995.
86. *Kpakpa Désenchanté* (Lomé, Togo), 18 May 1994, p. 5; *Idem*, 24 April 1995, p. 7.
87. Chabal and Daloz, *Africa Works*, p. 160.
88. *Kpakpa Désenchanté* (Lomé,Togo), 24 April 1995, p. 3.

Figure 4. "La bonne gouvernance expliquée en heures sup' à certains élèves butés", *Kpakpa Désenchanté* (Lomé, Togo), 10 December 1996, p. 3.

not improve the economic situation. The diplomat of the World Bank answers drily: "Privatize the Togolese people".[89]

In Figure 4, Eyadéma is depicted as a voracious dog with bared teeth. He watches as the French president Jacques Chirac points at a board. On it is written, "Practical work for good governance". Underneath these words is a chart that consists of two bones. Each bone is divided into separate portions – one "for the people" and the other "for myself". Eyadéma is angry because he will lose a significant bit of the "national bone". Chirac, the teacher, explains: "In the old days, you could eat 9/10 of the 'national bone' but now you can only bite half of it." In this lesson of fraudonomics, Eyadéma seems to obey the French president. As the inscription on his clothes indicates, Chirac is the "official sponsor" of Togolese politics. Despite the growling of the dog, Chirac's authority is uncontested.

During the 1990s, the phrase "good governance" became increasingly popular with the SAP. In the cartoon, Chirac no longer advocates for democracy as his predecessor did in 1990 at La Baule, but rather for good governance. In line with several other puns on the technical and political language of the adjustment, the concept of "good governance" represents another illustration of fraudonomics. The cartoonists hint sarcastically at the Newspeak of the

89. *Ibid.*

adjustment. Togolese officials integrated the rhetoric of the World Bank, IMF, and international donors into political communication. The journalists made puns on abbreviations, country rankings, or the use of arbitrary indicators.[90] In contrast to the Newspeak of the adjustment, the satirical newspapers used colloquial language or imitated wrong pronunciations. According to Orwell's definition, Newspeak contains no negative terms. For example, the only way to express the meaning of "bad" is through the word "ungood", while something extremely bad is called "doubleplus ungood".[91]

The animalization of the president as a salivating dog with pointed teeth was a figurative expression in many caricatures of the time. It also calls to mind George Orwell's *Animal Farm*, where the dogs are guards of the dictatorship.[92] The bone on the board illustrates the president's greed for the public budget. In contrast to Eyadéma's self-presentation as a charismatic peacemaker and father of the nation, the bloodthirsty dog was a common figure of speech that was used by regime opponents to denounce Eyadéma's personified propaganda.[93] The anthropomorphism might also be understood as revenge following the dehumanization of his dictatorship. Eyadéma's cult of hunting and nature preservation remained in the collective memory.[94]

CONCLUSION: FRAUDONOMICS AND CONTESTATION TODAY

This article has argued that cartoons fulfilled a political need in a time of acute disorientation. Cartoons perceived the structural adjustment and the authoritarian restoration as fraudonomics. They targeted the president, local politicians, businesspeople, and bureaucrats of the SAP institutions. The oppositional cartoons crisscrossed the economic and political sphere. Many cartoons testified the moral implications of the changing institutions and economic measures. Regarding the moral economy of the "adjustment people", this article has shown that the protests involved a much larger variety of actors and topics than expected.

This article has shown that the criticism of the early 1990s significantly destabilized the moral authority of the regime, which had to invent new

90. TVA (*Taxe sur la Chaleur Ajoutée*), *Kpakpa Désenchanté* (Lomé, Togo), 18 July 1995, pp. 4–6; BM ("*Banque Mortiale*" or PAS ("ça ne passe pas"), in Frère, *Presse et démocratie*, p. 269; "Togo as Last Country on the List of the IMF but also of Amnesty International", *Kpakpa Désenchanté* (Lomé, Togo), 18 May 1995, p. 5.
91. George Orwell, *Nineteen Eighty-Four* (London, 2007), pp. 338–339.
92. Orwell, *Animal Farm*, p. 112.
93. Toulabor, *Le Togo sous Eyadéma*, pp. 121–125, 300. Regime opponents named the president *Avusu*, meaning angry male dog in Èvegbe.
94. This representation is stressed in the novel by Ahmadou Kourouma, *En attendant le vote des bêtes sauvages* (Paris, 1998).

ways of legitimization. One must note that this period was a productive and creative moment in the demystification of Eyadéma's regime, which was also depicted in novels and theatre plays. For example, the writer Ahmadou Kourouma, who lived in Togo from 1984 to 1994, critically engaged with Eyadéma's biography and caricatured Eyadéma as the fictional President Koyoga.[95] A number of Togolese writers such as Kagni Alem, Kossi Efoui, and Sami Tchak, who all became famous for their literary works in the 1990s, were similarly successful in making the "real visible".[96]

However, a question remains: why did these critical discourses lose their contentious power? In terms of criticism, the period analysed in this article was one of liberalization. Yet, there is still a desperate need for the imagination of political alternatives in Togo, where Eyadéma's son Faure Gnassingbè has been in power since 2005. The current opposition press significantly lost both its quality and influence. Instead of the numerous satirical newspapers that existed during the 1990s, only one publication (*SIKA'A*) remains; although it seems quite isolated, monotonous, and futile in its denunciation of "Small Boy", the nickname of the current president. The former cartoonists and journalists interviewed for this article all live abroad, and work as fine artists, researchers, and consultants. Why did they stop denouncing the fraudonomics? The satirists faced the question of how to adapt to the changing political and economic landscape when the regime either conscripted or expelled any criticism. Today's situation shows a paradox of liberalization. It has never been as easy as it is now to express criticism, considering the vast landscape of social networks; so why does the liberalization of the media space not enable more liberated satirical protest?

---

95. Kourouma, *En attendant le vote*, p. 368.
96. Kangni Alem is a writer and founder of Atelier théâtre, Kossi Efoui was a leading activist and playwright during the 1990s, and Sami Tchak is a writer and sociologist.

IRSH 66 (2021), pp. 161–180 doi:10.1017/S0020859021000134

International Monetary Fund Riots or Nasserian Revolt? Thinking Fluid Memories: Egypt 1977[*]

MÉLANIE HENRY

IAAC/EHESS and ERC-DREAM project
CHS/Université Paris I Panthéon-Sorbonne
Paris, France

E-mail: Melan.henry@gmail.com

ABSTRACT: In recorded memory, the 1977 uprising in Egypt appears as the end of a cycle. Yet, at an international level, it marks the beginning of a wave of protest against International Monetary Fund measures. In this article, I study how communist memories of the uprising, which are the only ones recorded, have built up a disregard for 1977's "immature" insurgents. The article investigates how these narratives can inform us about the history of the uprising and argues that the search for a Cartesian-type collective subject among insurgents limits our understanding of the insurrection. It refers extensively to the Alexandria Arsenal, a state-owned shipbuilding company where the uprising began, and the relationship between this "vanguard" and the rest of the insurgents. It deconstructs the theoretical presupposition of an analogy between insurgents and a Cartesian subject that permeates the sources, and also the concepts of "collective memory" and "moral economy". This leads inevitably to the diagnosis of a defective subject. It favours the concept of "fluid memory" and highlights other "January 1977s".

"What was 1977?" is the rhetorical question posed by Ibrâhîm al-Bâz, student and Trotskyist, who was active during the uprising of 18–19 January 1977 in Egypt, before answering: "It was the last twitch of the dead man".[1] Indeed, in terms of recorded memory, 1977 was the final year in a cycle of social and political struggle in Egypt.

Yet, at an international level, 1977 may be seen as a beginning rather than an end. The massive protests of that year, which came shortly after those in Peru in 1976, began a wave of protest, which has not yet ended, against liberalization measures imposed by the International Monetary Fund (IMF) as a condition for accessing loans. It was the implementation of an IMF recommendation that

---

* I thank Jill McCoy for her translation and the ERC-funded project DREAM for their financial support.
1. Ibrâhîm Al-Bâz, Interview, 10 May 2013.

sparked the protests of 18 and 19 January. Public subsidies for twenty-five consumer products were halved "in order to tend towards real prices" and adjust to the rules of neoclassical doctrine. This measure was one of a series of liberal actions put into effect under President Anwar al-Sadat (1970–1981), the most emblematic being the economic open-door policy (the *infitâh*) of 1975. The year 1977 closed a period in national history while opening a period at the international level.

This paradox lies at the heart of this article and is resonant with the weak structuring of both academic and militant fields of modern austerity protests.[2] Reforms are considered to be an international phenomenon, whereas protests are seen as national – or even local. We will see how a "reformist" conception of social change, as examined in the typology of the sociologist Alain Roussillon,[3] is manifested in the reading of 1977 as an ending. Such a conception is part of a hegemonic discourse that relates to struggles in Egypt, the consequences and gaps of which we will also seek to analyse here.

Marxists and others on the left, those who created this discourse, are indeed at the heart of memories of the event. They were the only established political supporters of the protests. The Islamic movement, which was expanding in the 1970s, maintained good relations with President Sadat at the time of the uprising.[4] The movement was virtually absent from the protests, and there are no recorded traces of its possible involvement.[5]

The majority of protesters were not militants, although communists were accused of conspiracy. The communists defended themselves, thereby generating significant written traces. Some of them also shared their views on the event by writing its history, debating it, translating it into fiction, or recounting their experiences. Beyond the writings I used for the purpose of this research (published trial archives, articles from newspapers and journals, political essays, novels), this article is also based on an oral survey carried out in Alexandria, both an industrial hub and a university town, where the first demonstration took place on 18 January 1977 after news of the subsidy cuts had spread. My enquiry into the protests in Alexandria confirmed the general tendency to consider 1977 as an end date among militants and beyond.

---

2. John K. Walton *et al.*, *Free Markets and Food Riots: The Politics of Global Adjustment* (Oxford, 1994), p. 39.

3. Alain Roussillon, "Réforme sociale et politique en Égypte au tournant des années 1940", *Égypte/Monde arabe*, 199 (1994), pp. 18–19.

4. Islamist militants had indeed been released from prison en masse between 1971 and 1974 by Sadat to counter the influence of the left. It was not until November 1977 that relations between the Islamic movement and the President became tense over the peace process with Israel.

5. The presence of "religious elements" was witnessed in the attacks on nightclubs in the street of the Pyramids in Giza, Cairo. According to the General Prosecutor, no Muslim Brotherhood members were arrested during the uprising. Ahmad Sâdiq Sa'd, "Hâjatunâ Ilâ Istrâtîjîya Ishtirâkîya Jadîda. Qirâ' Thâniyya Fî Ahdâth Yanâyir 1977 [In Need of a new Socialist Strategy. Rereading the Events of January 1977]", *Al-Râya al-'arabiyya* (1988).

The leftists were imbued with the hopes of independence and social justice that the Nasserian experience had carried since the Free Officers coup in 1952, undermined by the 1967 defeat in the war against Israel. The militants maintained over time the idea that these revolts were transitory, and would potentially be replaced by more organized struggles, as in the orthodox Marxist interpretation.[6] From this standpoint, the 1977 uprising seems too spontaneous, violent, unconscious.

"Consciousness" was the watchword of these militants. The collective capacity of the oppressed to engage in successful protest, which gives their actions direction, depends on consciousness. This also distinguishes individuals who reflect from those who are "driven by their bellies". Thus, movements may fail if they are not fuelled by consciousness. Its centrality supposes an analogy between the collective subject of the protesters and the individual Cartesian subject, master of his consciousness. The Leninist party, the site of remembered struggle and democratic centralism, is built on such an analogy. But applying it to "revolutionaries", the masses who carry out revolutions, as opposed to "revolutionists",[7] the revolutionary militants, generates some blind spots.

This article asks how these militant narratives can inform us about the history of the uprising. Its purpose is to show that the search for a Cartesian collective subject among the insurgents, understood implicitly in both the actors' analysis and in many works of social science, limits our understanding of insurrections. This attempt at deconstruction builds on the idea that an insurrection, like an event, is plural. It considers the diversity and instability of the actors' intentions, both in the moment and retrospectively. To explore the more clouded aspects of the history of insurrection, it is productive to interrogate the resonances of an event with the political contexts that succeeded it.

We begin with the case of the Alexandria Arsenal, a state-owned shipbuilding company whose workers represented the vanguard of Nasserian hopes and who sparked the country's first protest on 18 January 1977. In combining approaches from social history of industry and conceptual history, we will describe the cultural and intellectual edifices that the world ending in 1977 had been built on. Following this embodied description of the relationship between the vanguard and the insurgents, the article will deconstruct the theoretical presupposition that the collective may be seen as a Cartesian subject, both in the actors' analysis and also in terms of the social sciences. We will see that this analogy leads inevitably to the diagnosis of a defective subject insofar as the insurgents are concerned. This logic, present in the sources, is reinforced by the notion of "collective memory",[8] as well as the concept of "moral

6. Walton, *Free Markets*, p. 3.
7. Hannah Arendt, *On Revolution* (London, 1963).
8. Maurice Halbwachs, *La mémoire collective* (Paris, 1997).

economy",[9] a determining notion in the study of modern austerity protests.[10] Finally, the article will highlight other "January 1977s" in the framework of contemporary history. It will favour the notion of "fluid memory",[11] as opposed to the too holistic "collective memory" of the event. Distancing the Cartesian reduction of the collective subject that emanates from this methodological pluralism will enhance understanding of the experience of the insurrectional event in two senses: how it was experienced by the participants, and how the event lives on.

ALEXANDRIA'S MARITIME ARSENAL: A SYMBOL

In 1977, the problem was that [...] we were running certain demonstrations like the one at the arsenal – the first in the country, we went out at 7 am – and the engineering school that joined them around 11 am or noon. These demonstrations were in the middle of others made up of millions of non-political people. There were very few of us [...], so you say, it's a hunger protest, there will be – you know cities –, thugs, needy people, there's going to be damage, etc. You're confused, because you want organized and politicized demonstrations but you find yourself with fire and destruction, where consumer cooperatives are being robbed and people are hungry, because they want to eat, it's only natural.[12]

We will see, beginning with the case of Alexandria's maritime arsenal, how a separation develops between conscious militants and those demonstrators who were driven by hunger, as described by Ibrâhîm al-Bâz in his account of the 1977 demonstrations.

According to police sources,[13] the first protests against subsidy cuts in Egypt began at the Alexandria Arsenal, a maritime factory that exemplified the Nasserian state's ambitions of economic development and social justice. In interviews with former workers and in two works by Ibrâhîm 'Abd al-Majîd,[14] who was an electrician at the arsenal before becoming a writer,

9. Edward Palmer Thompson, "The Moral Economy of the English Crowd in the Eighteenth Century", *Past & Present*, 50 (1971), pp. 76–136.

10. Walton, *Free Markets*, pp. 23–54.

11. The expression is developed from Michel de Certeau's work on the art of memory, understood as a fluid, interactive, and heterogeneous practice of time, space, and history. *The Practice of Everyday Life* (Berkeley, CA, 1988).

12. Al-Bâz, Interview, 10 May 2013.

13. 'Âdil Amîn, *Intifâdat Al-Qâhira Fî 18, 19 Yanâyir 1977. Hawâdith 19 Yanâyir 1977 Bi-l-Gîza. Qadiyyat Hizb al-'ummâl al-Shuyû'î al-Misrî. Qadiyyat Hizb al-'ummâl Wa-l-Hizb al-al-Shuyû'î al-Misrî Amâm al-Mahkama al-'askariyya al-'ulyâ* [Cairo Uprising of 18 and 19 January. Events of January 1977 in Giza. The Egyptian Communist Party Case. The Trial of the Workers Communist Party and of the Egyptian Communist Party] (Cairo, 2002), pp. 15–16.

14. Ibrâhîm 'Abd al-Majîd, *La Maison aux jasmins* (Arles, 2000); Ibrâhîm 'Abd al-Majîd, *Mâ Warâ' al-Kitâba. Tajribtî Ma'a-l-Ibdâ'* [Behind the Writing: My Experience of Creation] (Cairo, 2014).

the shipbuilding company appears as a place where "national consciousness" was performed. The fact that workers at the arsenal initiated the protest reinforces the powerful idea that the demonstrators of 18 and 19 January defended the "moral economy" built during the Nasserian period: a broad consensus, defended by the rioters but shared more widely, in the form of a moral contract between rulers and ruled.[15] This moral contract was called into question by the political reorientations undertaken by Sadat. The fact that the arsenal workers were the first to take to the streets on 18 January confirms their position at the vanguard of a national movement. But the exclusive dimension of this vanguard generates blind spots in our understanding of the 1977 uprising.

On the front lines

On 18 January, Mus'ad al-Tarabilî, engineer and communist militant, went to clock on and, as usual, "there were plenty of people, people talking amongst one another". But that morning, "people stayed, they didn't go to their workshops, they were saying [...] 'we must assert our rights! This action has to be reversed!'"[16] Mus'ad and Sayyid Mustafâ ("Berjo"), an electrician at the arsenal, were known locally for their political stance; naturally, the people turned to them. The slogans began to fly thick and fast: "Down with rising prices!" The Prime Minister was targeted by name: "Mamdûh Bey, oh Mamdûh Bey, a kilo of meat has gone to a guinea."[17]

The police report to the prosecutor commented that: "From factory to factory, they encouraged the workers to leave, which they did in small groups. They continued as far as the Bata Society."[18] The workers then moved towards the city centre, inciting residents and middle- and high-school students to block the street, according to Ibrâhîm 'Abd al-Majîd's novel based on the testimonies of former colleagues, which were collected in the weeks following the uprising.[19]

When they arrived at the Mahmûdiyya canal, which separates the peninsula of Alexandria from the industrial districts to the west of the city, the protesters faced the police, who were barring their route. Determined to continue, they routed the police, and several soldiers were thrown into the water. "The water level under the Chronogram bridge is not very high. They weren't seriously hurt; they did not fall a great distance", said Mus'ad.[20]

15. Thompson, "The Moral Economy".
16. Mus'ad Al-Tarabilî, Interview, 16 May 2015.
17. "Bi-al-rûh, bi-al-dam, hananzil al-as'âr"; "Mamdûh Bey, ya Mamdûh Bey, kîlû lahma baqâ bi-gînî." *Ibid.*
18. Amîn, *Intifâdat*, pp. 15–16.
19. 'Abd al-Majîd, *La maison*, pp. 52–53; Ibrâhîm 'Abd al-Majîd, Interview, 1 July 2014.
20. Al-Tarabilî, Interview, 16 May 2015.

This first event changed the tone of the popular demonstration. Here and there, there were clashes when central security forces intervened in the protesters' march. Mus'ad confirmed that his march was not responsible for any destruction of public or private property (buses, trams, cars, shops, consumer cooperatives where people used to buy subsidized products).

As in most major cities of the country, the processions marched through Alexandria all day. The police estimated that "at Tahrîr Square in Manshiyya, other workers from other factories joined them, and other individuals from various sections of the population, reaching a total of 10,000 people".[21]

Not far from this square, alongside the consular buildings and the courts, stands the old Alexandria Stock Exchange, which became the headquarters of the Arab Socialist Union, the single party built under Nasser. It was set on fire that day. In Cairo, clubs and luxury hotels in particular,[22] symbols of the debauchery of the rising élite, were targeted. Slogans denounced the global immorality of the "nouveaux riches", beneficiaries of the economic open-door policy that had been decreed in 1975:[23] "They dress in the latest fashion while we live ten in a room." "They drink whisky and eat chicken while the people starve."[24]

Nasser was omnipresent in the form of a portrait and a slogan, the simple chant "Nasser!". His supporters had been targeted by the "de-Nasserization" of the regime that had been set in motion by Sadat from 1971.[25] In their chant of "Nasser", the demonstrators were attacking Sadat's policy and legitimizing their own action, putting it under the patronage of the previous president, a monument of the imagined community.

The maritime arsenal: Symbol of a moral economy

For the Nasserian system's left wing, which published its views in the journal *Al-Talî'a* (The Vanguard), the arsenal was a spearhead. In 1961, at the beginning of the so-called socialist period, Nasser had made up for the lack of intellectuals in the ruling technocracy by freeing qualified communists from those with the most cultural and social capital. They provided ideological support

---

21. Amîn, *Intifâdat*, pp. 15–16.
22. Sa'd, "Hâjatunâ".
23. Yoichi Nakashima, "The Political Understanding of Al-Infitâh al-Iqtisâdî: A Case Study of Economic Liberalization in Egypt", IMES Working Papers Series, 12 (Tokyo, 1987).
24. "Malaff Ahdâth 18 wa 19 Yanâyîr [File of the Events of 18 and 19 January 1977]", *Al-Anbâ'*, December 1980.
25. On 15 May 1971, Sadat declared the "Corrective Revolution". Alain Roussillon, "Republican Egypt Interpreted: Revolution and Beyond", in M.W. Daly (ed.), *The Cambridge History of Egypt* (Cambridge, 1998), pp. 334–393.

for the country's development in *Al-Talî'a*,[26] where they called for the deep-ening of socialist logic, forging the "leftist" position. Mus'ad, who "could have been a technocrat",[27] fitted in well with this trend.

"This is not the story of a normal business, it is the story of the hope of the nation!"[28] summarized 'Abd al-Majîd, speaking of the arsenal. The techniques implemented in the state-owned business were developed in connection with the Soviet Union, and each year, a group of technicians and engineers spent nine months in Ukraine. With the 1977 protests, the arsenal workers were defending the "common good", as they also did by providing their share of industrial development.

Initially, I believed that there was a tradition of collective action at the arsenal, similar to that at the Helwan weapons factory, the other place where demonstrators emerged in the early morning on 18 January.[29] Its workers went on strike in 1968 to protest against the light sentences given to air force generals who were convicted of military misconduct in the war against Israel in 1967. On 21 February 1968, the same workers sparked off a large-scale protest, which included universities in particular.[30] In the early days of my investigation, I learned of memorable demonstrations organized by Alexandria's port workers in 1970 and 1974. They had insulted Sadat at the gates of his Alexandrian palace. In reality, the social status and protest tech-niques of these persons were at complete odds with those of the maritime arsenal's employees: they were dockworkers from the city's port. Untrained, older, newly arrived from their villages, or fleeing court sentences, the dockworkers were paid by task and had neither health insurance, nor paid leave.[31]

The arsenal workers, on the other hand, stood out in the industrial district of Qabbârî as being highly skilled and valued both symbolically and materi-ally. "I saw workers elsewhere, but they never had the consciousness of those at the arsenal", said Mus'ad. The company had been established in 1961, but eight years of preparation were necessary before the skilled labour and infrastructure were in place so that production could begin. Participants in a nascent collective, the 5,000 arsenal workers belonged mostly to the same age group, something that contributed significantly – according to

26. Roel Meijer, *The Quest for Modernity: Secular Liberal and Left-Wing Political Thought in Egypt, 1945–1958* (London, 2002).

27. Sayyid 'Berjo' Mustafâ Farrag, Interview, 26 May 2015.

28. 'Abd al-Majîd, *Mâ Warâ' al-Kitâba*, p. 64.

29. Amîn, *Intifâdat*.

30. Ahmed Abdalla, *The Student Movement and National Politics in Egypt, 1923–1973* (Cairo, 2008), p. 149.

31. Fathallah Mahrûs, Interview, 13 June 2015. He advised a strike leader and wrote an article on these struggles in an issue of the Communist Workers Party newspaper, the *Intifâd*.

Mus'ad and Sayyiḍ Berjo – to a feeling of community and general good relations. They were also close socially, as Mus'ad recalled:

> People got along, even engineers and laborers. There were friendships you would not have found in other places, where the engineers had to pay for their studies. Before Nasser, I could not have gone to school, [he] set up free education. You had people who came from the working classes, which ensured better relations with the laborers; there was no condescension or class-based tensions.[32]

The workers benefited from all the symbolic rewards of the Nasserist system: both "workers and artisans",[33] "well dressed and well educated",[34] they were famous in Alexandria. As a result, they worked "in a state of mind one only finds in armies at war".[35]

When conflicts emerged, they were settled within the work units – as they were minor and had to do with production-related issues. Well paid, highly valued, and part of a collective intelligence, the arsenal workers were the envy of Bata labourers and those of the oil industry. The arsenal's workforce had no reason to complain, explained Mus'ad. This, added to their "education", made possible what Mus'ad called "high consciousness": "with them, we could go beyond economic issues, we could talk about more than just stomach aches".[36]

Above and beyond "stomach aches"

This inferiority of "sector-specific demands" vis-à-vis "general demands" is a characteristic feature of workers' protests under Nasser, as exemplified by industrial wage strikes. To make themselves heard, workers maintained and even increased production rates, but refused to receive their wages.[37] The Trade Union Federation of Industrial Workers, created in 1957, the only union that structured workers, was designed to organize work in corporate terms rather than being contentious in its demands.[38] Workers and rural labourers formed a group that contributed to political decisions through making up fifty per cent of the National Assembly membership.[39] Through this, the Nasserist system institutionalized the political participation of workers and peasants,

32. Al-Tarabilî, Interview, 16 May 2015.
33. Abd al-Majîd, *Mâ Warâ' al-Kitâba*, p. 64.
34. *Ibid.*, p. 68.
35. *Ibid.*, p. 64.
36. Al-Tarabilî, Interview, 16 May 2015.
37. Fathallah Mahrûs, Interviews, June–July 2011; Françoise Clément, "Péripéties et vicissitudes de la libéralisation du marché du travail en Égypte", *Égypte/Monde arabe*, 20 (1994), 143–153.
38. Robert Bianchi, *Unruly Corporatism: Associational Life in Twentieth-Century Egypt* (New York, 1989).
39. Assef Bayat, "Populism, Liberalization and Popular Participation: Industrial Democracy in Egypt", *Economic and Industrial Democracy*, 14:1 (1993), pp. 65–87.

neutralizing social conflict. At the same time, any political acts apart from those that had been agreed by the regime were strongly repressed, which reduced the scope of potential action and redefined what was thinkable and what was unthinkable for political opposition groups, including the communists.

Nasser's policy was thus part of a "reformist thinking" of the social question: in conceptual, institutional, and social terms, it correlated the question of identity (ethnic, religious, or cultural) with that of knowledge and self-reform. This depoliticization of social change had been spreading through a range of political trends since the 1940s. Social policies were implemented with the overall aim of addressing all aspects of "Egyptian backwardness": spiritual; economic; legal; and even sanitary. Egypt was only one specific application of a universal programme. From this interpretative framework, based on European standards of "modernity", various intellectuals have assigned themselves a "critical function", both from the viewpoint of the colonial enterprise and from that of "'indigenous' responsibilities".[40]

This conception of social change permeated Mus'ad al-Tarabili's pronouncements, and gave the arsenal workers and students, who made generalized national claims in 1968 and 1972–1973, their status as the "vanguard" of the movement. The rest of the people who took to the streets on 18 January 1977 were "backward", "driven by their bellies".

In essence, this is the context of the 1977 uprising, which was rooted in hopes of independence and the Nasserian regime. That the Alexandria maritime arsenal acted as a driving force – the spearhead of modernity – in the 1977 uprising produces an effect of over-representation. Their model performance of the Nasserian moral economy makes sense when one considers their work experience as equivalent to an incorporation of the Nasserian state. They are the "vanguard" of the uprising, the metonymic receptacle of its consciousness.

THE INSURGENTS: A FAILING SUBJECT

The distinction between "conscious" militants and "unconscious" insurgents was a theme surprisingly shared by the supporters and detractors of the 1977 uprising. The regime denounced a communist plot that allegedly manipulated the masses. Leftists, authors of the memories of the event, defended their position, describing insurgents who were driven by social forces and unaware of their actions. The analogy between the Cartesian subject – endowed with duties, power, and knowledge – and the insurgent collective has long been a paradigm common to government and to Communists. In this reading, the insurgents appeared to be a "failing subject". This bias, consubstantial to the genesis of the sources, can be reinforced by later observers, based on

40. Roussillon, "Réforme sociale".

their use of the notions of "moral economy" and "collective memory" in their study of insurrections.

The "unconsciousness" of the insurgents

In a statement of 29 January 1977, Prime Minister Mamdûh Bey blamed the violence on an "insurrection of thieves" and on "communist elements wishing to manipulate the demonstrations by leading them to the public square and desiring to take control of the masses".[41] In the Egyptian press on 23 and 24 January, the involvement of the Soviets in organizing the riots was presented as obvious.[42] The courts did not hold the militants responsible for planning the events, and national security forces acknowledged that actions had not resulted from political activism.[43]

On the other hand, in the streets, the militants were trying to control the revolt. In Cairo, processions of workers and students came together to demand the withdrawal of measures imposed at the People's Assembly, not far from Tahrîr Square. In Alexandria, police sources mention a meeting with the city's governor.[44] Experienced militants demanded that protesters should limit their action to slogans and not cause material damage. This advice was sometimes ignored, and the voice of caution was generally overwhelmed.

The first writings on the uprising are by journalist Hussayn 'Abd al-Râziq, a senior member of the National Progressive Unionist Party, which emerged out of the left wing of the former single party that had been disbanded between 1975 and 1977. Râziq's book describes the "underlying causes" and the social forces that led to the "unplanned, spontaneous and global" movement.[45] Similarly, in *The House of Jasmine*, Ibrâhîm 'Abd al-Majîd explains the uprising: his account describes the structures that make history. In it, he uses typification, or the process of condensing the character traits of social groups into a single person. This process may be found in fiction, sociology, and history, though each genre gives it a different status.[46]

---

41. Hussayn 'Abd al-Râziq, *Misr Fî 18 Wa 19 Yanâyir. Dirâsa Siyâsiyya Wathâ'iqiyya* [Egypt on 18 and 19 January 1977: A Political Documentary Study] (Cairo, 1985).

42. Report from the Ambassador in Cairo to the Secretary of State in Washington of 24 January 1977. R 241431Z JAN 77. Available from: http://aad.archives.gov/aad/createpdf?rid=16925&dt=2532&dl=1629; last accessed 23 February 2021.

43. In reports 100 and 101 on the responsibility of the left in the events. "*Malaff Ahdâth 18 wa 19 Yanâyir* [File of the Events of 18 and 19 January 1977]", *Al-Anbâ'* (December 1980), "*al-Haqîqa wa-l-Târîkh*" [Truth and History], p. 22.

44. Amîn, *Intifâdat*, pp. 15–16.

45. Hussayn 'Abd al-Râziq, *Misr Fî 18 Wa 19 Yanâyir*, pp. 22–23.

46. Ivan Jablonka, *L'histoire est une littérature contemporaine. Manifeste pour les sciences sociales* (Paris, 2014), p. 67.

Too wrapped up in his physical life, the story's main character, Chagara, is not interested in the politics of his country.[47] Unbeknown to him, society's ills are nevertheless reflected in his physical and psychological state. On 18 January 1977, led by others, he is held in a kind of trance by events, and he regains consciousness only at the end of the day.[48] As such, Chagara stands for a people occasionally experiencing life as a collective group, but generally unaware of itself as a greater unity and only aspiring to prosaic goals (a salary rise, an apartment, etc.). Like a people as a whole, Chagara is driven by his political context. The political leader and the author, however, are conscious of what is taking place. Working, in their eyes, to "elevate the people's consciousness", they assume the insurgents are unconscious players.

The human sciences are not exempt from seeing in the insurgent collective a diminished subject that is made up of "unconscious" subjects. Objectivist analyses that explain insurrections but filter out the insurgents as individuals have been attacked for denying them rationality, as E.P. Thompson shows in his work on the moral economy of the crowd in eighteenth-century England, in which he describes insurgents' agency.[49] But instead of abandoning the paradigm of the Cartesian subject, the search for a "moral economy" can reinforce it, positing the "rationality" of the rioters. Thompson defended their rationality, as opposed to irrationality,[50] instead of questioning the relevance of the dichotomy. I have used this fruitful concept but question one aspect of it, pointing out that one may be tempted to integrate the insurgent collective to a narrative that does not make explicit that the group is not defined by a set of properties, and indeed is not a Cartesian subject.[51] I therefore agree with Achille Mbembe when he argues that the "rediscovery of the subaltern subject", in line with an "outdated Marxist tradition", has too often involved a search for the reflection of material conditions in the "subject's consciousness", leading to a reductive functionalism.[52] The main problem with this is that it may hinder listening to moral judgements or partisan projections.

---

47. Al-Majîd, *La maison*, p. 106.

48. *Ibid.*, p. 58.

49. E.P. Thompson explains that food riots usually arose in response to a regulated practice of protest, the purpose of which was to remind merchants and authorities of an earlier consensus, the paternalistic model, in which benevolence towards consumers was required in the market. The disappearance of these practices in the face of the introduction of modern forms of protest (centralization, industrial working class, party, union) has meant forgetting why they existed to begin with. What remains is "a spasmodic view of popular history" where "the common people can scarcely be taken as a historical agent before the French Revolution": Thompson, "The Moral Economy".

50. For instance, Edward Palmer Thompson, *Customs in Common* (London, 1991), pp. 258, 265, 302, 303.

51. Jacques Rancière, *Les mots de l'histoire* (Paris, 1992), p. 62.

52. Achille Mbembe, *On the Postcolony* (Berkeley, CA, 2001), p. 5.

Restoring the forgotten motives of rioters of the eighteenth century or the insurgents of 1977 does not mean that one should construe the motives of the collective formed on the streets as uniform so that it can be analysed – as one would an individual subject. Documenting the creativity of those who have acted consciously is, indeed, to contribute to the history of people's ability to act, as historian John Chalcraft argues.[53] The creation of groups that are consciously acting collectively is, moreover, congruent with revolutionary situations. Nevertheless, can the study of insurrections be limited to their intentional and conscious dimensions, as if they were all to be considered? Is the insurgent collective's ability to act not also a part of the heterogeneity of a movement in the process of being created? It is essential to take into account this multiplicity to examine the history of resistance to liberalization.

1977, final horizon in "collective memory"

With his founding notion of "collective memory",[54] Maurice Halbwachs considers the social conditions of memory production. Individual remembrance is linked to the memory of the social groups with whom experience is shared. This notion can, in turn, reinforce the paradigm of the collective as Cartesian subject and generate certain dead angles, among which is the notion that the 1977 uprising played an exclusively cycle-closing role.

However, the notion of "collective memory", inspired by historian Marie-Claire Lavabre,[55] reveals a hegemonic discourse on the uprising. The traces of the uprising were emblematic of the memory phenomenon because they contribute to a use of the past as a political resource. Proceeding by chronological, moral, or narrative simplification, relying on imprisonments, strikes, or deaths, the Alexandrian witnesses of the investigation matched their individual narratives with the so-called narrative of the groups to which they had belonged: the workers and/or political militants of the arsenal, the Communists of Alexandria, student militants, and so on. The result was a common chronology that gave meaning to the 1977 uprising. A surprisingly stable "collective memory" was thus at work. The congruence between the events at the arsenal, the insurrection of 1977, and Nasserian hopes is so striking that it becomes disturbing: this is a result of the event's being analysed in terms of "collective memory". Indeed, the convergence of notions forged around this concept generates coherence and stability in social science narratives. This relationship to culture, consisting of determining its rules rather

---

53. John Chalcraft, "Thinking Subaltern Activism and Popular Politics in the Middle East and North Africa in Gramscian Perspective", paper presented at the Gramsci in the Middle East: lessons from subaltern rebellions, Scuola Normale Superiore, Firenze, 2019.
54. Halbwachs, *La mémoire collective*.
55. Marie-Claire Lavabre, "Paradigmes de la mémoire", *Transcontinentales. Sociétés, idéologies, système mondial*, 5 (2007), pp. 139–147.

than interpreting its signs, makes it impossible to explore the intertwining of meaning in 1977.[56]

A component of stability, memory was made into a field of political action by communist militants in Egypt from 1995 onwards, the establishment of the Communist Movement Archives Committee until 1965.[57] This committee collected documentation and witness accounts relating to the communist movement until the pivotal date (1965) when the main communist organizations disbanded in order to lend support to Nasser. This date was later commuted in 1977.[58]

"Reform thinking" was also part of active remembrance. My interview with 'Abd al-Majîd attests to this. In his novels, he relays the history of the country in accordance with the doxa of the Egyptian literary field.[59] He assumes this responsibility because he believes that "normal people" do not have memory: their attention is too monopolized by daily obligations: eating; finding shelter; marrying one's children. From this perspective, memory is consciousness. Collective history and individual history occupy parallel worlds that only enlightened beings can bring together.

Following 18–19 January, the measures were withdrawn but the great neoliberal disruption continued, producing the change that conferred on the 1977 uprising its status as the end of an era. Ibrâhîm al-Bâz:

> Most people saw in 1977 a rebirth of the movement, a new beginning, and the starting point of a rapid chain of events that would lead us to a revolution. And the truth, what we discovered afterwards, when we stood back and looked at the events, is that 1977 was what? The last twitch of the dead man.[60]

The years 1967–1977 were a period of intensified protest, of increased unofficial trade union militancy, and of a growth in communist organizations. The latter worked hard to increase their presence. The important presence of their slogans in the 1977 demonstrations and the fact that these were regularly reused was a commonly cited signification of their effectiveness. An important moment in the local establishment of communist groups had taken place just a few months before, during the campaign for the legislative elections of 1976, with the independent candidacy of five communists and

---

56. Clifford Geertz, "Thick Description. Towards an Interpretive Theory of Culture", in *The Interpretation of Cultures: Selected Essays* (New York, 1973).

57. Didier Monciaud, "Un travail de mémoire de la gauche égyptienne", *Cahiers d'histoire. Revue d'histoire critique*, 86 (2002), pp. 115–123.

58. Hannân Ramadân, coordinator of the gathering of additional witness accounts for the Center for Arab and African Research in Cairo, which hosts the committee's research, Interview, 9 May 2013.

59. Samia Mehrez, *Egyptian Writers between History and Fiction. Essays on Naguib Mahfouz, Sonallah Ibrahim and Gamal al-Ghitani* (Cairo, 1994); Richard Jacquemond, *Conscience of the Nation: Writers, State, and Society in Modern Egypt* (Cairo, 2008).

60. Al-Bâz, Interview, 10 May 2013.

many leftist Nasserists. Barely a few months after the events, the president of the Unionist Party, Khâlid Muhyî al-Dîn, said that 1977 represented the departure of the Marxists who were still present in institutions, despite Sadat's efforts to eliminate them.[61]

After his liberation from prison in 1977, Mus'ad al-Tarabilî's whereabouts were strictly controlled. He was arrested again in 1979, 1980, and 1981. He stopped fighting in 1981 and went to work abroad, receiving a higher salary for the same job. His journey ended in 2012, when I met him, on his return from five years spent in China. "I abandoned great hopes in favour of what I could accomplish. I did not want to lose on all fronts, personally and collectively. Rather than great hopes, I focused on what I knew how to do, I trained a lot of people. I built my life."[62]

Increasing emigration was key to the disintegration of the militant world. Thanks to measures put in place under Sadat, it became more common to emigrate: there were about 100,000 workers abroad in 1973 and almost 3 million in 1984.[63] Families also relied more frequently on the resources of a parent who was abroad.[64]

As a result of the 1977 repression and the oil boom, labour demonstrations ceased for a while and did not resume until 1983–1984.[65] More generally, the conditions for collective action evolved with the arrival of President Mubarak in 1981. Sadat had alienated diverse opponents, as illustrated by the arrest of more than a thousand workers' association, political, and religious figures on 5 September 1981. Mubarak immediately released most of them and softened his relations with intellectuals. He proceeded in the same way with the Unionist Party, the legal left, which was increasingly favouring stability over protest.[66] Clandestine communist organizations languished, sometimes preferring militant actions in "civil society".[67]

The frozen aspect of memories of the events of 1977, like the enduring "haunting" of Nasser,[68] were reinforced by the living conditions and militant

---

61. Khâlid Muhyî al-Dîn, "Recenti Sviluppi Democratici in Egitto e l'Assemblea Nationale 1977 Progressista Unitaria", presented at the conference "La Sinistra egiziana e le prospettive del socialismo nel mondo arabo", Rome, 1977, pp. 7–13, quoted by Gennaro Gervasio, *Al-Haraka al-Markisiyya Fî Misr 1967–1981* [Marxist movement in Egypt 1967–1981] (Cairo, 2010), pp. 119, 240–247.
62. Al-Tarabilî, Interview, 16 May 2015.
63. Mostafa Kharoufi, "L'*Infitâh*' et l'envers du décor", *Tiers-Monde*, 31:121 (1990), pp. 209–215.
64. Proof of this may be found in the massive increase of currency transfers into Egypt. Sixty-nine million dollars in 1973 became 3.9 billion dollars in 1984. Kharoufi, "L'*Infitâh*'.
65. Omar El Shafei, *Workers, Trade Unions and the State in Egypt, 1984–1989* (Cairo, 1995).
66. Marsha Pripstein Posusney, *Labor and the State in Egypt, 1952–1994: Workers, Unions, and Economic Restructuring* (New York, 1997), p. 36.
67. Dina El Khawaga, "La génération seventies en Égypte. La société civile comme répertoire d'action alternatif" in Mounia Bennani-Chraïbi *et al.* (eds), *Résistances et protestations dans les sociétés musulmanes* (Paris, 2003).
68. Sara Salem, "Haunted Histories: Nasserism and the Promises of the Past", *Middle East Critique*, 28:3 (2019), pp. 1–17.

life in the 1980s and 1990s, by the memory initiatives undertaken by communist militants, and by the notion of "collective memory". Because this establishes a close link between a community endowed with memory and subject – in the sense of *cogito* – the notion of "collective memory" tends to reify social groups.[69] However, beyond the fact that all groups are always being defined, a wide swathe of the history of the insurrection resides in aspiring and short-lived collectives. Departing from a holistic approach to "collective memory" does not necessarily mean adopting a phenomenological reading of memory linked to individual experiences of the uprising.[70] On the contrary, the research methodology can be adapted to the fluidity of the uprising and the collectives that make it up.

A MANIFOLD INSURRRECTION

In order to reveal the other stories of the January 1977 uprising, one has to break with the quest for a single meaning of the event and a self-conscious insurgent subject. This approach may generate an element of chaos, given that it requires the event to be seen from multiple points of view and temporalities: this diversity makes it difficult to prioritize elements of analysis. Sociologist Charles Kurzman affirms that all insurrectional moments share the element of confusion. Confusion, however, is a single horizon only to the extent that the only alternative to a study of the subjective experience of events is an objective study, a search for the causes of revolution.[71] If we do not wish to apply a holistic and causal approach to writing the history of groups, how is it possible to restore the multiplicity of an event without giving up on producing a consistent historical account?

Instead of contrasting insurgents' perspectives of the event with a teleological reading, which would inscribe the event in a later process that is necessarily unknown to the actors, I prefer to weigh the anchor with regard to the event's future. A history of the manifold event is thus made by jumping back and forth between the eras, ever conscious that it does not have an end point. Subsequent revolts express the elements that were contained in the 1977 uprising: "bread idiom",[72] democratic expectations, the will to overthrow the regime. These later revolts therefore make it possible to highlight aspects of

---

69. Jocelyne Dakhlia, *L'oubli de la cité* (Paris, 1990), p. 11.
70. Claude Romano, "La phénoménologie doit-elle demeurer cartésienne?", *Les Études philosophiques*, 100:1 (2012), pp. 27–48; Paul Ricoeur, *Memory, History, Forgetting* (Chicago, IL, 2009).
71. Charles Kurzman, "Can Understanding Undermine Explanation? The Confused Experience of Revolution: Systems and Mechanisms", *Philosophy of the Social Sciences*, 34:3 (2004), pp. 328–351.
72. Mélanie Henry, "Le 'trésor' révolutionnaire. Insurrections et militantismes à Alexandrie en 1946 et en 1977 (Égypte)" (Ph.D., Université d'Aix-Marseille, 2018), p. 227.

the original event that were previously difficult to describe. This is particularly true of the 2011 uprising.

A counterpoint to leftist accounts

As told by the left, the protests of 1977 circumvented partisan and union political intermediation, as did many protests of the neoliberal era.[73] The protesters did not set up institutions that would allow dialogue and did not intend to take power. What was immature in the eyes of leftist militants was also a rejection, as shown by the avoidance of actions created by official organizations (the General Federation of Egyptian Workers' Unions, the Rally party) and unofficial ones (underground parties and unionists).

On 18 January, unionists and political protesters reflected a desire to see their powerful demonstrations bear fruit. To do so, they consolidated and institutionalized a space of protest within the sphere of their daily actions. Despite the fact that experienced militants demanded that protesters limit their action to spoken slogans, police stations were set on fire.[74] The burning of the headquarters of the Arab Socialist Union in Alexandria probably indicated the rejection of the party that controlled all authorized political life.

In the previous two decades, a considerable part of trade union unrest had been conducted in parallel with the official organization, the General Federation of Egyptian Workers' Unions, and was often aimed against it.[75] However, it was an intervention framework for left-wing activism.

The attitude of the federation towards liberal reforms recalled the ambivalent relation of Communists toward the uprising.[76] Federation president, Salâh Gharîb, had been in favour of the economic open-door policy in April 1975, but pressure from left-wing trade unionists had nevertheless led to the adoption of a reduced version of the measures. The "openness" was seen as a necessity for economic growth, but care had to be taken to preserve the "socialist trajectory".[77]

On the evening of 18 January, the federation leadership denounced the government measures. During their first meeting with Sadat since 1973, the

---

73. Richard Stahler-Sholk *et al.*, "Introduction: Globalizing Resistance: The New Politics of Social Movements in Latin America", *Latin American Perspectives*, 34:2 (2007), pp. 5–16.
74. *Ibid.*
75. Bianchi, *Unruly Corporatism*, p. 143.
76. Gamal Abdel Nasser Ibrahim, "Représentation syndicale et transition libérale en Égypte. Lecture des élections de 1996", *Égypte/Monde arabe*, 33 (1998), pp. 181–223.
77. Protesters succeeded in causing the creation of a committee designed to formulate their recommendations on the *Infitâh*. In October 1976, the Ethical Code of Unionized Work – formed out of the committee's work – was made public in *The Workers*, the Federation's weekly newspaper. Marsha Pripstein Posusney, "Labor as an Obstacle to Privatization: The Case of Egypt", in Iliya F. Harik *et al.* (eds), *Privatization and Liberalization in the Middle East* (Bloomington, IN, 1992), pp. 85–105, 83.

president agreed in principle to all of their requests and undertook to consult them on all legislation concerning workers. As a result, the 1977 uprising made it possible to reassert the federation's status while consolidating its internal leadership position through repression of the union's left wing.[78]

This tendency to break the rules of dialogue between authorities and representative bodies – a tendency found during the "IMF revolts" as well as during the 2011 and 2019 uprisings – can be seen as a sign that a new vocabulary is emerging. It may also be seen as a sign of a lack of interest in "democracy" and/or a desire for effective representative democracy and/or a desire for radical regime change.

Open interpretations

In general, the problem with a teleological reading of the event – and with attributing meaning to any event in a historical chain of events – is that the era in which the actors perceived the event is not considered. Instead of favouring synchronic sources and references known to the actors, one might examine the event from the point of view of its futures. Some features of the event appear retrospectively because they are expressed in fits and starts. The relatively recent character of the 1977 episode, which belongs to a "contemporized past",[79] makes it possible to use the insurrection's existing presences in order to better grasp it. The break with the political system in 1977 displays several characteristics when compared with subsequent events.

The 2005 and 2017 protests over the price and distribution of subsidized flour suggest that a silent tradition, a "bread idiom", was carried over from the January 1977 uprising. Though the uprising did not curb liberalization, it did lead to government reconsideration of the issue of subsidies as early as 19 January; and this was obviously not forgotten. The case of the 2017 protests is salient.[80] Limited to a certain number of towns, they had an ordered structure. Government and police managed road blockades calmly, in contrast to the fierce crackdown on all social and political protest after the summer 2013 coup d'état. Since January 1977, the threat of insurrection has been known to all. As such, protesters have hoped they would be heard playing the first notes of the melody: a route to dialogue has been established. This resonance in the twenty-first century reveals a dimension of the 1977 uprising: it

---

78. Posusney, *Labor and the State*, pp. 23, 25.

79. Jan Assman and John Czaplicka, "Collective Memory and Cultural Identity", *New German Critique*, 65 (1995), pp. 125–133, p. 129.

80. Since a 2014 reform, there have been cards with chips that have allowed holders to access subsidized products, but the system has not yet been implemented throughout the country. There have been consumer complaints that provisioning problems have resulted from the distribution of the cards.

inaugurated a kind of revolt that is in itself interpellation and negotiation with the state.

The political scientist Larbi Sadiki establishes links between "bread revolts" and "democratic achievements" in the 2000s when examining cases of "democratization", which he recognizes as fragile, in Sudan (1985), Algeria (1988), and Jordan (1989). Food insecurity, dramatized by the symbol of bread (*al-'aish*, in Egyptian Arabic, literally meaning life) and engendered by liberal measures, represents a denial of democracy. According to the moral contract of the "bread democracy" widely diffused in the Arab world in the period following independence, the people gave up political rights in favour of social rights: the vote versus bread. Bread protests, that "discontinuous practice of democracy",[81] herald a period of democratization: bread versus the vote. Circumvention of the regime's rules for the political game resulting from independence thus appears as a desire for democracy that, for Sadiki, assumes the form of representative democracy. This analysis would refer to a reformist – as opposed to a revolutionary – dimension of the 1977 protests.

For a segment of the Egyptian Far Left, the 1977 demonstrators' violent acts prove a radicalism that political militants have been unable to grasp. In his 1988 text, Ahmad Sâdiq Sa'd challenged the criticism of the Unionist party, which he described as "reformist", lagging behind popular radicalism. The same idea is supported by Tamer Wageeh and Hossam el-Hamalawy, both journalists and trained politically in the Revolutionary Socialist Tendency movement, which emerged in the 1990s during the break with the Egyptian radical left's history. Though for the Egyptian Communist Party the enemy was limited to "the clientelist wing of the regime",[82] these militants held that an overthrow of the regime was possible.

In a text published shortly before the protests of 25 January 2011, the intellectual 'Adil al-'Umrî condemned the inability of experienced militants and intellectuals to defend the insurgents' justified recourse to violence. He distinguished himself from the previously cited authors in saying that "intellectuals – including from the left wing – are incapable of recognizing, much less understanding, that the masses are larger and more powerful than those they imagine".[83] For al-'Umrî, Marxist and Nasserist intellectuals had accepted the "insurrection's failure because it did not envision toppling the regime and replacing it with a new, acknowledged socialist one".[84]

81. Larbi Sadiki, "Popular Uprisings and Arab Democratization", *International Journal of Middle East Studies*, 32:1 (2000), pp. 71–95.
82. Hossam El-Hamalawy, "1977: The Lost Revolution" (Cairo, 2001).
83. 'Âdil al-'Umrî, "*Qirâ'a Mukhtalifa Li-Intifâdat 18 Wa 19 Yanâyir*" [Another Reading of the Uprising of 18 and 19 January], *Al-Bûsla*, 2011.
84. *Ibid.*

Echoes throughout time

The period beginning in 2011 brought about a redefinition of Egypt's recent history. Nevertheless, in this troubled context, the hegemonic interpretation remained relatively stable. In view of the deconstruction presented in this article, it appears that these testimonies could be read differently. Instead of a reliable memory, the search for a *fluid memory* – that is to say, closely dependent on unstable enunciation – could reveal how the present modifies what we perceive from the past.

It was not uncommon for witness accounts to clash. The analogy between 1977 and 2011 appeared in various ways: a confusion between eras, an association of ideas bringing about a shift from one to the other, whether explicit or implicit, and even true constructions. The witnesses most attached to an internally coherent narrative were not exempt from the effects, sometimes surreptitious, of present hopes about past experience.[85]

CONCLUSION

In conclusion, the analogy between the acting group and the Cartesian subject generated a monolithic understanding of the 1977 uprising. From an emic perspective, according to the logic of "reformist thought" in the Roussillon sense, militants who produce sources and workers at the arsenal identified signs of "backwardness" in their compatriots. Though this "vanguard" may have lost its status during the "de-Nasserization" of the state apparatus and the transition to a new "moral economy" from the 1980s onwards, its ideology has persisted in memories of the event and in a leftist political culture. It even seemed to be emboldened as the world of hope that arose before 1967 sank during the 1980s, and the past was converted into militancy in the 1990s. From an etic perspective, the notion of "collective memory" reinforces the monolithic character of these readings because it highlights the stable dimensions of memory and is connected to institutionalized collective groups. Thompson's concern with restoring rationality to the insurgents is accompanied by the use of an analogy between insurgents and the conscious subject. It thus perpetuates standards of modern struggles such as the party and the union, making the insurrection appear to be a form of "bankrupt" mobilization.

Through a deconstruction of 1977 as the end of a cycle, this article has sought to point out how to make visible other dimensions of the revolt. I have proposed that we study how eras collide and how fluid memory works on events, all the while considering the futures of events as resources

---

85. Mélanie Henry, "Fathallah Mahrûs (1936–2016): L'imagination rebelle d'un ouvrier communiste alexandrin", *Égypte/Monde Arabe*, 17 (2018).

to understand their plurality. Retrospectively, this uprising resonated with other historical events, alternately highlighting the desire for democratic reform, the establishment of a "bread idiom" understood by rulers and ruled alike, and even a desire for regime change. These re-readings provide hints towards the competing logics that were contained in the 1977 event.

From 25 January onwards, there was talk of a "revolution" and signs that certain actors wanted to inaugurate. This movement combined a leaderless dimension and extreme fluidity with the affirmation of a revolutionary identity. Indeed, the 2011 uprising led to the creation of associations, parties, and unions, but, like many of the popular movements of today, it only became institutionalized at its margins. The uproar of the counter-revolution initially reinforced the diagnosis of an absence of "revolutionaries" amid reluctance to engage with the political game.[86] But the 2019 demonstrations – in Algeria, Sudan, Iraq, Chile, and so on – have, in turn, created a retrospective inauguration point. The power of these movements recalls the possibility of the emergence of a new narrative of the 1977 uprising, which, far from suggesting immaturity, would become a sign of revolutionary approaches to come.

---

86. Asef Bayat, *Revolution without Revolutionaries: Making Sense of the Arab Spring* (Stanford, CA, 2017).

IRSH 66 (2021), pp. 181–214 doi:10.1017/S0020859021000183
© The Author(s), 2021. Published by Cambridge University Press on behalf of the
Internationaal Instituut voor Sociale Geschiedenis

Democracy and Adjustment in Niger:
A Conflict of Rationales

VINCENT BONNECASE

Institut des mondes africains
5 cours des Humanités
93300 Aubervilliers, France

E-mail: vincent.bonnecase@cnrs.fr

ABSTRACT: In the early 1990s, Niger saw growing anger towards the military regime in power, not only because of police violence, but also due to its economic and social policies, particularly its first structural adjustment programme. After several months of revolts, the regime fell, giving way to a democratic government in 1991. Under pressure from international financial institutions, the new government quickly embarked on the same economic and social path as the previous one and adopted an adjustment policy, resistance to which had played a fundamental role in its accession to power. The government faced increasing street protests, and was overthrown by the army in January 1996, with most of the population not mobilizing to protect the democratic institutions. This article examines the conflicts of rationales that marked these few years, and shows how, by whom, and to what extent these rationales were opposed in practical terms. It also offers a social history of the adjustments by looking at how they were received by the people. By so doing, it looks back at a moment that has profoundly marked Niger's recent history: in this country, as in others, the adjustments have reconfigured rivalries, produced violence, and left an indelible mark on the political imaginary up to the present day.

The National Conference of Niger, which was meant to lay the foundations for a democratic regime in the country, took place between 29 July and 3 November 1991. It brought together representatives from various sections of Nigerien society and was the culmination of several years of mobilization against the violence of the existing military regime and its economic and social direction. The reduction in public expenses that followed the signature of an initial structural adjustment programme (SAP) with international financial institutions in the early 1980s had led to major demonstrations that were

* I am grateful for the comments shared by the participants of the workshop that we organized on this Special Issue at the International Institute of Social History, especially Leyla Dakhli and Sidy Cissokho.

violently repressed by the authorities. Demonstrations increased in the early 1990s, when the government announced new austerity and liberalization measures and the adoption of a new SAP. It was therefore not unexpected that the delegates to the National Conference would reject any new adjustment policy in 1991, at the same time as the country was undertaking a process of democratization. The first free, multi-party elections in the country's history were held in February 1993. A few months later, the elected government, which was made up in part of people who had marched against the military regime and its liberalization policies in the previous decade, announced that negotiations with the financial institutions would be restarted with a view to adopting a new SAP. When the devaluation of the CFA franc led to a sudden increase in prices in January 1994, the social climate became plagued with deep tensions, intensified by partisan struggles. The new regime was overturned by the army in January 1996, with most people not mobilizing to protect the democratic institutions.[1]

This story brings others to mind. In the early 1990s, many countries in sub-Saharan Africa experienced social revolts against authoritarian regimes that had imposed structural adjustments, which produced democratization processes, the pursuit of adjustments by the democratically elected governments, and the overturn of those elected governments a few years later.[2] Parallels can also be drawn with the Arab Spring revolts that broke out in 2011, founded on aspirations for democracy and improved living conditions, but leading to great disappointment and eventually the restoration of authoritarian rule. As far as Europe is concerned, it might be reminiscent of the trajectory of Greece in 2015, at least in its early stages, when it experienced significant social movements and the installation of a new government that ultimately was forced to bend to international demands and establish a policy that its members had fought against before coming to power.

Every story has its own specific elements, but there is one that links them all: they bring different opposing rationales into play. In the 1990s, a return to an adjustment policy seemed to many Nigeriens to be inconsistent: how could a democratic government that had just been installed close down public services, reduce wages, devalue the currency, increase prices, and generally do the opposite of what it had been elected to do? At the same time, the adoption of an adjustment programme seemed to the international financial institutions to be extremely rational, given the catastrophic state of Nigerien public expenses: how could a poor country continue to spend more than it earned? It is not a question of treating these different rationales – economic and political – as separate, watertight spheres: military coups d'état could also

1. For a political history of Niger written by one of its most prominent actors of the 1990s, see André Salifou, *L'Histoire du Niger* (Paris, 2011).
2. Pearl T. Robinson, "The National Conference Phenomenon in Francophone Africa", *Comparative Studies in Society and History*, 36:3 (1994), pp. 575–610.

have an economic cost, as prior debates on the relationship between democracy and development suggest.[3] It is more a question of anchoring them within actual rivalries in order to see how, by whom, and in what form they were strenuously contested during the democratization process of the 1990s, before "the right thing" was imposed. This will lead us to reflect more generally on the question of rationality and politics. While the idea that there are no other possible policies – the famous "there is no alternative" – has lent legitimacy to the adoption of liberal economic reforms in many democratic societies for about forty years, it is important to see how what is rational from one standpoint can seem totally absurd from another, and how what are perceived as legitimate rationales may be the result of conflicts and power relations.

In this article, I will also seek to provide a social history of adjustments, with a particular focus on how they have been received by the people, following the "politics from below" approach.[4] Structural adjustment programmes have been subjected to numerous critical interpretations of their social effects, in particular through the prisms of education or health.[5] Their propensity for making the poor even more fragile has been widely highlighted, including – retrospectively – by the people who initiated them.[6] However, this critical interpretation, which is based on sources mobilized by international institutions to understand the effects of their policies, has essentially remained a history from within.[7] There are scarcely any popular histories of adjustments that might make it possible to reflect on how they were connected to local political dynamics, and in particular to aspirations for democracy.[8] It is to this area of thought that this article wishes to contribute, starting with the case of Niger, where adjustments have reconfigured antagonism, produced violence and left traces in the political imaginary in a way that still seems particularly enlightening today.

3. Seymour Martin Lipset, "Some Social Requisites of Democracy: Economic Development and Political Legitimacy", *The American Political Science Review*, 53:1 (1959), pp. 69–105.
4. Jean-François Bayart, Achille Mbembe, and Comi Toulabor, *Le politique par le bas en Afrique noire. Contribution à une problématique de la démocratie* (Paris, 1992).
5. See, for example, Hélène Charton and Sarah Fichtner (eds), "Faire l'école", *Politique africaine*, 139: Special Issue (2015); Laëtitia Atlani-Duault and Laurent Vidal (eds), "La santé globale, nouveau laboratoire de l'aide internationale?", *Revue Tiers-monde*, 215:Special Issue (2013), pp. 7–164.
6. Joseph Stiglitz, *La Grande Désillusion* (Paris, 2002).
7. Jeffrey Chwieroth, *The Capital Idea, the IMF and the Rise of Financial Liberalization* (Princeton, NJ, 2010).
8. While there is a significant body of research on the economic effects of democracy, it is far more unusual to ask what liberal economic policies have done for democracy in Africa. On this question, see Ernest Harsch, "Structural Adjustment and Africa's Democracy", *Africa Today*, 40:4 (1993), pp. 7–29; Mojúbàolú Olúfúnké Okome, *A Sapped Democracy: The Political Economy of the Structural Adjustment Program and the Political Transition in Nigeria, 1983–1993* (Lanham, MD, 1998); Kwame Boafo-Arthur, "Ghana: Structural Adjustment, Democratization, and the Politics of Continuity", *African Studies Review*, 42:2 (1999), pp. 41–47.

This work is based on a number of different forms of research conducted in Niamey over a period of ten years, the most recent of which, in 2019, specifically examined the association between democratization and structural adjustments. I have relied on written Nigerien sources, in particular the transcriptions of the discussions at the National Conference, and the press, which was opening up with unprecedented pluralism at the time: these archives reflect not only social mobilizations and grand political plans, but also the general atmosphere and sentiment, and a spirit of the time made up of hopes, expectations, and disappointments. I will also draw on interviews conducted with individuals who took part in the social struggles of the 1980s and 1990s, in particular members of associations and trade unions, as well as people who did not belong to political organizations but who experienced the moment through discussions on street corners and events in their daily lives.[9] Using these different sources as my starting point, the challenge, from a narrative standpoint, is to tell a story with an unhappy ending, albeit one punctuated by moments of popular joy. While inviting an "eventful conception" of temporality,[10] I will also focus on each of these moments individually, without interpreting them in the light of what happened later.

WHEN "ADJUSTED" PEOPLES ASPIRED TO DEMOCRACY

In present-day Niamey, it is not easy to imagine a time when, for a large number of Nigeriens, democracy offered the prospect of not only greater participation in political life by everybody, but also an improvement in living conditions. It is more common to recall the democratization of the 1990s as a catastrophe from this standpoint. In order to imagine a moment such as this, one must plunge back into the social revolts and everyday discontent that marked the end of the authoritarian regime, distinguishing between this story and the memories its protagonists may have of it, informed by what happened subsequently. More broadly, contrary to any retrospective constructivism, it means asking what makes it possible from the sources to understand

---

9. A large part of the interviews with members of trade unions and political organizations took place around Alternative Espaces Citoyens, many of whose members had mobilized in the years between 1980 and 1990, and maintained a relative distance from government matters. My interviews with non-militants were carried out in two working-class districts: the one I was living in, Kirkisoye, on the outskirts, and the other where I spent a good number of days, the Petit Marché district, in the centre.

10. William Sewell, "The Temporalities of Capitalism", *Socio-Economic Review*, 6:3 (2008), pp. 517–537. See also the exhortation to take "what is going on" and "currently emerging situations" seriously and question restoring authoritarianism in Amin Allal and Marie Vannetzel, "Des lendemains qui déchantent? Pour une sociologie des moments de restauration", *Politique africaine*, 146 (2017), p. 27.

what other futures might have been possible and envisaged by those who lived through those times.[11]

The torments of the "conjoncture"

At the beginning of the 1980s, Niger was under an authoritarian government. The single-party regime that had been established under President Diori Hamani at the time of independence was overturned by a coup d'état in 1974, and the country passed into the control of a Supreme Military Council (CMS) led by Lieutenant Colonel Seyni Kountché until 1987. During this period, visible protests were limited: opposition parties were banned, mobilizations were strictly monitored, and the workers' unions, which were part of the Union des Syndicats des Travailleurs du Niger (USTN), practiced "responsible participation", to use its leaders' terminology.[12] This did not prevent ordinary anger from being displayed towards the regime, although its forms and purposes are hard to decipher because it was essentially situated outside the most expected political spaces, and cannot be inferred from mobilizations.[13]

We will begin with the fact that the 1980s corresponded with a period of greater material difficulties for the Nigerien working classes, compared with the second half of the 1970s. Following the fall of President Diori Hamani, the country's economy had enjoyed a relative boom thanks to uranium, its main extractive resource, exports of which had quadrupled, with prices rising to five times between 1974 and 1980. In the first place, this benefited foreign companies, which owned almost seventy per cent of the share capital of the uranium mines, but it also translated into a significant increase in the Nigerien state's resources, enabling it to build schools and clinics, support manufacturing, and develop public services, while also greatly increasing wages, with the minimum wage more than doubling over five years.[14] By contrast, some data identify a stagnation, or even a deterioration, in living conditions in the 1980s. Whereas the number of primary school teachers doubled between 1975 and 1980, it increased by just twenty-five per cent between 1981 and 1986, which only made it possible to keep the average number of pupils per class at forty-three.[15] The number of Nigerien doctors peaked in

11. Frederick Cooper, *Le colonialisme en question. Théorie, connaissance, histoire* (Paris, 2010), p. 29.
12. Mamadou Gazibo, "Gloire et misère du mouvement syndical nigérien", *Politique africaine*, 69 (1998), pp. 126–134.
13. By investigating ordinary anger without inferring mobilizations or collective action, I am pursuing an approach I used in my work in Burkina Faso. See Vincent Bonnecase, *Les prix de la colère. Une histoire de la vie chère au Burkina Faso* (Paris, 2019), pp. 11 ff.
14. Emmanuel Grégoire, "Niger. Un état à forte teneur en uranium", *Hérodote*, 142 (2011), p. 211.
15. "Direction de la Statistique et de la Démographie", *Annuaire statistique. Séries longues* (Niamey, 1991), p. 65.

1980, and fell during the remainder of the decade, while the number of nurses grew slower than the population.[16] Domestic household water consumption, which increased steadily during the 1970s, fell suddenly in the 1980s, while a drop in food production led to a famine in the middle of the decade.[17]

The 1980s was also the exact period when an SAP was implemented in Niger. Faced with a decline in the price of uranium, the Nigerien government saw its external debt quadruple between 1980 and 1982, becoming a third of the country's gross domestic product.[18] This led Niger to enter into negotiations with international financial institutions, which, following a process of ideological transformation, had made liberalization the first condition for the development of the African continent.[19] In 1982, an initial "stabilization programme" signed with the IMF imposed significant budget cuts and economic liberalization measures, while allowing the government to restructure its external debt. Four similar agreements were signed between 1983 and 1986, which, taken as a whole, constituted Niger's first SAP.[20]

While this period has remained in the collective memory as a time of great difficulties, there is nothing to indicate that the Nigerien people attributed their problems to the adjustment policies at the time. The first SAP was barely mentioned in the press, except retroactively some years later,[21] and the very concept of "adjustment" was still unknown to many people.[22] It was another term with economic connotations that became used as a popular way to describe the difficulties affecting the population, or the "conjuncture" ("downturn"). Initially used by Nigerien political leaders to mean an "economic downturn" after the years of development supported by income from uranium, "conjuncture" rapidly became part of the vocabulary of daily life. One also sees it being used in the press and in university writings from the early 1980s,[23] as well as in ordinary, everyday conversations, including those in Djerma, Tamasheq, and Peul (the country's main languages). Everyone used the word "conjuncture", even if they did not speak French. In the words of a retired former government official, "everyone [understood]

---

16. *Ibid.*, p. 51.

17. *Ibid.*, pp. 97 and 136.

18. *Ibid.*, p. 221.

19. Dieter Plehwe, "The Origins of the Neoliberal Economic Development Discourse", in Philip Mirowski and Dieter Plehwe (eds), *The Road from Mont Pelerin: The Making of the Neoliberal Thought Collective* (London, 2009), pp. 238–279.

20. Salifou, *Histoire du Niger*, p. 291.

21. "Conférence débat sur la situation socio-économique du Niger. Une politique d'ajustement est incontournable", *Le Sahel*, 23 April 1990.

22. According to my interviews, no one recalled having heard any talk of adjustment when the first SAP was implemented in the 1980s, while the second SAP was immediately popularized as such in the 1990s.

23. Archives Diplomatiques, Nantes (hereafter, AD), Niamey-105, USN, "Le Niger à l'heure de la conjoncture", 18 March 1983.

everyone who said, 'there's the *conjoncture*', 'there's the *conjoncture*'".[24] The great popularization of the word in Nigerien society showed a popular propensity for appropriating economic objects and giving them a new meaning associated with its own reality.[25]

Not everyone shared the same concept of what the "conjuncture" was, however. Everybody had had a particular experience of it, even though one person's memory would partially reflect someone else's and produce a shared memory for both of them. One of its great manifestations, which is cited repeatedly, is that "there was no money" or that "it wasn't circulating".[26] In the 1980s, the "conjuncture" therefore became a customary reason for rejecting requests for material assistance from one's family circle. A usual way of addressing these requests was to say in Haoussa: "abokina yanzou babou koudi, conjoncture tche" ("My friend, there's nothing, there's a downturn").[27] This lack of money in circulation limited opportunities for remunerative business activities as well as informal solidarity relationships, which was inconsistent with people's moral representations of the proper functioning of the economy.[28]

Another way in which the "conjuncture" manifested itself markedly was through price increases or, more covertly, through operations aimed at camouflaging the increase by changing the weight or volume of consumer goods. Hence the "conjuncture" is sometimes recalled as a moment when litres stop being "real litres" and kilos stopped being "real kilos".[29] These operations left a trace in the vernacular names given to consumer goods. The best-known example is the bottle used for Braniger, the most widely consumed beer in the country: in 1986, it went from 66 to 48 centilitres with no change in price, which led its consumers to call it "the conjuncture".[30] Another example was bread: consumption had increased since the 1970s under the influence of international aid, but its per-unit price was changed regularly by official decree. Today, if one asks a bread seller for a "quarter of a baguette", he cuts it into three pieces and takes a piece: in other words, a whole baguette is made up of three "quarters" (both in French and in the local languages). This can lead to assumptions about the past, as we see in this interview with a man who was born during the "conjuncture", and his wife:

24. Interview with D., a former public official, Niamey, 6 March 2019.

25. Jane Guyer, *Marginal Gains: Monetary Transactions in Atlantic Africa* (Chicago, IL, 2004).

26. Interviews in the Petit Marché district of Niamey, March 2019.

27. Interview with D., a former public official, Niamey, 6 March 2019.

28. Jane Guyer, Kabiru Salami, and Olusanya Akinlade, "'Kò s'ówó'. Il n'y a pas d'argent!", *Politique africaine*, 124 (2011), pp. 43–65.

29. Vincent Bonnecase, "Politique des prix, vie chère et contestation sociale à Niamey. Quels répertoires locaux de la colère?", *Politique africaine*, 130 (2013), p. 108.

30. 2019 saw the end of the "conjuncture" as a bottle of beer: Braniger went out of business.

Me:	How many quarters are there in a loaf of bread?
The wife:	Three.
Her husband interrupts:	No, no, four. "Quarters" means that it's divided into four.
She replies:	Yes, but there are three quarters in a baguette, no? I'm talking about bread. As for the rest, I don't know [laughter]. Maybe when you were small, baguettes were bigger.[31]

One last frequently cited manifestation of the "conjuncture" was the increased difficultly in attaining salaried status, which has a tangible and moral resonance that goes beyond just the salaried workers. After independence, the development of salaried employment gave rise to strong expectations, not only because its tangible repercussions had multiplied due to redistribution, but also because it supported shared ways of expressing expectations of justice from the authorities, particularly in urban spaces.[32] The "conjuncture" years corresponded to a period when these salary resources dried up: while the number of salary earners quadrupled in the private sector during the 1970s, it declined in the 1980s.[33] The number of government employees increased tenfold between 1961 and 1984, before stagnating.[34] Even today, this drop in salary resources is still remembered – through repeated failures to pass the civil service entrance examinations, the scarcity of offers of employment, or the loss of a family member's job – as is the resentment this caused towards the regime of the time.[35]

The fact that this decade-long downturn period meant years of material problems was nothing exceptional in itself: the previous decade had also been noteworthy for the most significant episodes of drought and famine since the beginning of the twentieth century, which associated the whole of Sahel with great poverty in collective perceptions for many years.[36] What was new about the 1980s, which led to the popularity of the word "conjoncture", was more the fact that a central significance in these problems, which were experienced by most people on a daily basis, was attributed if not to the direction of the economic policies, then certainly to the economy itself.

31. Interview with R. and K., residents of Kirkisoye, 12 March 2019.
32. Bonnecase, *Les prix de la colère*, pp. 170–191.
33. Direction de la statistique et de la démographie, *Annuaire statistique*, pp. 76–77.
34. *Ibid.*, pp. 82–83.
35. Interviews in the Petit Marché district of Niamey, March 2019.
36. Vincent Bonnecase, *La pauvreté au Sahel* (Paris [etc.], 2011).

Economic anger, political anger

Although this powerful economic resentment translated into only a limited number of protests in an extremely authoritarian context, they were not totally non-existent. At the time, the principal protest force was the Union des Scolaires Nigériens (USN). Formed in 1960, it initially brought together the country's college and high-school students, as well as Nigerien students abroad. With the opening of the University of Niamey in 1973, the USN experienced a growth that led to a larger number of strikes and protests in the country that went far beyond teaching issues.[37] A study of these mobilizations reveals an increasingly close association between challenging the repressive dimension of the military government and its economic direction in the context of the adjustments: the USN played an important role in this combined rejection of authoritarianism and liberalization policies during the 1980s.

The tracts written by the USN offer a good overview of its activities. They were carefully collected by the French consular services as part of the surveillance of the former colony, making it possible to utilize them today to gauge the evolution of the union body during a period of adjustment. In the 1970s and 1980s, the tracts focused on living conditions, not only in schools and universities, but also in the country as a whole due to the impact of repeated droughts. Significantly, the most important movements led by the USN in this period took place in 1973, 1976, and 1983, all years of significant national food shortages.[38] During these years, the image of a "hungry people" was a recurring one in the tracts distributed in Niamey, along with scholarships, student housing, and the organization of examinations. This image had a literal significance in the country as a significant segment of the population suffered from hunger and malnutrition, but it also had a more metaphorical meaning, in that the authorities' responsibility for the production of food and the image of the granary state are a fundamental register of political legitimacy.[39]

In the 1980s, the government's economic direction, apart from the question of people's living conditions, became a more significant motive for mobilizations by school and university students. The first stabilization programme, which was signed with the International Monetary Fund (IMF) in 1982, imposed significant budget cuts for the civil service. The effects of this were immediately visible in the education sector: the government adopted a declaration known as "Zinder", which proposed that the State's education costs be

---

37. On the history of the USN, see Tatiana Smirnova, "Student Activism in Niger: Subverting the 'Limited Pluralism', 1960–83", *Africa*, 89 (2019), pp. 167–188; Tatiana Smirnova and Camille Noûs, "La violence comme mode de régulation politique. La CASO et les mobilisations étudiantes dans le Niger des années 1990", *Politique africaine*, 157 (2020), pp. 223–232.

38. Boureima Alpha Gado, *Une Histoire des famines au Sahel. Étude des grandes crises alimentaires (xixe–xxe siècles)* (Paris, 1993).

39. Vincent Bonnecase, "Faim et mobilisations sociales au Niger dans les années 1970 et 1980. Une éthique de la subsistance?", *Genèses*, 81 (2010), pp. 5–24.

transferred to the parents of pupils and to local governments.[40] This was when the World Bank and the IMF made their first appearance in USN tracts, signalling a notable development in its discourse. Although it had always had an international dimension, France had been the focus of criticism up to that time, whether it was a question of its "companies [giving up] the country to imperialism",[41] its "neo-colonial" government,[42] or its head of state, who was presented as the "President of the French Republics of Africa".[43] In the early 1980s, the Bretton Woods institutions became a new target of the USN, which accused the CMS of "delivering the country bound hand and foot into the jaws of the IMF" after it signed a new stabilization agreement in 1983.[44]

This new development overlapped with a growing rejection of authoritarianism, while Seyni Kountché's regime hardened its attitude towards protests. In May 1983, against the backdrop of the rejection of the Zinder declaration, the USN's mobilizations gave rise to extensive repression. Starting from a highly localized conflict,[45] they led to the largest protest demonstration Niamey had seen since independence, bringing together "a thousand people",[46] according to the French Embassy, and "several thousand" according to the USN.[47] The authorities reacted violently: dozens of students were imprisoned in a military camp, while others were forcibly recruited into the government administration and sent to regions far from the capital. One of them, Amadou Boubakar, died during interrogation due to "isolation after a slightly overlong march", according to the official version relayed by the French Ambassador, so that there was "no reason to doubt it".[48] This repression put an end to the USN's demonstrations for several years. Officially, it was dissolved, but it continued its struggle against the reductions in public expenses and government violence, the central focus of tracts that continued to be written clandestinely.

"Structural adjustment" was still a relatively abstract notion, however, even among the most militant pupils and students. The latter saw the changes in

40. Conseil national pour la société de développement, *Conférence-débat sur l'école nigérienne. Déclaration de Zinder* (Niamey, 1982).

41. AD, Niamey-105, Association des élèves du lycée national, untitled tract, 22 February 1973.

42. AD, Niamey-105, USN, tract entitled "Échec à la coopération!", 20 January 1972.

43. AD, Niamey-105, USN, Lomé Section, open letter to President Diori, 3 February 1972.

44. AD, "Le Niger à l'heure de la conjoncture".

45. The invalidation of the theses of around twenty students by the École Supérieure d'Agronomie had led to a protest by their colleagues and, as a response, the temporary total closure of the college by the authorities, followed by solidarity mobilizations in other establishments.

46. AD, Niamey-106, letter from the French Ambassador to Niger to the Minister of Foreign Affairs, 13 May 1983.

47. AD, Niamey-105, USN, tract entitled "A la mémoire des scolaires martyrs", 1 May 1985 (handwritten).

48. AD, Niamey-106, letter from the French Ambassador to Niger to the Minister of Foreign Affairs, 13 May 1983.

economic policies through their daily realities far more than through the prism of an ideological struggle against liberalism. Immediately after the signature of the stabilization programme, the Nigerien government put a stop to free school supplies in primary schools and decided to end boarding at colleges and high schools, which was a very real penalty for all the young people who needed to find accommodation because they had come from their villages to study in the city. A similar measure that has remained in the memory shows the way in which liberalization policies were perceived in practice as being relevant to both a new economic direction on the part of the government *and* the brutality of power:[49] stopping boarding meant both reducing public expenses and putting an end to potential hotbeds of dissent in the country, because it was often in these places that pupils and students met to write their tracts and prepare their demonstrations.

The implementation of a policy to ease tension by General Ali Saibou, who came to power after the death of Seyni Kountché in 1987, encouraged renewed mobilizations. Local chapters of the USN, which no longer had any legal existence, re-formed in schools and universities. The Union des Etudiants Nigériens de l'Université de Niamey (UENUN), in particular, became the spearhead of the protest movement. The Nigerien government therefore embarked on the "Education III" project, which was established in 1987 by the World Bank for sub-Saharan countries, and which led to new budget reductions in the education sector.[50] The criteria for granting scholarships were revised to be more selective, and the "programme policy", which guaranteed that students would be recruited into government jobs when they went to university, was abandoned. This had a powerful impact because of the challenges access to the Civil Service by a family member posed for his or her family. This project gave greater visibility to the role of international financial institutions in the country's economic policies. As the country's first independent newspaper explained some years later: "The World Bank entered the Nigerien vocabulary at the time of Education III."[51] Aside from the education issue, economic liberalization became the target of USN tracts, which castigated a "structural adjustment policy [that] leads to the privatization of a certain number of companies and state offices and to the closure of certain sectors that are judged by the international financial bodies to be unprofitable".[52]

At the end of the day, the mobilizations of the 1980s reveal the tangible profile the adjustment gradually acquired among the people who were most invested in the protests within Nigerien society, as well as the political meaning they initially attributed to it. As we know, in many countries, the new liberal doxa was imposed in authoritarian contexts, "the export of liberalism" by

---

49. Interviews at Alternative Espaces Citoyens, Niamey, March 2019.
50. World Bank, "Education III" project (Washington, 1987).
51. "La Banque mondiale prête à aider le Niger si…", *Haské*, 17 December 1991.
52. AD, Niamey-105, USN / UENUN, " Lettre ouverte au chef de l'État ", 23 January 1989.

international institutions having preceded the call for democracy.[53] It is also important to understand, however, what this chronology means through people's representations: in Niger, neoliberal policies were *first* seen as the product of a military regime before *later* being associated with democracy.

From anger to revolt: 1990

On 9 February 1990, Niger experienced a day of insurrection that undoubtedly marks the history of the country to this day, first because of the bloodshed (three demonstrators killed by soldiers and many others injured), but also because of its effects: the day played a key role in the democratization of the country. It was therefore an "event": that is, to use Sewell's approach, facts that modified the structure of the society within which they were produced.[54] By retracing what happened on that day, the various motives that drove its participants, the elements that made it possible, and its immediate ramifications, it becomes possible to show that the revolt was against both authoritarianism and structural adjustment, to the point where it is difficult to distinguish which of them inspired the protesters that year.

At the beginning of 1990, the student activism led by the USN was thriving. Among the most common issues of concern were rejection of the Education III project promoted by the World Bank and the question of scholarships, accommodation, and employment opportunities, as well as political freedoms and rejection of the brutality of the military regime, memories of which were very much alive on the university campus. General assemblies were held in an area that had been baptized "Place AB" in memory of Amadou Boubakar, who had been killed in 1983. A large demonstration was planned for 9 February 1990 in defence of a five-point platform of demands that included access to university works for all students, access to registration, teacher recruitment, the withdrawal of the Education III project, and legal recognition of the USN, which was still officially banned.[55] One of the practical challenges for the organizers was how to cross the bridge linking the University District on the right bank to the rest of the city. Many saw it as an "insurmountable obstacle":[56] in previous years, students had made a habit of crossing it by night in small groups on the eve of demonstrations and then assembling in Place de la Concertation, which began to emerge as a "place of anger".[57]

53. Yves Dezalay and Bryant Garth, *The Internationalization of Palace Wars: Lawyers, Economists, and the Contest to Transform Latin America States* (Chicago, IL, 2002).
54. William Sewell, "Historical Events as Transformations of Structures: Inventing Revolution at the Bastille", *Theory and Society*, 25:6 (1996), pp. 841–881.
55. Archives of the UENUN, University of Niamey (hereafter, AU), "Plateforme revendicative du 8 décembre 1989".
56. Interview with T., a former Secretary-General of the UENUN, 7 March 2019.
57. Hélène Combes, David Garibay and Camille Goirand, (eds), *Les lieux de la colère. Occuper l'espace pour contester, de Madrid à Sanaa* (Paris, 2015).

On the morning of 9 February, there was a widespread feeling of danger on campus: in addition to the memory of Amadou Boukaré, the fate reserved for similar demonstrators on the continent was a feature of all the discussions. Less than a year earlier, the repression of a demonstration in Lubumbashi in Zaire had led to the death of a student (according to the official report).[58] Some elected "to drink [...] a litre of whisky or pastis before days of action, [as that] gives you more courage on the marches".[59] In the centre of the city, an initial gathering in Place de la Concertation was dispersed at dawn with truncheons, and the bridge was guarded by around a hundred police officers, who were ordered not to let the demonstrators through.[60]

When the demonstrators arrived at the police barrier, a delegation asked the officers to allow them through, but the authorities refused, instead ordering them to disperse. Tear gas was used, and the students responded by throwing rocks and Molotov cocktails, while covering their faces with wet handkerchiefs so they could breathe.[61] The police called in reinforcements from the Republican Guard, the Gendarmerie, and the Fire Service, in line with the "foreseen plan of action", as those responsible for operations in the field explained later.[62] The troops opened fire. For many students, it was the first time they had heard the crack of gunfire, and when they saw demonstrators falling, they understood that they were real bullets.[63] Panic set in, and the demonstrators retreated towards the university campus. Three protesters were killed on the bridge: Alio Nahanchi; Maman Saguirou; and Issaka Kaïné.

The day was a tipping point in protests against the regime. After what the government organ called a "regrettable blunder",[64] protests intensified and spread to other sectors of society. The three students who had been killed on 9 February were buried the following day, after a silent march that included not only students, but also their families and parent associations, as well as locals who had no ties to the victims. Some people recall that as their first demonstration, although they were just children at the time.[65] On 16 February, there was another protest march, which the USTN joined, marking a turning point in the history of the country's biggest workers' trade union. This demonstration was given a religious dimension, with the trade unionists referring to a Muslim practice of reciting verses from the Koran in memory of the dead a week after their deaths. This allowed people to express their "support along

58. Interview with A., a former member of the USN, Niamey, 2 March 2019.
59. Interview with I., a former member of the USN executive, Niamey, 7 March 2019.
60. National Archives of Niger, Niamey (hereafter, ANN), 11W8.12, National Conference of Niger, discussions on 20 August 1991 dedicated to 9 February 1990.
61. Interview with M., a former member of the USN, Niamey, 3 March 2019.
62. ANN, 11W8.12.
63. Interview with T., a former member of the USN, Niamey, 3 March 2019.
64. "Une bavure regrettable", *Le Sahel*, 7 March 1990.
65. Interviews in the Petit Marché district of Niamey, March 1990.

the way, murmuring 'Allahou Akbar'".[66] Although many do not recognize themselves in this practice, because a good number of trade unionists looked more to historical materialism than they did to spirituality,[67] it nonetheless contributed to the expansion of a struggle to which everyone was able to attribute their own meaning.

The shift also lent support to the very purpose of the mobilizations. Up to that time, it had been above all about opposing the violence of the regime while struggling for better living conditions. After 9 February, the establishment of democratic institutions became a full-blown cause. It was driven by a favourable international climate due to similar struggles taking place in neighbouring countries, led by Benin, where a National Conference declaring itself to be sovereign had just been formed.[68] The mobilized populations referred primarily to local realities, however. Although the university year was declared to be "white" (meaning that no diplomas would be validated), students and workers increased the numbers of demonstrations to denounce the government's responsibility for the "massacre of 9 February", while also demanding political openness. Ali Saibou's government was obliged to retreat in the face of these protests, giving the USN legal recognition and allowing greater freedom of expression. In May, the first independent newspaper, *Haské* ("Clarity" in Haoussa) saw the light of day. On 15 June 1990, the Higher Council for National Orientation, the country's principal government authority, recommended a revision of the Constitution with a view to the development of democratic pluralism.[69] It was five days before the Franco-African Summit in La Baule, which went virtually unnoticed in Niamey.[70]

The demand for democracy, however, was closely linked to material expectations that expressed themselves through an increasingly widespread rejection of structural adjustment policies, even as pressure from international financial institutions increased. After a visit to Niger by a World Bank-IMF mission, the prime minister announced the adoption of a framework economic policy document in September 1990, prior to the signature of a new SAP calling for the "reduction of the wage bill", "the privatization of public enterprises", and "the dissolution of those for which it has been determined that there is no possibility of a turnaround".[71] The protests against the regime, where it was now possible to hear slogans like "the SAP will not pass!",[72] multiplied and

---

66. "Les commémorations du 9 février", *Haské*, 1 April 1991.
67. Interview with I., a former member of the USN executive, Niamey, 7 March 2019.
68. Richard Banégas, *La démocratie à pas de caméléon. Transition et imaginaires politiques au Bénin* (Paris, 2003).
69. "Multipartisme et développement", *Le Sahel*, 2 July 1990.
70. This summit, during which François Mitterrand stipulated that French aid to Africa would now be contingent on the adoption of democratic reforms, would sometimes be put forward as one of the main factors behind the democratization of the continent.
71. "Programme d'ajustement structurel. L'envers et l'endroit", *Le Sahel*, 18 September 1990.
72. Interview with former members of the USN, Niamey, March 2019.

increasingly radical methods were adopted. In Niamey, road transport trade unions blocked traffic, leading to violent clashes between the police and protesters, several of whom were arrested.[73] In other towns, students attacked symbols of the state, including the police station in Maradi, which was stoned, and the Court in Arlit, which was attacked with clubs.[74] For its part, the USTN organized a five-day inter-profession strike, during which Niamey saw its largest protest since independence. Some days later, Ali Saibou proclaimed a multi-party system, and announced that a National Conference would shortly be summoned. *Haské* enthusiastically proclaimed that these were "days that will turn everything around":

> Today's establishment of a multi-party system in Niger is the result of the pressure put on the government by the latest five-day strike. The strike is, of course, part of a series of protest movements driven principally by the trade unions and students, the most dramatic of which was the massacre of 9 February. But due to the extent of its outcome (a virtually total paralysis of all the country's activities) and the demonstration of strength to which it gave rise (almost a hundred thousand people took to the streets in Niamey alone), [this mobilization] shows that the social instability is [...] an expression of profound discontent.[75]

At the beginning of the 1990s, virtually the whole of sub-Saharan Africa experienced a wave of democratization following the events in Niger. Contrary to analyses that stress the role played by exogenous factors, from the fall of the Berlin Wall to the summit in La Baule, it is now acknowledged that these transformations were more fundamentally related to local dynamics that revealed the historical narrative of democratic practices on the African continent.[76] However, only very rarely has any study had the objective of studying the actual course of mobilizations (especially if one makes a comparison with what was done at the same time in other parts of the world, in particular Eastern Europe), or studying the "crowd" phenomena taking place in the streets, almost experimentally revealing how these mobilizations can "take off" and, in a manner of speaking, "stick".[77] In the case of Niger, a new look at this process clearly reveals a close connection between democratic struggles, state violence, and structural adjustments, to the point where rejection of the SAP became an important element of political legitimacy for those who took to the streets against the military regime.

---

73. "Altercations entre syndicalistes et 'briseurs de grève'", *Haské*, 30 August 1990.
74. "Débordement de manifestants à Maradi et à Arlit", *Haské*, 15 November 1990.
75. "Les cinq jours qui firent tout basculer", *Haské*, 15 November 1990.
76. Jean-François Bayart, "La démocratie à l'épreuve de la tradition en Afrique subsaharienne", *Pouvoirs*, 129 (2009), pp. 27–44.
77. Michel Dobry, "Les causalités de l'improbable et du probable. Notes à propos des manifestations de 1989 en Europe centrale et orientale", *Cultures & Conflits*, 17 (1995), p. 2.

THE FALL

From 29 July 1991 to 27 January 1996: these two historic dates are barely four and a half years apart. The former is when the Nigerien Conference opened at a time of shared optimism,[78] while the latter is the date of a military coup d'état that led to a sense of resignation, and even drew some support among a good part of the population.[79] Here, it is not a question of putting the internal and external causes into perspective – following a dialectic of inside and outside – in the fall of Nigerien democracy less than five years after it had been established. The issue is to show that this emerging democracy saw immediately what was possible, albeit impeded by the liberal economic policy that was imposed on it, not only because it limited the ability of the new leaders to act, but also because it conflicted with the political imaginaries that had led to the social revolt against the military regime in the first place.

Starting from joy

It was a beautiful scene, so much so that some spectators report that its main protagonist slightly overplayed his role.[80] It was 15 August 1991 and André Salifou had just been appointed to lead the presidium charged with coordinating the work of the National Conference. He rose to speak to thank his opponent, who had withdrawn in his favour. His voice broke, and he crouched down and hid his eyes while the over 1,000 delegates who had gathered in a packed sports hall stood to applaud.[81] The scene reveals a particular moment in Nigerien history, one charged with emotion, which is not easy to retrace if one only uses oral memories. When this moment is invoked in the streets of Niamey, the accounts related about it often devalue or deride it. What took place later influences these accounts, because we know what happened after the conference, i.e. four and a half years of social tension, opposition along party lines, and disappointments, culminating in a coup d'état. When listening to various sources, the whole problem lies with recreating the emotional tone of the initial moment without weighing it down with the feelings that came later.

78. Élodie Apart, "Les modalités de la transition démocratique au Niger: l'expérience de la conférence nationale", in Bernard Salvaing (ed.), *Pouvoirs anciens, pouvoirs modernes de l'Afrique d'aujourd'hui* (Rennes, 2015), pp. 153–167.
79. Patrick Quantin, "Retour sur l'analyse d'un coup d'État", *Politique africaine*, 62 (1996), pp. 113–116; Emmanuel Grégoire and Jean-Pierre Olivier de Sardan, "Le Niger. Mise au point et suite", *Politique africaine*, 63 (1996), pp. 136–141.
80. Discussion at LASDEL, 1 March 2019.
81. This scene can be viewed in the first minute of the documentary *La Conférence nationale. 98 jours de vérité*, which Mahamane Mamadou made about the conference. A significant part of the discussions was filmed by the Office de Radiodiffusion et de Télévision du Niger (ORTN). Available at: https://www.youtube.com/watch?v=hNiiW5F6CkI; last accessed 25 February 2021.

In the months preceding the conference, events that would have seemed unthinkable just a few years earlier reflected people's high spirits. One of the most remarkable of these was the women's marches demanding a greater place in future debates. When the National Committee for the Preparation of the National Conference (CNPCN) met in May 1991, it had only one female participant, who resigned in protest against the male hegemony. A large march organized on 13 May from Place de la Concertation brought thousands of women together (see Figures 1 and 2). There were banners that read "No to the Conference without women", "Discrimination" and "We defend our rights".[82] Four days later, a group of women blocked the discussions at the CNPCN, booing the participants who were already in the building and preventing others from accessing it. One of the initiators of this action, who was a trade unionist, castigated the idea that a preparatory committee should only include men on the pretext that it was "technical".[83] Six new women were eventually admitted to the committee.[84]

The selection of the delegates to the National Conference was also a matter of controversy at times. At the end of its work, the CNPN called for 1,204 delegates representing the political parties, the trade unions (nearly all of which were affiliated with the USTN or the USN), employers, and the government.[85] Although most of the delegates were selected internally by their own organizations, their selections also gave rise to public opposition, particularly as regards the representatives from the so-called rural world. The CNPN had only provided for sixty-four delegates for each of the country's rural districts, explaining that the farmers were "politically unorganised, and therefore fragile and easily corrupted" by the government.[86] They were the only members of the National Conference whose representation was territorial rather than organizational. In certain districts, there was a rivalry among farmers caused by the ongoing transformations and cooperatives, which were the main organized rural structures and answered to the prefectures. The delegate from Gouré, Aliou Aboubakar, explained that he had succeeded in having himself appointed before the cooperatives from the district tried to send their own candidate to Niamey. At the conference, he became the best-known representative of the rural world, to the point where he pursued his future political career under the name "Monde Rural", which he kept until the end of his life.[87]

82. I am basing this on photos that appeared in *Le Sahel* and *Haské*.

83. "Madame Bagna Aissata Fall, présidente du Comité de coordination des femmes pour la participation à la commission préparatoire de la conférence nationale", *Haské*, May 1991.

84. "Les travaux de la commission reprennent dans la sérénité", *Le Sahel*, 20 May 1991.

85. ANN, 1W1.1, Conférence nationale, Acte fondamental, "Statuts", 20 July 1991.

86. ANN, 1W2.2, National Conference, summary report for 1 August 1991.

87. Interview with Aliou Aboubakar, known as Monde Rural, a former rural world delegate at the National Conference, Niamey, 15 August 2009.

Figures 1 and 2. Women's demonstration before the National Conference. Photographs published in *Haské*, 1–30 May 1991 and *Le Sahel*, 14 May 1991.

Figures 1 and 2. Continued.

On 29 July 1991, President Ali Saibou "declared the conference of the living forces of the nation open".[88] It rained hard that day. A USN representative who was staying on the university campus alongside delegates from the rural world recalls them showing their joy, mocking a military regime that was able to block everything, "even the rain for the harvests".[89] The following day, the headline in *Haské* read "How great democracy is", while discussing the "conference of every hope", with photos showing the smiling faces of women and men with raised fists.[90] Even the government organ *Le Sahel* had to acknowledge that "joy could be read on every face".[91] On the second day, the National Conference declared itself sovereign, thereby relegating Ali Saibou and his government to the background.[92] The Seyni Kountché Sports Complex, where the conference was held, was renamed the Stade du 29 Juillet, while the crossroads giving on to the Niger Bridge was named Place des Martyrs in memory of the great demonstration that had been brutally suppressed a year and a half earlier.[93]

Apart from these most significant initial decisions, the period of the conference was characterized by a totally new kind of freedom of expression in a country where one might have been afraid of picking up a tract a few years earlier. As the co-founder of the first Nigerien satirical magazine, *Le Paon africain*, recalls, "[p]eople were not afraid to talk; it was new. Even [in government bodies] there was a free tone; you could find caricatures of the Head of Government [...]. It had never been seen before".[94] That an acting president should have to step aside before a conference that proclaimed itself sovereign, that a head of state should be obliged to explain his actions, that military officers could be challenged by civilians – these were all things even the most optimistic activists would not have been able to imagine at the beginning of the decade.[95] Even those who are now the most critical of the conference retain a lingering sense of how exceptional it was, which permeates their interviews almost in spite of themselves. An elderly inhabitant of the area

88. ANN, 1W3.1, National Conference, opening address by Ali Saibou, the President of the Republic, 29 July 1991.
89. Interview with M., a former USN delegate at the National Conference, Niamey, 2 March 2019. This ironic attribution of responsibility for the climate echoed a previous one: in 1974, during a drought, the CMS had invested in aeroplanes that allegedly stimulated clouds to artificially cause rain ("Pluies provoquées. Le directeur de la météorologie nationale parle des conditions de réussite de l'opération ", *Le Sahel*, 3 July 1974).
90. "Que c'est beau la démocratie", *Haské*, 8 to 16 August 1991.
91. "Le grand départ", *Le Sahel*, 30 July 1991.
92. "La conférence nationale s'autoproclame souveraine", *Le Sahel*, 31 July 1991.
93. ANN, 1W1.37, National Conference, act naming various public places and buildings in the urban community of Niamey, 30 July 1991.
94. Interview with A., a journalist and cartoonist, Niamey, 1 March 2019.
95. Interview with I., a former member of the USN executive, Niamey, 7 March 2019.

around the Petit Marché started out talking about "deceit" and "settling accounts" before comparing the National Conference of Niger to those taking place in other West African countries at the same time:

> Ours was an exceptional conference. It wasn't like the others. [...] It lasted at least, almost three months. It was the longest, longer than Benin or Mali. In Lomé [Togo], when it began, it was one month. Only one month. Eyadema said: "One month, and that's all, and your sovereignty, that's in the hall down there, and it stays down there". Here, they sacked the President of the Republic. They got someone else. The President of the Republic didn't represent anything. The President was separate. They did what they liked.[96]

Of course, the conference did not enjoy the same reception from every sector of society in 1991. It was monitored especially closely at the university, where students decided to remain on campus for the entire summer. General meetings were arranged in the evenings to talk about the discussions of the day and prepare for the next one with the USN representatives. As one explained, "we built fires in front of the buildings, we drank tea, we quoted Che Guevara and Marx, and we had the feeling that we were heirs to the revolutionaries".[97] Civil servants, even those who worked far from Niamey, also followed the Conference very closely. Many said they had listened to the meetings on the radio every day, including one teacher in a village in the centre of the country: "All the civil servants had a lot of hope", he explained, and "this did not only include the civil servants, as their wages helped many family members to live, apart from their wives and children".[98] The widespread distribution of newspapers also testifies to the interest these workers took in the discussions that were under way: the circulation of *Haské* reached 15,000 copies during the National Conference (compared with 5,000 earlier), figures that no Nigerien news organization has ever seen since.[99]

The welcome the conference received went beyond the social classes who were originally the most directly concerned, however, this is harder to measure. The Office de Radiodiffusion et de Télévision du Niger (ORTN) broadcast the meetings daily in the country's various national languages, which enabled those who did not speak French to follow the discussions. What was new about these broadcasts compared to the usual news relays needs to be assessed. Up to then, it had little room for the unexpected, because it was monitored and censored by the authorities, and when something unexpected arose that might cause problems for the government, it took days for news to spread throughout the entire country, as the (fixed) telephone system was

---

96. Interview with S., a former soldier, Niamey, 5 March 2019.
97. Interview with A., a former member of the USN, Niamey, 4 March 2019.
98. Interview with W., a former teacher, Niamey, 28 February 2019.
99. Marie-Soleil Frère, *Presse et démocratie en Afrique francophone. Les mots et les maux de la transition au Bénin et au Niger* (Paris, 2000), p. 124.

underdeveloped.[100] The National Conference gave many Nigeriens the chance to learn about things in real time for the first time in the country's history. The extraordinary return of a former adviser to Kountché who had left to take refuge in Belgium after an attempted coup d'état aroused especially keen interest, to the point where audiocassettes of his declarations would be sold in the country's markets the following year.[101] Across the whole country, revelations about the past and decisions to be taken on the future were the subjects of informal discussions. It was in this context that "fada", or informal meeting groups of young people, developed. The word refers more to a subordinate position than to a certain age range – where everyday events and politics were discussed over tea.[102]

The anticipated decisions included both the implementation of democracy and the direction to be taken by economic policies, as rejection of the structural adjustment had played a significant role in the fall of the military regime. At the conference, the SAP went through numerous interventions, beginning with Ali Sabou's opening address, in which he justified its adoption even before declaring the meeting open.[103] Conversely, every – or nearly every – party rejected it in its general policy statement, in particular the Parti Nigérien pour la Démocratie et le Socialisme (PNDS), the party that would win the legislative election a year later, which submitted "the unsuitability of the economic model proposed by the Bretton Woods institutions" as evidence.[104] The statement by Amadou Cissé, a World Bank official speaking in the name of the international organizations, was one of the only ones to be heckled, if we are to believe the messages from the rapporteurs, who took note of everything that happened in the hall in the same way as they did with discussions in the National Assembly.[105] One whole day, 2 October 1991, was dedicated entirely to the adjustment. The rapporteur-general introduced discussions by stating that "the plenary assembly has not provided sufficient concrete alternative measures to the structural adjustment, whereas the public finance deficit is estimated to be 100 billion CFA francs".[106] The participants who took turns at the podium advocated counting on the

100. There was one fixed telephone line for every 570 inhabitants at the end of the 1980s (Direction de la statistique et de la démographie, *Annuaire statistique*, p. 141).

101. Interview with B., a DVD seller in the area of the Grand Marché, Niamey, 3 March 2019; "Bonkano prêt à débarquer à Niamey", *Sahel Dimanche*, 11 October 1991.

102. Florence Boyer, "'Faire fada' à Niamey (Niger). Un espace de transgression silencieuse?", *Carnets de géographes*, 7 (2014). Available at: https://journals.openedition.org/cdg/421; last accessed 18 January 2021.

103. ANN, 1W3.1.

104. ANN, 1W4.15, National Conference, general policy statement of the PNDS-Tarayya, 12 August 1991.

105. ANN, 1W5.18, National Conference, speech by Amadou Cissé, World Bank official, undated.

106. ANN, 1W9.6, National Conference, report of discussions of 2 October 1991.

country's own resources, including taxing the informal sector, renegotiating uranium prices, recovering debts incurred by domestic companies with the state, and, above all, recovering funds diverted by senior members of the military regime. At the end of the day, the Chair of the Economic Committee reached the following conclusion:

> the structural adjustment in its current form is rejected by a majority, and the discussions have only confirmed this. Together with the structural adjustment, lowering of the wage bill, privatization of domestic companies and staff reductions are also rejected.[107]

The National Conference ended on 3 November 1991. In his closing speech, the new Prime Minister, who was elected by the delegates to lead a transition government until the elections, stated that the conference had "achieved [...] cardinal reforms that will make Niger a country that has signed an unlimited lease with democracy".[108] One might find these words ludicrous today, in a country that saw three military coups d'état and a constitutional coup in the twenty following years. However, apart from the fact that other futures might have been possible, one might also view the Nigerien National Conference as the culmination of social struggles that could never have been predicted to be possible a few years earlier. This moment needs to be interpreted in relation to its past, not only to what came after. As the Nigerien political scientist Malam Souley Adji remarked when suggesting that we look at how this event was perceived at the time it unfolded: "The important thing is that it happened, because [that it would happen] was not at all evident. The fact that things didn't work later is a different story."[109]

TINA in Niger

A public debt can be measured, but how is it possible to measure the cost of popular disaffection with a regime that emerged out of social movements? On the one hand, there are the cold, hard facts of budget statistics that clearly show what needs to be done, while on the other there are things that cannot easily be quantified, such as political feelings and social violence. By putting into effect a liberalization policy similar to the one that had been put in place at the end of the military regime, the government that emerged from the National Conference did what budgetary rationality, with the support of international financial institutions, instructed it to do. But it also dismissed

---

107. ANN, 1W9.6, National Conference, speech by Jackou Sanoussi, Chair of the Economic Committee, 2 October 1991.
108. ANN, 1W3.4, National Conference, speech by Cheiffou Amadou, transitional Prime Minister, 3 November 1991.
109. Discussion with Malam Souley Adji, lecturer and researcher in political science at the Université Abdou Moumouni, Niamey, 14 March 2019.

the exercise of power by people whose roles had been decisive in the democratization process, and who expected something quite different from it. If one looks at the forces at work, one might say retrospectively that there was no alternative to this political decision (the famous TINA),[110] *if* one clearly understand it as the outcome of a power relationship: after the fall of the military regime, several different rationalities that opened up to a number of possible ones stood in opposition to each other in Nigerien society.

In the wake of the National Conference, the transition government enjoyed the benefit of a social truce with the trade unions, but not a financial truce with its funders. Barely a month after the conference had ended, the IMF decided to suspend its support for the country, taking the view that it had breached the structural adjustment agreements entered into with the previous government. This led to reprisals from a number of financial partners: the cost of debt service, which represented over half the state's tax revenues, suddenly increased by twenty per cent, and in 1992, the Nigerien government had to repay 11 billion CFA francs that had not been budgeted for at the beginning of the year. More fundamentally, Niger found itself "almost entirely cut off from the various [forms of] budgetary aid that had previously enabled it to attend to its most urgent matters", in the words of a study carried out for the OECD.[111] The consolidation of public accounts was the first task the Nigerien authorities set themselves. The resources the National Conference had counted on to carry out this consolidation turned out to be far smaller than it had initially hoped, however. Renegotiation of uranium prices with foreign companies was a failure, and prices continued to fall.[112] The approach taken to recover the funds diverted by former dignitaries, which had raised so many expectations, did not have the expected returns.[113] The only significant windfall came from international aid. The Nigerien government's recognition of Taiwan – which is still recalled today by the evocative phrase "Taiwan or chaos" – had an immediate impact, although it did not offset the reduction caused by the break with international financial institutions.[114]

At the outset, the regime was supported by the principal social forces involved in the National Conference, as witnessed by the reactions to a military uprising in February 1992. Troops took over the national radio and the airport, arresting four ministers and the President of the High Council of

110. TINA is an acronym for "there is no alternative", a phrase originally associated with British Conservatives during the Margaret Thatcher era.
111. Ann Vourc'h and Laina Boukar Moussa, *L'expérience de l'allégement de la dette du Niger*, working document no. 82 (OECD, 1992), p. 29.
112. "Fixation du prix de l'uranium: l'échec", *Le Républicain*, 28 January 1992.
113. "Commission crime et abus. La montagne a accouché d'une souris", *Le Sahel*, 9 June 1993.
114. "La semaine de vérité", *Haské*, 1 December 1992. Today, the phrase "Taiwan or chaos" is commonly attributed to Mohamed Bazoum, the Minister of Foreign Affairs in the transition government, although he denies using it.

the Republic to demand that one of their own be freed and that their back wages be paid.[115] In response, the USTN organized a "dead city" day – that is, a total halt to all business activities – in Niamey. The same evening, a crowd of thousands of people, including workers and students, in support of the new regime gathered in Place de la Concertation, where they stood up to the soldiers, who fired into the air to disperse the crowd.[116] When the night ended, the mutineers freed their prisoners and returned to their barracks. According to the government newspaper, the mutiny "made it possible to revitalize the spirit of the National Conference: […] popular meetings organized throughout the country, a two-day strike and dead city operations allowed the democratic forces (associations, political parties and trade unions) first to save, and then even possibly to take back control of, the democratic process".[117]

In fact, however, the "spirit of the National Conference" was already long gone, and democratization was proceeding in a context of growing tensions associated with the government's budgetary policy. While a new Constitution was submitted in 1992 for a referendum, there was a growing number of strikes and demonstrations to protest against unpaid salaries in the civil service. The threat that examinations in the education sector would be invalidated, which was brandished by the government at the end of the year to stop the strikes, led to an escalation of the protests. In January 1993, thousands of demonstrators, including students, parents, and teachers, gathered in Place de la Concertation to proclaim their rejection of the "white year". Government and police vehicles were damaged and the courtyard of the presidential palace was invaded by demonstrators, who forced the main door open, leading the police to intervene with truncheons and tear gas.[118] It was one month before the presidential election and the general election between the Mouvement National pour la Société de Développement (MNSD), which had emerged out of the former military regime, and the main parties of the National Conference, which had joined together in the Alliance des Forces pour le Changement (AFC), whose principal political slogan was "*Canji!*" ("change" in Haoussa). The adjustment hung over the campaign, even as the Nigerien state was under pressure from international financial institutions. Just before the elections, "guidelines", including a salary freeze and another reduction in public spending in particular, were "made known to the transition

115. The High Council of the Republic, of which André Salifou was the President, was the legislative body of the transitional institutions responsible for monitoring the political directions defined at the National Conference. The imprisoned soldier was Captain Maliki Bouraima, who had been involved in a bloody expedition against the Tuareg rebellion in May 1990.
116. "La folle nuit", *Haské*, 13 March 1992.
117. "La leçon", *Le Sahel Dimanche*, 6 March 1992.
118. "L'année blanche consommée", *Haské*, 28 January 1993.

government by the IMF".[119] Without advising people how to vote, the USN warned voters against any step backwards in this tract:

> Niger is preparing for the first presidential elections in its history. [...] Our country is embarking on a decisive phase towards pluralist democratization. [...] For the USN, the MNSD [would represent] a backward step for our country. For the USN, the return of the MNSD means the SAP, catastrophe. [...] It would be the first sign of a return to the old order.[120]

What made this tract special is that it was undoubtedly one of the last political leaflets in which it was still possible to associate the adjustment with the "old order" of the military regime. The AFC defeated the MNSD in the elections, and the new government took office in April under the leadership of Mahamadou Issoufou. A month later, he announced budget economy measures, while also indicating his willingness to reach an agreement with the World Bank and the IMF. Civil service salaries were frozen, even though several civil service bodies were already facing significant arrears. The retirement age was reduced, which was viewed as social regression in Niger. The high school and university academic years were also declared "white", because teachers had been on strike for too many days.[121]

These decisions, which were taken by the first democratic government in the country's history immediately after its election, consummated the break with the social forces that had led the struggle against the military regime. It also led to a radicalization of protest methods. In May, university and high-school students, members of the USN, attacked the headquarters of the political parties making up the AFC, destroying all of them except one, which was protected by militants armed with batons, and bows and arrows.[122] In June, the energy sector trade unions began an indefinite strike after a World Bank manager announced that it was "unfortunately obliged to suspend disbursements in the electricity sector" in order to defend the "rationale of the adjustment". "This depends above all on the Nigeriens", the manager explained in the Nigerien press.[123] In July, there was another military uprising in Zinder, the country's second largest city, where the Prime Minister was paying a visit. Soldiers tried to arrest him in order to have their back wages paid and to obtain better treatment. As a reaction, a meeting was organized in Place de la

---

119. "Redressement économique et financier. Les préalables au PAS", *Le Républicain*, 12 November 1992.

120. AU, USN, tract entitled "Le nouvel ordre", 21 February 1993.

121. "Programme d'urgence de l'AFC. Intention et réalité", *Haské*, 14 May 1993; "Déclaration de politique générale de Mahamadou Issoufou", *Le Sahel*, 24 May 1993.

122. "Mise à sac des sièges des partis politiques membres de l'AFC. Les scolaires renouent avec la violence", *Le Sahel*, 19 May 1993.

123. "'L'ajustement n'est qu'une gestion maitrisée de l'économie d'un pays'", déclare le responsable du département Sahel de la Banque mondiale", *Le Républicain*, 24 June 1993.

Concertation to "save democracy", but this time it only involved the AFC parties: the trade unions had given up the fight.[124]

In fact, it was the government's economic policy rather than the democratic institutions that now became the central issue for social struggles. These struggles indirectly opposed the protagonists of unequal forces. On the one hand, the trade unions battled against the liberalization policies imposed by international financial institutions, while their field of action was being limited by their own government. In September, a law authorized "the collective or individual requisitioning of civil servants in the event of strikes triggered in a vital strategic sector". Unionists were now "obliged not to undertake anything that might frustrate the provision of a minimum level of service".[125] This law also restricted the purpose of strikes to professional interests, which led the government newspaper to proclaim that "every strike of a political nature is illegal".[126] On the other hand, the international institutions and Niger's principal funders multiplied their injunctions to pursue economic orthodoxy. In October, the French Minister of Finance demanded the "return of all African countries into the international financial community", announcing that "not even one cent will be paid to countries that have not made the necessary effort to obtain the signature of an agreement with the Bretton Woods institutions".[127] At the heart of this long-distance struggle was the SAP, which was now a frequent presence in daily discussions far beyond militant circles.[128] Cartoons on the adjustment became more frequent in the newspapers, like the one in which a man explains that he is going to have to choose between the television and condiments (see Figure 3): the SAP itself had become a subject of public debate, and even more, one of the favoured prisms through which to understand the country's political development.

There are different ways to describe these few years in Nigerien history. One is to explain that the initial objective of the transition government to count on domestic financial resources alone was profoundly absurd, given the country's debt ratio and its dependence on outside aid. The other is to take the view that the Nigerien government could not commit itself to a policy the questioning of which had played a fundamental role in its accession to power – and also in the production of political legitimacy – without cutting itself off from the social bases that had striven the most for democratization and still

124. "L'objectif des mutins à Zinder. Abattre le Premier ministre", *Le Républicain*, 15 July 1993.
125. "Présidence de la République du Niger, ordonnance du 3 septembre 1993 portant réglementation du droit de grève dans la fonction publique", *Journal officiel de la République du Niger*, 1993.
126. "Toute grève à caractère politique est illégale", *Le Sahel*, 7 September 1993.
127. "Économie. FMI, passage obligé", *Haské*, 1 October 1993.
128. Interview with B., an English teacher, Niamey, 2 March 2019.

Figure 3. Structural adjustment through a press cartoon in 1993. Cartoon published in *Haské* on 13 October 1993.

remained indispensable to the functioning of an under-administered state.[129] Whatever the version may be, what emerges on both sides is an impression of a conflict of rationales – or absurdities, depending on the point of view one chooses – that cross through the political struggles during those times.

129. In 1990, the Nigerien state had a little more than 37,000 permanent and auxiliary civil servants, or 4.5 civil servants for every 1,000 inhabitants. By comparison, France had seventy-six civil servants per 1,000 inhabitants, only counting permanent staff; even that number is quite low for Europe (Institut national des statistiques et des études économiques, *Annales statistiques de la fonction publique, 1945, 1969, 1989*, Paris, 1992; Institut national de la Statistique, *Annuaire statistique du Niger, 1990–2006*, Niamey, 2007).

From devaluation to demobilization

In the end, it was the IMF that won. In 1994, Niger returned to a new round of negotiations with international financial institutions that ended with the signature of a "confirmation agreement" in March, just after the CFA franc had been devalued two months earlier.[130] This return cannot be the only explanation for the military *coup d'état* in 1996. However, it had a lasting effect on the devaluation of the democratic ideal, while also coinciding with extensive political demobilization, which, as has been shown in other contexts, *also* obeys a form of rationality.[131]

The decision to devalue the CFA franc, which was made official by the West African Heads of State in Abidjan on 11 January 1994 in the presence of the French Minister of Cooperation and the Managing Director of the IMF, caught the Nigerien population completely unawares. There had been no debate in Niger on this measure, which had a powerful effect on daily lives, even though the country had just had its first free elections. Even the very idea of a devaluation had only appeared in the Nigerien press a few weeks earlier, and only a few people understood the meaning of the word in the streets of Niamey.[132] The Nigerien historian Boureima Alpha Gado, who had been a delegate at the National Conference, wrote a column in *Haské* with the evocative title "It's democracy that's being devalued".[133] The measure immediately resulted in a considerable increase in the prices of consumer products, despite government decrees that allegedly froze prices, and in a lack of cash and food, as retailers suspended transactions while they waited for prices to go up even more.[134] The shock affected everyone's spirit: devaluation is one of those events that do not occur very frequent in one's lifetime, but everyone remembers where they were when they found out about it. This is what one resident of Niamey, who was ten years old at the time, had to say about it:

> I was small, I remember, we were sent to the mill [to grind millet]. [...] When we arrived, the guy said: "Ah, there's devaluation now, and prices have doubled". We didn't understand any of this [...]. We said: "OK, here's what we've been given". [*He thinks*] It should have been 25 francs, because I had a hundred francs for four *tias* to be ground. The guy said: "The prices have doubled. I'm not going to do it like that". At this point, an old man heard us. He listened calmly and didn't

130. "1994. Les repères de la vie économique nationale", *Le Républicain*, 5 January 1995.
131. On democratic disaffection in Europe, see Céline Braconnier and Jean-Yves Dormagen, *La Démocratie de l'abstention. Aux origines de la démobilisation électorale en milieu populaire* (Paris, 2007).
132. "Dévaluation du CFA. A quoi s'attend le Niger?", *Le Républicain*, 23 December 1993.
133. "C'est la démocratie qu'on dévalue", *Haské*, 14 January 1994.
134. "Des commerçants spéculateurs", *Haské*, 14 January 1994. According to official statistics, the average price increases reached thirty-five per cent in 1994, before continuing at a lower rate in the four following years (Bonnecase, "Politique des prix, vie chère et contestation sociale à Niamey").

say anything. And when he saw the guy insisting, he came over and said: "Ah, it's because they are young that you're cheating them. The devaluation doesn't affect you at all. Because up to now, the diesel you're paying for hasn't changed. So it doesn't affect you. You need to grind it like that". [*He laughs*]. The guy was ashamed, and he did it like that. He paid the price I wanted. That's really what I remember.[135]

In addition to the many tensions in everyday interactions, devaluation coincided with an increase in violence during mobilizations. Just before it was made official, small groups of pupils and students armed with rocks and Molotov cocktails stoned government buildings and burned vehicles belonging to international organizations.[136] The protests went on for several months before they were brutally put down by the police. On 10 March 1994, the police went on to the university campus, where students were preparing a demonstration. One student, Harouna Tahirou, was killed when a tear gas grenade was fired straight at his head.[137] This drew a strong reaction at the university and in the rest of the city. Some of the students who had been recruited by the PNDS at the time of the National Conference burned their cards in public.[138] Others delivered an ultimatum demanding the resignation of the Mayor of Niamey. An open letter was written for the attention of "Monsieur le criminel" to denounce his responsibility for Tahirou's death, as well as the fate reserved for the political forces that had worked the hardest for the democratization process: "You say we worked together for change. No: WE worked for change, but you, you are just an opportunist who came from nothing, who kills our militants as a way of thanking us."[139] This death, which occurred just three years after 9 February massacre, had a lasting effect on the students in view of its similarity to the excesses of the military regime. A portrait of Tahirou (see Figure 4) still hangs in front of the UENUN offices today.

In contrast to what had happened three years earlier, however, Tahirou's death did not lead to a rally of dissatisfied people or create the potential conditions for a political crisis.[140] In the months that followed, the workers' unions increased the number of demonstrations demanding wage increases

135. Interview with R., a resident of Kirkisoye, Niamey, 28 February 1991.
136. "Étudiants en furie", *Haské*, 14 January 1994.
137. "La mort de l'étudiant Tahirou Harouna. Il faut dédramatiser la situation selon le préfet-maire Souleymane Abari", *Le Républicain*, 17 March 1994.
138. Interview with T., a former member of the USN, Niamey 3 March 2019.
139. AU, USN-UENUN, "Lettre ouverte à Souleymane Abari Dan Bouzoua, préfet maire de la communauté urbaine de Niamey sortant, futur résident du camp pénal de Kollo", 22 March 1994.
140. See Michel Dobry's proposed analysis of a "fluid situation", in which various categories of society intermingle in multi-sector mobilizations, which makes it hard for governments to predict the behaviour of actors and creates potential conditions for political crises: Michel Dobry, *Sociologie des crises politiques. La dynamique des mobilisations multisectorielles* (Paris, 2009), p. 125 *et seq.*

Figure 4. Portrait of Tahirou hanging in front of the UENUN offices. Photo: author.

that would make it possible to face the price increases, before beginning an "indefinite strike" on 1 June 1994. The strike lasted fifty-five days, the longest the country had ever seen, but it ended in failure.[141] The students clearly leaned towards demobilization too, even though it was the worst year they had seen since the beginning of the decade in terms of the deterioration in living conditions and physical repression of protesters. A final general meeting was organized in July 1994 on the Niamey campus, just before the end of the university year. According to the handwritten notes taken by the secretary of the meeting, there was a very lively debate on the tactics to be adopted:

141. "L'USTN lâche prise!", *Haské*, 27 July 1994.

The differences emerged in broad daylight when the question was asked about the method to be adopted for the struggle. Some believe that blocking the bridge on the road leading to the campus was a measure of no consequence, because those who would suffer the most would be the people whose support we needed, and not the government. This is why they decided that the best method would be to organize a march and a sit-in at the Prime Minister's office. If the police intervened, we should withdraw and block the bridge. [...] This demobilization is [...] a real handicap for the movement. [...] In the face of this paradox between growing misery and the demobilization, or even the resignation of the base, there was a tendency towards resignation. [...] In any event, it would be perilous to continue with the movement with a number of comrades that borders on the shameful and the ridiculous. This is even more justified in the case of arrests, when all our comrades risk being left to their own destiny.[142]

Most of the people who attended this general meeting had experienced the victorious mobilizations that had led to the fall of the military regime a few years earlier and the effervescent spirit of the National Conference. Some years later, the era of the possible had ended; it was a time of disillusionment, including among the social groups who had initially been the main drivers of the democratization process. This was symbolized in 1995 by a cartoon that appeared in *Haské* (see Figure 5), which is emblematic of the opening up to pluralism. It shows two women reminiscing, "in Kountché's time, [they had] real peace", before saying "all democracy has brought us is broke guys".[143]

On 27 January 1996, Colonel Ibrahim Maïnassara Baré, the Chief of Staff, seized power in a coup d'état.[144] The National Assembly was dissolved, political parties were suspended and a state of emergency was proclaimed. This coup undoubtedly did not represent the inevitable culmination of this story; other outcomes had been possible. It also took place within a shorter timeline marked by the exacerbation of partisan struggles in 1995, which led to the regime's institutions being blocked.[145] It was not a return to the past in the strict sense of the word, as if nothing had happened in the past five years, and the new head of state was quick to give a democratic form to his seizure of power by promising early elections. On the other hand, it marked an evaporation of the political aspirations that had developed at the beginning of the decade: in Niamey, no one took to the streets to defend the government under attack, unlike in February 1992 and July 1993. By contrast, the international

---

142. AU, USN-UENUN, summary of discussions held on 19 July 1994 (handwritten).

143. "Awa et Mariama. 'Ah cette démocratie'", cartoon, *Haské magazine*, special edition no. 2, 1995.

144. "Le Conseil de salut national prend le pouvoir", *Le Sahel*, 29 January 1996.

145. In September 1994, Mahamadou Issoufou resigned as Prime Minister, and the AFC broke up. In January 1995, a general election was won by the MNSD, whose leader, Hama Amadou, became Prime Minister. There followed a year of cohabitation during which the President and the Prime Minister continued to argue about the limits of their respective roles. See Grégoire and Olivier de Sardan, "Le Niger. Mise au point".

Figure 5. Democracy through a press cartoon in 1995. Cartoon published in *Haské* magazine, special edition no. 2, 1995.

financial institutions energetically condemned the coup d'état. The day after, Boukary Adji, who had been responsible for implementing the first SAP under Kountché, was named Prime Minister.[146] He would be succeeded by Amadou Cissé, soon after the latter had led a mission to the World Bank to finalize the implementation of the second SAP,[147] which was ready to be signed.

---

146. "M. Boukary Adji, nouveau Premier ministre", *Le Sahel*, 1 February 1994.
147. "Ajustement structurel. Les dessous de la bonne note", *Le Républicain*, 28 September 1994.

CONCLUSION: RATIONALITY AND ABSURDITY IN POLITICS

A number of questions arise on the conclusion of this story that go beyond the case of Niger alone.

The first regards what populations revolt against, and what drives us as researchers to define it, what these populations explicitly define and what implicitly leads them to act. If we look at the meanings protestors attach to their actions, it is not truly possible to qualify the acts of revolt discussed in this article as "IMF riots", unlike in other countries at the time.[148] Even though the SAPs gradually revealed themselves to be a cause of the anger in Nigerien society, everybody saw their existence much more through concrete realities than through the prism of an ideological struggle against external forces. All along, it was "the state" rather than "international organizations" or "liberalism" that was the preferred target of popular anger, and in this respect it appears to be fairly nation-centric and state-focused, as was the case with other movements I have studied in West Africa.[149] However, this does not mean that the adjustment did not work as a backdrop to this anger even more than I had imagined before I began this research. In this respect, it is undoubtedly an important part of the social history of other African revolts, one that it is important to investigate further.

The second question touches on the political economy of democracy as it has affirmed itself in Africa in the past forty years or so. In a good number of African countries, the political liberalization of the 1990s went hand-in-hand with economic liberalization. There was nothing obvious about this convergence: it was even quite paradoxical for the time, including economically, if one considers the increasingly powerful voices that made democratization an important condition for development.[150] As it happens, liberalization weakened the nascent democracies, and if these voices are to be believed, it had an adverse effect on the economy. The most important thing, however, is that liberal reforms had *already* been under way before the political regimes became democratic in many parts of the continent, and even played an important role in the protests against the authoritarian regimes, as in Niger. In other words, when the years of democratization are today commonly devalued on the streets of Niamey, Bamako, and Ouagadougou as having led to a privatization of the state, a loss of the old rules, and a deterioration in living conditions, it is doubly unjust: on the one hand the transformations people blame were already under way, and on the other there was nothing a

148. John Walton and David Seddon (eds), *Free Markets and Food Riots: The Politics of Global Adjustment* (Oxford, 1994).
149. Bonnecase, *Les prix de la colère*, pp. 255 ff.
150. Amartya Sen, *Development as Freedom* (Oxford, 1999).

priori that made it inexorable for the new regimes that were born out of the social revolts to pursue them.

The third question, which is more controversial and more subjective, concerns the rationale used by the international financial institutions. It is admitted that "things are more complicated than people may believe" and that there is no reason to question the morality of events in a scientific article. Notwithstanding this, when I returned to this moment in Niger's history and decided to look at the sequence of events in depth from the perspective of the sociology of the events, I was surprised to discover the extent to which this story, although it had a clear rationale from an accounting perspective, also simultaneously harboured elements that might legitimately seem absurd if one adopts the point of view of the rebels and their aspirations for democracy. I was also surprised to discover how closely the most violent moments of repression by the Nigerien state during this period were connected with the chronology of the adjustments, to the point where it is hard not to think that the international financial institutions co-produced the conditions that made this violence possible, even though it was not their intention to do so. Finally, I was surprised that today, these somewhat strange actions – increasing the burden of debt just after democratic institutions had been installed, forcing devaluation the day after unprecedented free elections – do not seem to be more absurd, not only from the standpoint of the material consequences, but also through the prism of the deep traces they left in political imaginaries and the practical impact this could have. Considering that conflicts of rationales such as this are always possible, it seems to me to be important to reflect on it.

IRSH 66 (2021), pp. 215–238 doi:10.1017/S0020859021000146

A Well-Adjusted Debt: How the International Anti-Debt Movement Failed to Delink Debt Relief and Structural Adjustment

HÉLÈNE BAILLOT

CESSP, Université Paris I Panthéon-Sorbonne
Paris, France

E-mail: hbaillot@gmail.com

ABSTRACT: This article analyses the process by which the issues of debt and structural adjustment were redefined by a plurality of actors, from institutional experts to activists, during the 1980s and 1990s. Although it mainly focuses on the 1990s, when the Jubilee 2000 campaign emerged, blossomed, and died, it takes into account the institutional mobilization preceding it. It then points to the need to think about the dynamics of competition and the division of labour among international players. While the leading Jubilee 2000 coalition in the Global North opposed debt on economic and religious grounds, African anti-structural adjustment programme (SAP) activists who joined the Jubilee Afrika campaign promoted an alternative framework: according to them, debt was not just economically "unsustainable"; it was first and foremost "illegitimate", as were any conditions attached to its reduction, beginning with the implementation of SAPs. The story of the anti-debt campaign is the story of their failure.

The Greek sovereign debt crisis emerged at the end of 2009: the new government of Georges Papandréou announced a budget deficit of 12.7 per cent, an amount that far exceeded those stated by his predecessor, thus unveiling the long-time masking of Greek public accounts. As a result, credit rating agencies downgraded Greek debt, which lost its triple A mark, and Greek debt obligations flooded the secondary debt market without finding any buyers. In April 2010, with a public debt amounting to 350 billion euros, that is, 150 per cent of the country's GDP, Greece was on the verge of defaulting. Its government turned to the International Monetary Fund (IMF) and the European Union (EU), who agreed on an initial bailout programme. Reaching the amount of 110 billion euros, a loan was granted in exchange for the implementation of structural reforms: a wage freeze in the public sector; pensions cuts; and a steep rise in VAT. In the following years, two further bailout programmes were signed, leading to major protests and social unrest throughout the country. In April 2015, early parliamentary elections brought to power the leftist coalition Syriza, and a few months later the Greek parliament established the Truth Committee on Public Debt, whose mandate was to investigate the origin and contraction of Greek public debt. Chaired by Zoe Konstantopoulo (who then served as head of the Hellenic Parliament) and scientifically coordinated by Éric Toussaint (head of the Committee for the Abolition of Illegitimate Debt (CADTM)), the committee issued a report stating:

> The [adjustment/bailout] programs consist of neoliberal policy measures that involve deep spending and job cuts in the public sector, extended deregulation of the private sector, tax increases, privatizations, and structural changes (misleadingly called "reforms"). These internationally imposed measures, supposedly aimed at reducing the country's budget deficit and public debt to sustainable levels, have pushed the economy into a deep recession – the longest recession experienced in Europe during a period of peace. Millions were thrown into poverty, unemployment, and social exclusion, while human rights, particularly economic and social rights, were grossly undermined. Public services and infrastructure such as schools, hospitals, courts, and municipalities around the country have been merged, shut down, or otherwise suffocated, in order to achieve fiscal targets specified by the creditors that have been widely criticized as unacceptable and unrealistic.[1]

The entanglement of public debt and structural economic reforms, of which the Greek case is a cruel example, is not new, and one can only be struck by the similarities between the situation faced by some European countries in the aftermath of the financial crisis of 2008 and the situation encountered by a majority of African countries some thirty years ago. Throughout the 1980s and 1990s, many African countries, facing outstanding levels of debt, were compelled to implement structural adjustment programmes (SAPs) under the auspices of the IMF and the World Bank. Inspired by the Washington Consensus, such programmes featured national currency devaluations to enhance export earnings and discourage imports, the privatization of government-controlled industries and services, and cuts in government budgets.[2]

Launched in 1996, Jubilee 2000 was the first transnational anti-debt campaign. Gathering activists from the Global North and the Global South, its goal was to achieve massive debt reduction for poor countries by the end of the year 2000, as per the biblical principle of jubilee. While activists mostly focused on debt, a peculiar level of attention was given to the issue of SAPs. Campaigners demanded that debt cancellation take place "under a fair and transparent process" and with no attached conditionalities (i.e. the implementation of structural adjustment policies in southern countries benefiting from debt relief agreements). Their mobilization resulted in concrete outcomes with

---

1. The Truth Committee on Public Debt, *Preliminary Report*, 18 June 2015, p. 7.
2. Yves Dezalay and Bryant Garth, "Le 'Washington Consensus'", *Actes de la recherche en sciences sociales*, 121–122 (1998), pp. 3–22.

the launch, in June 1999, at the G7 Cologne summit, of a new international debt relief initiative: the enhanced Heavily Indebted Poor Countries initiative (HIPC II, Figure 1).[3]

Not surprisingly, the "success" of Jubilee 2000 lies at the heart of the scholarship on the campaign: scholars who became interested in Jubilee were mostly driven by the same incentive, that is, underlying factors leading to success.[4] Coming from diverse backgrounds – political economy, political science, and anthropology – they offered rich and diverse analytical frameworks to understand why Jubilee achieved what it did. Although they produced a rich corpus that shed light on different facets of this transnational movement, they did not avoid some shortcomings. Firstly, they tended to forget, or at least to downplay, the fact that the issue of success was highly controversial within the Jubilee movement itself. If some activists rejoiced in the campaign's results, others, mainly from the Global South, denounced HIPC II as a "cruel hoax". Of course, the existence of conflicting interpretations among activists is not uncommon – other articles gathered in this Special Issue show it well – and social movement scholars have long shown that movement participants may have different perceptions of what counts as success.[5] But the split that hit Jubilee 2000 just a few months after the Cologne agreement turned it into a paradigmatic case of a conflicted campaign;[6] in November 1999, southern activists gathered in Johannesburg and decided to continue the mobilization on their own under the new banner of Jubilee South. Secondly, while acknowledging that Jubilee was a genuine transnational campaign, scholars tended to mainly focus on northern activists; field research was mostly conducted in the United Kingdom, where the international secretariat of the campaign

---

3. For a study of the way in which measurements of over-indebtedness have been constructed, used, and modified in the context of multilateral initiatives for Heavily Indebted Poor Countries (HIPC), see Marc Raffinot, "Mesurer le surendettement des pays à faible revenue. Technique, éthique ou politique?", *Revue Tiers Monde*, 1 (2013), pp. 51–70.

4. See, for example, André Broome, "When Do NGOs Matter? Activist Organizations as a Source of Change in the International Debt Regime", *Global Society*, 23 (2009), pp. 59–78; Joshua W. Busby, *Moral Movements and Foreign Policy* (New York, 2010); Paula Goldman, *From Margin to Mainstream: Jubilee 2000 and the Rising Profile of Global Poverty Issues in the United Kingdom and United States* (Ph.D., Harvard University, 2010); Noha Shawki, "Issue Frames and the Political Outcomes of Transnational Campaigns: A Comparison of the Jubilee 2000 Movement and the Currency Transaction Tax Campaign", *Global Society*, 24 (2010), pp. 203–230.

5. Marco Giugni, "Was it Worth the Effort? The Outcomes and Consequences of Social Movements", *Annual Review of Sociology*, 24 (1998), pp. 371–393.

6. Some works, mostly coming from scholars involved in the anti-debt movement, have nevertheless dealt with this important issue: Elizabeth Donnelly, "Proclaiming Jubilee: The Debt and Structural Adjustment Network", in Sanjeev Khagram, James V. Riker, and Kathryn Sikkink (eds), *Restructuring World Politics: Transnational Social Movements, Networks, and Norms* (Minneapolis, MN, 2002), pp. 155–180; Jean Somers, "The Dynamics of South/North Relationships within Transnational Debt Campaigning", *Interface*, 6 (2014), pp. 76–102.

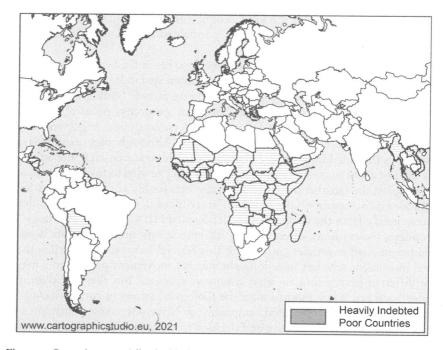

Figure 1. Countries potentially eligible for debt relief under the HIPC II initiative (1999).

was based, and in the United States, where the IMF and World Bank are head-quartered. As a result, the participation of southern campaigners in the anti-debt movement, especially African activists, remains largely overlooked, a fact that reminds us that the sociology of transnational social movements is still mainly focused on Western civil societies – despite some commendable exceptions.[7]

Drawing on field research conducted during my Ph.D. thesis in the United States and United Kingdom as well as in Uganda and the Philippines between 2011 and 2017,[8] this article aims at presenting and analysing some important

7. Franklin D. Rothman and Pamela E. Oliver, "From Local to Global: The Anti-Dam Movement in Southern Brazil, 1979–1992", in Jackie Smith and Hank Johnston (eds), *Globalization and Resistance: Transnational Dimensions of Social Movements* (New York, 2002), pp. 115–132; Lesley J. Wood, "Bridging the Chasms: The Case of Peoples' Global Action", in Joe Bandy and Jackie Smith (eds), *Coalitions Across Borders: Transnational Protest and the Neoliberal Order* (Lanham, MD, 2005), pp. 95–117; Janet Conway, *Edges of Global Justice: The World Social Forum and Its "Others"* (London [etc.], 2012); Johanna Siméant, Marie-Emmanuelle Pommerolle, and Isabelle Sommier (eds), *Observing Protest from a Place: The World Social Forum in Dakar (2011)* (Amsterdam, 2015), pp. 137–156.
8. Hélène Baillot, *"Nous ne devons rien, nous ne paierons rien". Jubilee 2000 et la redéfinition du mode de problématisation de la dette des pays pauvres (1996–2000)*, (Ph.D., Université Paris I Panthéon-Sorbonne, 2017).

controversies that surrounded the construction of poor countries' debt as a public problem. To do so, it mostly relies on a large range of militant sources gathered from Jubilee USA, Jubilee UK, Jubilee Uganda, and Freedom from Debt coalitions (in the Philippines); minutes of meetings, flyers, newsletters, advocacy materials, faxes, and emails were systematically collected over the period 1996–2000. A careful analysis of this rich documentation along with interviews conducted with former Jubilee activists helped me better understand not only the different positions national Jubilee coalitions had on debt, but also how their positions evolved over time. It also gave me a good sense of the tensions that arose between the different coalitions, especially although not exclusively between northern and southern campaigners.

As I will demonstrate in this article, those tensions, which eventually led to a split between northern and southern campaigners, were not merely over the question of numbers (i.e. how much debt relief should be granted), but arose from a difference in underlying principles. While the leading coalitions in the Global North mainly opposed debt and structural adjustment on economic and religious grounds, African activists who joined the Jubilee Afrika campaign promoted an alternative framework: according to them, debt was not just economically "unsustainable"; it was first and foremost "illegitimate", as were any conditions attached to its reduction, beginning with the implementation of SAPs. Debt thus became a metaphor to denounce the long-term and ongoing domination of the Global North. This was especially the case as many African activists increasingly expressed the feeling that the domination of the Global North was being reproduced within the Jubilee 2000 campaign itself. While truly transnational, Jubilee 2000 remained dominated by northern coalitions, especially Jubilee UK and Jubilee USA. It is thus essential to pay particular attention to the issues of power imbalances and division of labour among international activists. Only through such a lens can we better understand how and for whom debt and structural adjustment became – and remain – an issue.

Although this article mainly focuses on the 1990s, when the Jubilee 2000 campaign emerged, blossomed, and died, it also takes into account the institutional mobilization that immediately preceded it. While often considered to be activists' "adversaries", experts in economics working for international organizations played an important role in framing debt and structural adjustment as a problem.

HOW POOR COUNTRIES' DEBT AND STRUCTURAL ADJUSTMENT BECAME A PUBLIC PROBLEM: THE EARLY STAGES

Before anti-debt activists launched massive protests in the inner cities of Birmingham or Cologne, and before they started widely circulating petitions in favour of debt relief, experts, and consultants, acting from within the institutional framework, were the first to seize upon the debt issue and to frame it as a problem. Their mobilization, although confined to bureaucratic arenas, paved the way for Jubilee 2000 and provided anti-debt activists with solid economic expertise, on which they heavily relied.

The role of institutional experts in the early problematization of debt and structural adjustment

In the early 1990s, the international financial institutions expressed great relief that the international systemic crisis they had feared had not occurred. Severe economic and financial difficulties faced by many South American countries in the wake of Mexico's sovereign default appeared to have been overcome thanks to the launch of two massive rescue plans,[9] that is, the Baker and Brady plans (1985 and 1989), both designed by the United States Treasury.[10] But while the World Bank and the IMF were celebrating victory,[11] other institutional actors started expressing their concerns: according to them, the economic and financial crisis, far from being over, was now striking another group of states, namely the heavily indebted poor countries. Among the institutional actors who first coined poor countries' debt as a problem were experts and consultants working for United Nations agencies such as the United Nations Development Programme (UNDP), the United Nations Conference on Trade and Development (UNCTAD), and the United Nations Children's Fund (UNICEF). One can also mention the role of experts working for national aid agencies such as the Swedish International Development Authority (SIDA) as well as for a few think tanks active in the field of international development, including the Institute of Development Studies or the Institute of Policy Studies, both headquartered in the United Kingdom. Although quite diverse, they shared common characteristics and can be considered as a small elite of development economists. Trained at some of the most prestigious universities (such as Yale, Cambridge, MIT, and the London School of Economics), they tended to circulate widely across the private and the public sector, across states and international organizations, and among non-governmental organizations (NGOs) and think tanks. Stephany Griffith Jones, for example, before joining the Institute of Development Studies where she worked on poor countries' debt crisis, started her career in 1970 at the Central Bank of Chile and then worked at Barclays Bank International in the UK. In the meantime, she acted as a consultant to

9. Vinod K. Aggarwal, "Interpreting the History of Mexico's External Debt Crises", in Barry Eichengreen and Peter H. Lindert (eds), *The International Debt Crisis in Historical Perspective* (Cambridge, 1989), pp. 140–188.
10. Marc Raffinot, "Dette des pays émergents. Traitements innovants et multiplication des crises", in Marc Raffinot, *La dette des tiers mondes* (Paris, 2008), pp. 77–90; Tony Killick and Simon Stevens, "Mechanisms for Dealing with Debt Problems", in Zubair Iqbal and Ravi Kanbur (eds), *External Finance for Low-Income Countries* (Washington, DC, 1997), pp. 145–174.
11. World Bank, *World Debt Tables* (Washington, DC, 1989).

governments and to international organizations including UNICEF and the World Bank. Another example is Percy Mistry, who, after serving as a financial analyst at the World Bank for fifteen years (1971–1986), worked as a consultant for various international organizations and as an adviser on matters of debt, macro-economic management, and structural adjustment for governments in Asia and Africa. At the same time, he pursued a successful career in the private sector, with such positions as CEO of Synergy Power Corporation, Senior Advisor to Europa Partners Ltd, and Director of the JP Morgan Emerging Markets Investment Trust. Trained at Cambridge and Yale, Richard Jolly, for his part, acted as economic adviser to the government of Zambia (1964–1966) before taking up the direction of the Institute of Development Studies (1972–1981). He then became Deputy Executive Director of UNICEF (1982–1996), a position he held when he seized upon the issue of debt and structural adjustment.

The involvement of these actors – described by Deacon and Hulse as "global social reformist[s]"[12] – in the issue of debt and structural adjustment emerged in a specific context. In the early 1990s, actors involved in the field of international development were facing a crisis of legitimacy. They had all seen their mission and their very reason for being questioned due to the poor results of the development policies conducted over the previous decade: economic stagnation, the dramatic rise of indebtedness, and the persistence of poverty were such that the 1980s had been qualified as a "lost decade" for development. Critical voices raised the inefficiency of international aid. Robert Cassen, a former World Bank senior economist, asked, sceptically, "Does Aid Work?" in a report on foreign aid that had a broad audience.[13] Furthermore, the 1980s were marked by the increasing power of international financial institutions (IFIs); the liberal turn taken by IFIs deeply affected the role of UN agencies, who saw their capacity reduced and their role marginalized on the international stage.[14]

It was therefore precisely in trying to defend the very meaning of their mission that experts working in the development field shaped debt and structural adjustment into a problem. If development policies did not achieve their expected positive effects, it was not because "aid doesn't work" but because other elements, lying beyond their scope, hampered its proper implementation, namely, debt and structural adjustment policies. By making debt a problem, they intended to transfer the responsibility for development failures to the two major international institutions in charge of dealing with international

12. Bob Deacon, Michael Hulse, and Peter Stubbs, *Global Social Policy: International Organizations and the Future of Welfare* (London, 1997).

13. Robert Cassen *et al.*, *Does Aid Work?* (Oxford, 1986).

14. Deacon, Hulse, and Stubbs, *Global Social Policy*; Yves Dezalay and Bryant G. Garth, *La mondialisation des guerres de palais. La restructuration du pouvoir d'État en Amérique latine, entre notables du droit et "Chicago Boys"* (Paris, 2002).

finance: the IMF and the World Bank. The construction of the debt problem during the 1980s and early 1990s must therefore be understood in the light of the dynamics of competition that opposed, within the international arena, a development pole, declining at the time, to a financial pole, led by the "Unholy Trinity",[15] which asserted a dominant position in a world marked by the end of the Cold War and the expansion of neoliberalism.[16]

The global social reformists experienced serious difficulties in making themselves heard by the IFIs officials, who, in 1989, were still asserting that "there [was] no generalized debt crisis".[17] For these institutions, who were in charge of managing poor countries' debt, to qualify the situation as a "debt crisis" would have meant accepting a share of responsibility, if not in the origin of the crisis then at least in its resolution.[18] That was a risk those institutions were not eager to take. To make their voices heard, the development experts participated in – and sometimes even organized – international conferences. From 7–10 July 1989, for example, Dubrovnik hosted the Conference on Future International Financial Monetary and Trade Cooperation for Development, where Steffany Griffith Jones, then a researcher at the Institute of Development Studies, was invited to speak. On 9–10 June 1992, Percy Mistry helped organize a workshop on the "Functioning of the International Monetary System" for the Forum on Debt and Development (FONDAD). Held at the Netherlands Ministry of Foreign Affairs in The Hague, the workshop included Stephany Griffith Jones along with John Williamson, the economist who coined the term "Washington Consensus", and Johannes Witteveen, a former IMF managing director. Another strategy was to write and disseminate reports. Some provided important ammunition for anti-debt activists, such as *Adjustment with a Human Face*, written for UNICEF by Andrea Giobanni Cornia, Richard Jolly, and Frances Stewart;[19] *Multilateral Debt: An Emerging Crisis?* written for FONDAD by Percy Mistry;[20] *A Way Out of the Debt Trap*, written for SIDA;[21] and the UNCTAD Annual Report 1993.[22] In spite of several important differences, all these reports shared a common central argument: the situation in poor countries, already very serious, was

---

15. Richard Peet, *Unholy Trinity: The IMF, World Bank and WTO* (London, 2003).

16. Bruno Jobert (ed.), *Le tournant néo-libéral en Europe. Idées et recettes dans les pratiques gouvernementales* (Paris, 1994).

17. *Ibid.*

18. David Ambrosetti and Yves Buchet de Neuilly, "Les organisations internationales au cœur des crises", *Cultures & Conflits*, 75 (2009), pp. 7–14.

19. Giovanni Andrea Cornia, Richard Jolly, and Frances Stewart, *Adjustment with a Human Face: Protecting the Vulnerable and Promoting Growth* (Oxford, 1987).

20. Percy Mistry, *Multilateral Debt: An Emerging Crisis?* (The Hague, 1994).

21. SIDA, *A Way Out of the Debt Trap: Proposals to Remove the Debt of the Poorest and Most Indebted Countries* (Stockholm, 1992).

22. UNCTAD, *Trade and Development Report* (New York, 1993).

worsening at an alarming rate. The total debt of sub-Saharan countries was such that it had become a major impediment to economic growth:

> A high level of debt has a generally detrimental effect on a country's macroeconomic situation inasmuch as it affects inflation, interest rates and exchange rates. A high level of indebtedness increases budget deficits, which may fuel inflation. A high rate of inflation leads to high interest rates, which can deter investments. The foreign exchange rate will then be difficult to defend. Economic problems and heavy indebtedness also lead to political unrest. All these factors discourage foreign investment.[23]

The act of "naming" the problem came along with the attribution of blame.[24] On that matter, all agreed on the fact that IFIs bore a great share of the responsibility and denounced "the pyramiding of multilateral debt",[25] which was deemed all the more problematic as international creditors imposed harsher condition on debtor countries than bilateral ones:

> The penalties for default or delay in making debt service payments to the IFI (and particularly to the World Bank and IMF) are severe. They can, for example, result in the suspension of debt relief agreements and the cessation of most new aid flows – not only from the multilateral institutions themselves but from bilateral agencies as well – thus resulting in cutting off the only lifeline that the poorest countries have opened to them for financing critical imports. Most developing countries have therefore chosen to continue paying multilateral debt service to the extent that they are able, even when it absorbs a large portion of any new credits or grants they might receive from any source.[26]

In the various reports, the global social reformists also criticized the design of SAPs. Poorly conceived, they proved to be inefficient in improving the economic performance of indebted countries:

> The economic outcomes of these loans and the programs they financed have not yet generated the levels of sustainable growth required, nor sufficiently enhanced export earnings, to cover the additional debt service burdens imposed, as quickly as had been anticipated when these loans were made.[27]

Worse, SAPs were held responsible for the increase in the outstanding debt:

> Between 1980–87 the outstanding stock of multilateral (including IMF) debt to sub-Saharan Africa increased by some \$25 billion, most of it applied to lending for structural or sectoral adjustment. Between 1987–92, the debt stock increased by roughly a further \$16 billion while total debt service obligations to multilateral

23. SIDA, *A Way Out of the Debt Trap*, p. 10.
24. William L.F. Felstiner, Richard L. Abel, and Austin Sarat, "The Emergence and Transformation of Disputes: Naming, Blaming and Claiming", *Law and Society Review*, 15 (1980–1981), pp. 631–654.
25. Mistry, *Multilateral Debt*, p. 9.
26. *Ibid.*, p. 16.
27. SIDA, *A Way Out of the Debt Trap*, p. 12.

institutions (including the IMF) were about $2.4 billion higher; having increased from under $1 billion in 1980 to nearly $3.4 billion in 1992.[28]

In their reports, the global social reformists advocated in favour of debt relief for the poorest countries and insisted on the importance of multilateral debt relief. From different angles, they also called for reform in the design of SAPs. Experts at SIDA, for example, requested a revision of the economic policy calendar: for major reforms to be fruitful, indebted states should be given more time to repay their loans. For their part, UNICEF experts advocated for better inclusion of the most vulnerable people in the design of SAPs and called for "adjustment with a human face".[29]

The mobilization of these development experts, although muffled and confined to bureaucratic arenas, attracted attention from World Bank and IMF officials, who, in September 1996, agreed on the launch of a joint programme: the Heavily Indebted Poor Countries initiative (HIPC). The intent of this initiative was to provide an exit from the rescheduling process by reducing debt to "sustainable" levels so that it was not an impediment to growth. But while the HIPC initiative opened the way for the reduction of multilateral debt, it also strengthened the link between debt reduction and structural adjustment. Indeed, in order to benefit from debt relief under HIPC, a country had to demonstrate its strong commitment to major IMF and World Bank economic reforms for at least six years (qualifying period).

The global social reformists thus opened a breach into which Jubilee 2000 activists stepped. They also developed and circulated solid economic expertise on debt and structural adjustment in poor countries, on which Jubilee activists heavily relied.

The emergence of a transnational social movement against the debt:
The birth and rise of Jubilee 2000

Launched in 1996, Jubilee 2000 was the first international campaign advocating for the cancellation of the public debt of the poorest countries. Initiated by international NGOs, anti-poverty groups, and church-related agencies such as Tearfund and Christian Aid, Jubilee 2000 called for the "cancellation of the backlog of unpayable debt for the world's poorest countries – which either cannot be paid or can be paid only with enormous human suffering".[30] To achieve their goals, Jubilee 2000 activists engaged in advocacy and intense lobbying with international financial institutions and the heads of state of the most industrialized nations. Along the way, the campaign gained the

---

28. Mistry, *Multilateral Debt*, p. 17.
29. James P. Grant, "Introduction", in Giovanni Andrea Cornia, Richard Jolly, and Frances Stewart, *Adjustment with a Human Face*, p. 4.
30. Jubilee 2000 Coalition, *How It All Began: Causes of the Debt Crisis*, 1998. Jubilee UK archives, Newcastle.

endorsement of several celebrities. Bono, Bob Geldof, Youssou N'Dour, Giorgio Armani, to mention a few, took active part in the campaign by attending protests, creating and selling T-shirts in favour of debt relief, or organizing concerts. At the 1999 Brit Awards ceremony, Jubilee 2000 was honoured with the Freddie Mercury Award and received the public support of Keith Flint, David Bowie, and Bono. The latter even took part in the international Jubilee 2000 delegation invited to meet with Pope John Paul II.

In May 1998, a large protest was organized in Birmingham that was attended by about 70,000 activists. In June 1999, 40,000 demonstrators formed a human chain around Cologne, Germany, and a petition with 17 million signatures in favour of debt relief (the largest petition in history at the time) was presented to the heads of state of the most industrialized countries:

> We, the undersigned, believe that the start of the new millennium should be a time to give hope to the impoverished people of the world. To make a fresh start, we believe it right to put behind us the mistakes made by both lenders and borrowers, and to cancel the backlog of unpayable debts of the most impoverished nations. We call upon the leaders of lending nations to write off these debts by the year 2000. We ask them to take effective steps to prevent such high levels of debt building up again. We look for a new beginning to celebrate the millennium.[31]

Heavily relying on the expertise produced by the "global social reformists", Jubilee 2000 campaigners mostly framed the debt as an economic issue. Debt was considered as "unsustainable" and Jubilee 2000 campaigners advocated in favour of debt relief on such grounds. Some Jubilee 2000 campaigners also relied on religious arguments and called for "debt forgiveness". In December 1999, for example, Jubilee USA organized a candlelight vigil:

> Candles placed within paper bags bearing the names of the indebted countries targeted for debt forgiveness by the J2000 campaign will be lit one by one. As each country's candle is lit, a prayer will be offered for the people there and for the forgiveness of the country's debt.[32]

While Jubilee 2000 cannot be confined to a religious campaign, one must acknowledge the central position of churches and faith-based NGOs in the birth and rise of the Jubilee movement. Jubilee USA, one of the most important national coalitions (not least because of its proximity to the IMF and World Bank headquarters and the US Congress) comprised many of the larger US national churches (the Episcopal Church, the Methodist church, the National Catholic Conference of Bishops, and the Presbyterian Church), as well as Christian relief agencies (Catholic Relief Services and Lutheran World Relief) and faith-based NGOs such as Bread for the World, an ecumenical Christian advocacy NGO, and the Center of Concern, a Jesuit think tank.

---

31. Jubilee 2000 petition. Jubilee UK archives, Newcastle.
32. Interview with Marie Dennis, Maryknoll Office for Global Concern/Jubilee USA, Washington, DC, June 2011.

The notion of Jubilee itself comes from the Bible, from the book of Leviticus, and describes an event that occurred every fifty years when slaves were freed, land was restored, and debts were cancelled. The idea of linking debt relief to the new millennium and the religious idea of Jubilee was proposed in the early 1990s by Martin Dent, a British professor at Keele University.[33] Together with Bill Peters, a former British ambassador to Uruguay and High Commissioner to Malawi, Martin Dent started promoting the Jubilee principle that he considered a "Theological Help in an Urgent Crisis".[34]

While debt was the main focus of the Jubilee campaign, campaigners also took on the issue of SAPs. In its advocacy work, the Jubilee 2000 international secretariat devoted significant attention to the issue of structural adjustment through the perspective of "debt conditionalities". For example, the main booklet of the campaign, *The Debt Cutter Handbook*, included a double page on the issue of SAPs. A paragraph entitled "SAPping the Poor" described such programmes as "IMF economic policies imposed by western creditors whose ultimate purpose is (a) to generate hard currency to repay debt and (b) to open up developing country markets to foreign imports".[35] Because of the strong presence of faith-based organizations, SAPs were even criticized with the help of religious arguments. Participants in Jubilee 2000 religious workshops were invited, for example, to "compare the provisions in the biblical texts to the structural adjustment policies of the international financial institutions", in which "the poor pay the debt as governments cut the lifelines of health, education, basic food subsidies and ultimately, hope".[36]

From its inception in London in 1996, Jubilee 2000 was intended to become a transnational campaign. Its founding members, as well as its first funder,[37] considered that only a worldwide movement would be able to put efficient pressure on the decision makers concerned with the debt issue, that is, G7 countries and IFIs. Priority was given to two paths of internationalization: the G7 countries themselves and the poorest indebted countries. As for the first, the young secretariat of Jubilee 2000 thought that pressure would be more efficient from the "inside", that G7 leaders would be more responsive

33. Baillot, *Nous ne devons rien, nous ne paierons rien*, pp. 289–318; Goldman, *From Margin to Mainstream*, pp. 56–72.
34. Martin Dent, *Jubilee 2000: A New Start for Debt Ridden Developing World*, 8 May 1998, p. 9. Jubilee UK archives, Newcastle.
35. Jubilee 2000 UK, *The Debt Cutter's Handbook* (London, 1996), p. 32. Jubilee UK archives, Newcastle.
36. Rev. Rebeca Dudley, "Debt as a Challenge to Faith", in Jubilee 2000 UK, *The Debtcutter Handbook* (London, 1998), p. 2.
37. The £50,000 grant provided by the Tudor Trust to the emerging Jubilee 2000 in 1996 was conditioned on the internationalization of the movement. Jubilee UK, *Notes of a Meeting Held at the Tudor Trust*, London, 6 March 1996. Jubilee UK archives, Newcastle.

if their own constituencies were nationally involved.[38] During the years 1996 and 1997, Jubilee expanded to Germany, the United States, and Canada. Churches and international organizations such as Oxfam, Tearfund, and Action Aid, who were part of the secretariat of Jubilee 2000, played a key role in this process.[39]

As for the second, the secretariat of Jubilee 2000 considered that getting southern indebted countries involved would help legitimize the anti-debt movement in the eyes of northern campaigners; they believed that only transnationalization would help bring some moral suasion to a campaign that otherwise would run the risk of appearing as another movement for the poor without the poor. Because Africa was considered the continent most victimized by globalization, most concerned with indebtedness, and most affected by unfair economic policies imposed by the World Bank and the IMF, the secretariat worked hard to get African countries on board.

In 1999, Jubilee 2000 was a loosely affiliated campaign of around sixty national coalitions. But as the campaign was gaining momentum, tensions appeared, especially although not exclusively along the North–South divide.[40] While the leading coalition in the North mostly opposed debt and structural adjustment on economic and religious grounds, African activists who joined the Jubilee Afrika campaign started to promote an alternative framework. Debt was not just economically "unsustainable"; it was first and foremost "illegitimate", as were any conditions attached to its reduction, beginning with the implementation of SAPs.

"DON'T OWE! WON'T PAY!" AFRICAN ANTI-SAP ACTIVISTS WITHIN THE JUBILEE CAMPAIGN

While most academic works devoted to Jubilee 2000 tend to adopt a monolithic approach, thus insisting on the "success" of the movement, a greater inclusion of southern activists in the analysis shows that the issue of structural adjustment was highly controversial within the anti-debt campaign. As shown in the following section, tensions, even leading to a split between northern and

---

38. Tim Green and Sam Clarke, "Achieving Debt Relief by 2000: Jubilee 2000 and a New Debt Coalition", discussion paper for Jubilee 2000 Board, 1 May 1997. Jubilee UK archives, Newcastle.
39. *Ibid.*
40. While it is essential to intend to establish major trends within the Jubilee movement, one must not fall into caricature. A detailed analysis of anti-debt activists shows that dividing lines within the movement were quite blurred and cannot be simplified to a clear North–South opposition. Some organizations, although based in the Global South, were more in line with the positions held internationally by leading coalitions in the Global North (i.e. Jubilee UK and Jubilee USA) than with the ones of their southern counterparts. This is the case, for example, of Jubilee Uganda, whose founders, mostly former members of the Government of Uganda with close links with the World Bank and the IMF, were not ardent defenders of anti-imperialism and pan-Africanism.

southern coalitions, did not result from a question of number but rather over underlying principles.

"Illegitimacy" versus "unsustainability": The promotion of alternative frameworks on debt and structural adjustment

The launch ceremony of the Jubilee Afrika campaign took place in April 1998 in the capital of Ghana, Accra. This event, supported by Jubilee UK, which helped establish a Jubilee Afrika secretariat, was a crucial step in the process of internationalization of Jubilee 2000 as it officially marked the involvement of African activists in the international Jubilee 2000 movement. The African – or even pan-African – dimension of the campaign was verified by the participants' countries of origin;[41] only Northern Africa was absent from the ceremony, which appeared as a predominantly sub-Saharan event. Delegates came from religious organizations and churches, grass-roots organizations, development NGOs, trade unions, and political parties. For three days, African activists as well as a few international delegates attended conferences and participated in workshops to discuss the debt crisis.

Analysing the speeches delivered in Accra as well as the content of the advocacy material produced by southern coalitions gives us a good sense of how African activists framed the issue of debt and structural adjustment and to what extent these framings were different from the ones of the leading coalitions in the Global North. The major observation relates to the type of arguments developed by the different coalitions to contest international debt policies. While Jubilee USA and Jubilee UK advocated in favour of debt relief on the basis of religious and moral arguments, Jubilee Afrika mobilized primarily on historical and juridical grounds. Debt was not just "unsustainable", it was first and foremost "illegitimate". In support of their claims, African activists multiplied references to history, in particular to the periods of the transatlantic slave trade and colonization. In his keynote address at the Accra Conference, South African Archbishop Ndungane of Cape Town, who played a major role in the fight against apartheid, drew a parallel between the number of victims of slavery and of debt bondage:

> It has been pointed out that in the course of the Atlantic trade in slavery 24 million people were placed in servitude. More than one and half million were thought to have died as they crossed the Atlantic Ocean. The United Nations Development Program has argued that today's debt bondage can directly account for the death of millions of children.[42]

---

41. The ceremony gathered delegates from Ghana, Angola, Burkina Faso, Burundi, the Democratic Republic of the Congo, Sierra Leone, Kenya, Mali, Mozambique, Liberia, Nigeria, Rwanda, Senegal, South Africa, Tanzania, Uganda, and Zimbabwe.
42. Rev. Njonkonkulu Ndungane, "A Clean Slate: Africa Springboard to Hope", in Jubilee 2000 Afrika Campaign, *Conference Report*, April 1998. Jubilee USA archives, Washington, DC.

While some national debts had been directly inherited from the colonial period,[43] these references were primarily symbolic; debt was used as a metaphor to denounce relations of domination that were still ongoing.

Although African activists raised concerns about poverty, their discourse did not descend into pessimism. African countries were not presented as "intrinsically poor" but as having been damaged by the iniquitous policies imposed over the years by the West:

> It has often been said that Afrika is poor. What nonsense! It is not Afrika that is poor. It is the Afrikans who are impoverished by centuries of exploitation and domination – so correctly said Osagyefo Kwame Nkrumah in his address of 8th August 1960 to the National Assembly as the then First President of the Republic of Ghana.[44]

In order to celebrate African agency, the discourse of activists was full of references to major Black historical figures, from heroes and martyrs of African independences struggles, to pan-Africanist leaders, to African-American civil rights activists.[45] We found, for example, references to Mwalimu Nyerere, Patrice Lumumba, Queen Mother Moore, and Kwame Nkrumah. One of the most visible figures was Thomas Sankara, whose powerful speech against the debt hold in Addis Ababa was frequently reproduced in Jubilee Afrika advocacy material.

By making a detour through history, African activists, whose profiles will be examined below, insisted on the responsibility of former colonial powers in the impoverishment of Africa – former colonial powers, who, at the time of the campaign, were also some of the major bilateral creditors of African countries. Such a transfer of responsibility allowed activists from the Global South to go further in their claims and to turn the basic accounting question "who owes who?" upside down. On the basis of history, southern countries would not owe anything to northern creditors. If anything, they were owed. As a result, African activists did not just ask for debt "relief" or debt "forgiveness", as the leading Jubilee coalitions in the North did. They demanded "total debt cancellation" for all African countries (Figure 2).

This claim came along with a firm stance on structural adjustment. Because debt was considered "illegitimate" in the first place, no conditions were to be attached to its cancelation. African activists thus called for "the scrapping of

---

43. This was, for example, the case of the newly independent Democratic Republic of the Congo, which had to assume an important share of the debt contracted during the colonial period: "Le contentieux belgo-congolais", *Courrier hebdomadaire du CRISP*, 15 (1965), pp. 1–25.

44. Kofi Klu, "Jubilee 2000 Afrika campaign: In Making Debt Cancellation Serve the Purpose of Poverty Eradication", paper for the conference "Poverty in Africa: A Dialogue on Causes and Solutions", Center for the Study of African Economies, Oxford, 15–16 April 1999.

45. Marie-Emmanuelle Pommerolle and Johanna Siméant, "African Voices and Activists at the WSF in Nairobi: The Uncertain Ways of Transnational African Activism", *Journal of World-Systems Research*, 16 (2009), pp. 82–93, quotation on p. 91.

Fig. 2 Demonstration organised by the Kenyan Jubilee 2000 campaign.
Source: advocacy.international.co.uk.

the HIPC initiative" and for the "immediate termination of the conditions
attached to all the internationally designed debt relief mechanisms tying this
to further economic adjustment".

In order to better understand the positions defended by Jubilee Africa, one
must briefly discuss the social trajectories of the actors who served on its
board. Such a focus is justified by the fact that this group was at the core of
the Jubilee movement in Africa. They were the ones who, with the help of
the Jubilee 2000 international secretariat in London, organized the conference
in Accra and, later, coordinated the activities of the many member organizations at a continental level. Biographical data collected by the Jubilee 2000
international secretariat shows that the African secretariat was a small group
of around ten individuals, mostly coming from Ghana (hence the Afrika spel-
ling with a k) but also from Côte d'Ivoire and Nigeria. Although diverse in
age, gender, and country of origin, they all had elitist profiles – as is often
the case for the most internationalized activists;[46] most of them attended university, the majority of them studying law while others studied political science, journalism, or sociology. Significantly, the secretariat included three
jurists, two journalists, and two teachers. Another distinctive feature is that
Jubilee Afrika members shared similar ideological backgrounds: they were
all anti-imperialist, Marxist, and pan-Africanist intellectuals. At the time of

46. Anne-Catherine Wagner, "Syndicalistes européens. Les conditions sociales et institutionnelles
de l'internationalisation des militants syndicaux", *Actes de la recherche en sciences sociales*, 155
(2004), pp. 12–23.

Jubilee, all were political opponents of their national regimes. Affiong Southey, for example, had been a long-time advocate for the rights of the Ogoni people and a strong opponent of the Abacha regime in Nigeria. As for the Ghanaians, most of them initially favoured the military coups of General Jerry Rawlings (1979, 1981). Johnny Hansen, for example, had been Ghana's Minister of Interior. Delali Yao Klu, for his part, was one of the directors of the People's Defence Committee (PDCs) of the Volta Region, in charge of its press, information, and education. But both of them resigned in 1982 when the Provisional National Defence Council (PNDC) announced the signature of an SAP with the IMF, a decision they perceived as a betrayal. This leads us to their last common feature: all Jubilee Afrika secretariat members had played a leading role, within their respective national frameworks, in the protests against the implementation of structural adjustment programmes. Affiong Southey, for example, was one of the leaders of the National Association of Nigerian Students, and Iddrisu Fuseini was a leading member of the Transport Workers of the Trade Union Congress. Their opposition to neoliberal economic reforms appeared to be costly, and many of them were subjected to strong political pressure. Some were even forced into exile: Delali Yao Klu fled to Togo and Nigeria before returning to Ghana in the early 1990s, and Affiong Southey and Kofi Klu fled to the United Kingdom where they were granted refugee status.

For these activists, the emerging Jubilee 2000 campaign provided an unexpected opportunity to reinvigorate the struggle against the economic reforms induced by the SAPs while benefiting from international resources, audience, and protection. In their view, debt and structural adjustment programmes needed to be tackled side by side, as two faces of the same coin. But as the year 2000 approached, opportunities for African activists to oppose economic reforms imposed by IFIs within the anti-debt movement narrowed; at the international level, the issue of SAPs faded into the background as Jubilee 2000 leaders decided to focus their efforts on obtaining concrete debt relief agreements. The legislative strategy adopted by Jubilee USA embodied the directions taken by the anti-debt campaign. As shown below, its analysis allows us to get a better handle on the conflicts that divided anti-debt activists using a concrete case.

Structural adjustment: A bone of contention within Jubilee 2000

In the years following the launch of Jubilee 2000, the issue of structural adjustment tended to become a major bone of contention between southern and northern campaigners. As explained in the first section, it would be unfair to say that Jubilee activists in the North did not care about structural adjustment reforms. They did. But as the campaign advanced and as the year 2000 approached, Jubilee 2000 leaders tended to favour intense direct lobbying with G7 finance ministers and IFI officials, a choice that generated fierce

debates among northern campaigners in the North but which, above all, precipitated the rupture with their southern counterparts. Jo-Marie Griesgraber,
current executive director for the New Rules for Global Finance Coalition and
former executive-committee director of Jubilee USA, remembers:

> We had a terrible struggle inside the group as to how to go about it. Especially
> when it looked like we were beginning to make progress and that it was really
> becoming an issue with legs, going to make a difference [...] how to articulate
> that? Should we go and just say cancel it, no conditions and cancel the debt
> now? Or say, well, that's not possible, so we will have to recognize that there
> will be some conditions on debt reduction, and it will be debt reduction not com-
> plete cancellation.[47]

In the United States, internal discussions resulted in the creation of a "legislative group" whose main goal was to pass legislation in favour of debt relief in
the US Congress. As Gerald Flood, a senior policy adviser for the US Catholic
Bishops Conference and prominent member of Jubilee USA, explained, "[w]e
wanted to get something substantial by the end of 2000".[48] For a few months,
members of the legislative group met on average once a week to draft the bill.
Because they "felt that realistically, getting the Congress, the Administration,
the G7, the IMF and the World Bank to agree to scrap the initiative and start
afresh would be an impossible task", they decided to focus on "amending the
existing framework", that is, the HIPC initiative, by shortening the waiting
period for countries to receive debt relief, redefining debt sustainability, and
broadening the eligibility criteria. Rather than trying to delink debt and structural adjustment, legislative group members chose to speak in broad terms of
changing the nature of conditionality to have a greater focus on poverty reduction. Introduced in Congress by Representative Jim Leach (R–Iowa) on 11
March 1999, the bill provoked indignation and anger among anti-debt activists, especially (but not exclusively) in the Global South. Thus, at a conference
held in Montreal in October 2000, Ann Pettifor, a member of the Jubilee international secretariat and director of the Jubilee 2000 campaign, expressed her
disapproval of the Jubilee USA strategy:

> In the UK we avoided "playing god" by backing particular debt relief initiatives;
> or by listing countries that required debt cancellation. While we did produce a list
> for guidance, and as a way of highlighting the inadequacies of creditor initiatives,
> we argued strongly that decisions about eligibility had to be taken by independent
> arbitrators. This approach did not always prevent us from making errors.
> However, it did protect us from the approach followed by our friends in the US
> coalition who fell full [*sic*] of NGO lobbyists ("ledgers") on Capitol Hill who

47. Interview with Jo-Marie Griesgraber, Center of Concern/Jubilee USA, Washington, DC,
June 2011.
48. Interview with Gerald Flood, US Catholic Bishops Conference/Jubilee USA, Washington,
DC, June 2011.

promoted debt relief initiatives (notably the Leach Bill) acceptable to Republican Senators (because the Bill endorsed structural adjustment programs), but which were inimical to southern civil society. It helped to split, turn off and immobilize campaigners in the US and divided the movement internationally.[49]

For their part, Jubilee African activists intended to impede the passage of the law by addressing a letter to US congressional representatives in which they laid out the reasons for their opposition to the "Leach Bill":

> We appreciate the efforts of legislators like Representative Jim Leach, and commend them for their leadership on this important issue. However we must point out that Mr. Leach's legislation contains a fatal flaw: it leaves multilateral debt relief in the hands of the International Monetary Fund (IMF) and continues to enforce the current link between access to multilateral debt relief for impoverished countries and compliance with harsh IMF structural adjustment austerity programs [...] We respectfully ask that the US Congress decline to support the multilateral debt proposal contained in the bill sponsored by Representative Leach. While undoubtedly well-intentioned, these provisions would eventually have an adverse impact in Africa and in other impoverished regions of the world.[50]

Affiong Southey and Kofi Klu (members of the Jubilee Afrika secretariat) were among the signatories, along with Dennis Brutus (a well-known anti-apartheid activist and honorary president of Jubilee Afrika) and Guillaume Soro (then General Secretary of the Student Federation of Ivory Coast – FESCI).

The tone was more virulent when criticisms were directly addressed to Jubilee USA activists. As shown by the following email, criticisms concerned both the content (a bill that did not oppose structural adjustment) and the form (the lack of coordination with southern activists):

> It is unthinkable for any campaign using the banner "Jubilee" and/or debt cancellation to propose to those who claim to be our creditors that they should continue on with policies and conditionalities such as Structural Adjustment Programs and HIPC which oppress us and literally cost us millions of lives each year. Likewise, it is unthinkable that any organization would propose legislation which reinforces and validates our oppression without first consulting with us and giving us the opportunity to oppose such legislation first, not after the fact.[51]

Over time, the feeling was exacerbated among African activists that the domination of the Global North – which the Jubilee 2000 international secretariat denounced in its advocacy material while talking about international economics – was being reproduced within the Jubilee network itself. Indeed, the Jubilee 2000 campaign encompassed strong divergences in terms

49. Ann Pettifor, "Jubilee 2000 and the Multilateral Institutions", paper presented at the International Forum, Montreal, 1–3 October 2000. Jubilee USA archives, Washington, DC.

50. Jubilee Afrika secretariat, "Letter to US Congress Representatives". Jubilee USA archives, Washington, DC.

51. Art Seroti, email to Jubilee USA, 6 April 1999. Jubilee USA archives, Washington, DC.

of power and resources between participants, here again especially though not exclusively between the Global North and the South.[52] While the Jubilee Afrika campaign struggled to make ends meet, Jubilee UK relied on a budget of £2 million. Gradually, a "We, people from the South" formed in opposition to a "Them, people from the North".

Jubilee South and the ongoing revolt of adjusted people

In June 1999, G7 leaders gathered in Cologne and agreed on a new debt relief initiative: the enhanced Heavily Indebted Poor Countries initiative, or HIPC II. This initiative marked a change in development paradigms; ownership, good governance, and the fight against poverty became the new pillars of the emerging post-Washington Consensus.[53] While this new rhetoric had concrete consequences – beginning with an increase in IFIs' legitimacy – its impact on international debt policies remained marginal.[54] HIPC II mainly consisted of an overhaul of the first HIPC initiative, which, while keeping the same general framework, aimed at providing "broader, deeper, and faster" debt relief. The specifics included an increase in the number of eligible countries, a shortening of the qualifying period from six to three years, and the sale of IMF gold to fund multilateral debt relief. As for the new focus on poverty reduction, governments seeking to benefit from debt reduction were required to adopt Poverty Reduction Strategy Papers (PRSPs).[55] Standardized both in form and in content,[56] PRSPs did not consist of a major reorientation of the policies promoted by structural adjustment packages. Liberalization and privatization remained the hallmarks, while the fight against poverty mainly consisted in the strengthening of safety nets for the most vulnerable.[57]

Although the campaign was not over at that time – the deadline had been fixed at the end of the year 2000 – the design of the new international debt relief

52. Tensions were also high between the two leading coalitions of the Jubilee 2000 campaign, Jubilee USA and Jubilee UK.

53. For a detailed analysis of the trajectories of the post-Washington Consensus in Mali, see Isaline Bergamaschi, *Le consensus post Washington au Mali. Trajectoires, usages et processus d'appropriation*, (Ph.D., Sciences Po, 2011).

54. Jean-Pierre Cling *et al.*, "La Banque mondiale, entre transformations et resilience", *Critique internationale*, 53 (2011), pp. 43–65.

55. Thomas Callaghy, *Innovation in the Sovereign Debt Regime: From the Paris Club to Enhanced HIPC and Beyond*, World Bank Operations Evaluation Department working paper, Washington, DC, 2004.

56. The staffs of the IMF and the World Bank produced guidelines to "help countries implement this new approach": IMF, IDA, "Poverty Reduction Strategy Papers – Status and Next Steps", 19 November 1999. Available online at: https://www.imf.org/external/np/pdr/prsp/status.htm; last accessed 23 February 2021; Brian Ames *et al.*, "Macroeconomic Policy and Poverty Reduction", *PRSP Sourcebook*, ch. 6, 2 April 2001.

57. Jeremy Gould, *The New Conditionality: The Politics of Poverty Reduction Strategies* (London, 2005).

initiative gave a good sense of what would be achieved by Jubilee 2000 campaigners. For southern activists, it proved that the strategy pursued by their northern counterparts and leaders in the global campaign was biased towards limited and non-radical changes.

And, indeed, Jubilee 2000 campaigners reacted very differently from the Cologne announcement. On the one hand, northern Jubilee coalitions were – with a few exceptions – lukewarm. Although they did not welcome HIPC II with enthusiasm, their criticisms focused mainly on the specifics: the new debt relief initiative did not go far enough. On the other hand, southern Jubilee coalitions denounced the initiative as a whole:

> Jubilee South sees nothing to welcome in this initiative. This Köln scheme, like its predecessors, refuses to acknowledge the moral dimensions of the debt crisis and the historical responsibility of the rich countries for the current state of affairs.[58]

Here, again, the question was not one of numbers but one of underlying principles:

> The Köln Debt Initiative does not offer relief for the 4.5 billion women and men in the South who suffer from debt domination. It makes a mockery of their right to a dignified life. "Expanded HIPC" means increased misery and debt for peoples of the south. "Expanded HIPC" means increased misery and debt for peoples of the South. HIPC is fundamentally flawed because it is linked to Structural Adjustment Programmes. These programmes have been shown to have a devastating human impact on account of diminished spending capacities for social services and job creation.[59]

Criticized for legitimizing debt, HIPC II was also accused of sowing division among the countries of the South by drawing a line between those who would benefit from debt relief and the others:

> We reject all schemes of the North that divide peoples of the South. We refuse to be categorized as "highly indebted poor countries" or "moderately indebted countries" etc., all of which do not reflect the real situation of impoverishment and the excluded and exploited people in ALL South countries.[60]

Southern activists felt "humiliated" and held northern campaigners responsible for what they considered a "failure":

> As often happens in history, good intentions are often marred by harsh realities in the ground. The movement failed to live up to the expectations of those who made the sacrifices. Charity is not always bad. But in this context, it provided the lenders with a high moral ground, and the borrowers a humiliating stance.

58. Jubilee South, "Jubilee South Rejects Köln Initiative as a Cruel Hoax", 18 June 1999. Jubilee USA archives, Washington, DC.
59. *Ibid.*
60. Jubilee South, "South–South Summit Declaration: Towards a Debt-Free Millennium", 21 November 1999, p. 3. Jubilee USA archives, Washington, DC.

The problem with the Jubilee 2000 Campaign was that its mainstream campaigners more unwittingly than intentionally, legitimized the debt and also by default legitimized the system that creates and perpetuates debt. Instead of challenging the debt and its underlying causes, the J2 campaigners focused on the numbers game, pushing for bigger and bigger amounts of "relief" thus, effectively, endorsing the notion that the debt was legitimate in the first place.[61]

Following the launch of HIPC II, tensions between northern and southern campaigners, already strong in the months preceding the G7 Cologne summit, resulted in a split within the Jubilee movement. In November 1999, a hundred southern delegates coming from Latin America, South East Asia, and Africa, as well as from the diaspora, gathered in Johannesburg where they decided to continue the struggle against debt and structural adjustment on their own under a new banner: Jubilee South.[62] The leading coalitions of Jubilee South were Jubilee Argentina, Jubilee South Africa, and the Freedom from Debt coalition (the Philippines). The Jubilee Afrika secretariat also played an important role in the birth of the movement, as did the DC-based coalition 50 Years is Enough. The platform it published clarified and developed its position: it urged southern countries "to call for debt repudiation, for restitution, reparations and repayment of the social, historical and ecological debt due to the South, for rejection of SAPs and other conditionalities and resistance to neoliberal economic policies".[63]

In spite of the split, Jubilee South activists intended to continue their collaboration with their northern counterparts. On 11–17 December 2000, they organized the first "South–North Dialogue". Held in Dakar, the event gathered a hundred anti-debt activists including delegates from Jubilee USA, Jubilee UK, and ErlassJahr (Germany). While the issues of reparations and repudiation remained contentious, all organizations agreed to work on the issue of debt illegitimacy. It is worth underlining that the CADTM, almost absent from the Jubilee 2000 campaign, lent its support to the organization of the South–North Dialogue. This close collaboration between Jubilee South and the CADTM continued after the campaign ended. Both organizations took an active role in the birth of the global justice movement, of which debt became a pillar.[64]

---

61. Jubilee South, "JNorth view from JSouth: Why Jubilee 2000 Failed", 12 February 2001. Jubilee USA archives, Washington, DC.
62. The creation of this new structure was the result of a process that took place over several months. Just a few months after the launch of Jubilee Afrika, members of an important Asian anti-debt network, a member of Jubilee 2000, the Asian Network on Debt and Development, gathered in Hong Kong to discuss the possibility of a South–South summit on debt. Around the same time, the head of Jubilee Nicaragua made its "Proposal for a South Jubilee".
63. Jubilee South, "South–South Summit Declaration", p. 1.
64. Laurence Caramel, "Les réseaux de l'antimondialisation", *Critique Internationale*, 13 (2001), pp. 153–161.

CONCLUSION

Establishing the relationship between the debt crisis in southern countries and the financial crisis of 2008 in the North resembles playing a game of mirrors. From one to the other, we find a common issue: debt, and especially indebtedness. Some institutions in charge of dealing with the debt are also present in both settings, including the G8 (G7 at the time of Jubilee 2000) and the IMF, which with the Greek debt crisis makes its return in Europe. Yet other institutions are specific to each situation: the World Bank, which played a central role during the 1980s and 1990s, was absent from the management of the European debt crisis, while the European Central Bank, absent in the case of southern countries, played a leading role in the European crisis. In both contexts, we also find public policy mechanisms which, although not exactly alike, show significant common patterns, beginning with the firm promotion – or rather imposition – of so-called structural reforms. The latter are driven and supported by common discourses: bilateral creditors and international financial institutions in both contexts insist on the responsibility of the borrowing states, the laziness of their populations, and the incompetence or even corruption of their governments. In the post-2008 European debt crisis, the derogatory – some have said "racist" – acronym PIGS (for Portugal, Italy, Greece, and Spain),[65] which was often used by financial, political, and media stakeholders, proved significant in this regard. Some NGOs or anti-debt networks are also present in the two pictures: the Jubilee Debt Campaign, ErlassJahr, Eurodad, and the CADTM, which strongly advocated during the 1990s in favour of the cancelation of the debt of southern countries, were still very much active in the post-2008 crisis. Eric Toussaint, who was involved in the campaign against debt and structural adjustment in the 1990s, is one of the most renowned activists of the anti-debt and anti-austerity movements in Europe. Lastly, we can underline the use of common arguments and concepts such as "odious" or "illegitimate" debt. Enshrined in argumentative chains rooted in history and morals, such notions, which activists are still using today, were initially forged to advocate in favour of the cancelation of the debt of southern countries owed to northern countries and international financial institutions.

Fifteen years after the end of Jubilee 2000, authors of the preliminary report of the Truth Committee on the Greek Public Debt provided "evidence of indicative cases of illegal, illegitimate and odious debts", and on this basis they "presented the options concerning the cancellation of debt" and called for the "repudiation and suspension of Greek sovereign debt".[66] Drawing on historical arguments, Greece's then-Deputy Finance Minister Dimitris Mardas

---

65. The use of the acronym goes back to 1979 and describes countries in the European Union considered to have troubled economies. It was then popularized by the financial press after 2008.
66. The Truth Committee on Public Debt, *Preliminary Report*, 18 June 2015, p. 4.

announced in April 2015 that, according to the country's General Accounting Office, Germany would owe Greece €279 billion in reparations for Nazi occupation during World War II.

Of course, the two "debt crises" are not the same – not least because European and African countries do not carry the same weight on the international scene. But at a time when sovereign debt has become one of the major constraints faced by European states, and when a large trans-party consensus agrees on the necessity of sharply reducing public expenditure, making a historical and geographical detour proved to be heuristic. Taking a step to the side offered the opportunity to question the idea of the ineluctability of debt and to understand that the debt problem is neither natural nor immutable.